Essays on
the American Constitution

Alpheus Thomas Mason

A Commemorative Volume in Honor of
Alpheus T. Mason

Essays on

the American Constitution

Edited by

Gottfried Dietze

Professor of Political Science
The Johns Hopkins University

PRENTICE-HALL, INC., *Englewood Cliffs, New Jersey*

125802

LIBRARY OF CONGRESS CATALOG CARD NO.: 64–19435

Printed in the United States of America

C–28353

PRENTICE-HALL INTERNATIONAL, INC., London
PRENTICE-HALL OF AUSTRALIA, PTY., LTD., Sydney
PRENTICE-HALL OF CANADA, LTD., Toronto
PRENTICE-HALL OF INDIA (PRIVATE) LTD., New Delhi
PRENTICE-HALL OF JAPAN, INC., Tokyo
PRENTICE-HALL DE MEXICO, S.A., Mexico City

Contents

vi

Alpheus Thomas Mason

An Introduction

This volume in honor of Alpheus Thomas Mason is a collection of essays written by former students who had the pleasure of learning from a great teacher, the privilege of working under a distinguished scholar, and the good fortune of being helped along by a friend. It is a genuine *Festschrift*: Not only is it presented to him to celebrate his 65th birthday. It also expresses the hope that he may take pleasure in the awareness that the free discussion which dominates his classes continues to prevail among those who were inspired by him and his work.

Princeton undergraduates recognized Alpheus T. Mason's merits in their own, unsilent way. When he was thirty-one and had been on the Princeton faculty for only five years, the senior class dedicated their year book to him with a handsome tribute. Year after year thereafter he was cited as "most inspiring teacher." Although his undergraduate courses are among the toughest in the university, they are among the most popular. Professor Mason's success as a teacher of undergraduates is matched by that as a teacher of graduate students. His are hard courses. There are few professors who, like him, require a research paper from every student every week throughout the semester. But if we students often groaned under the hard work, it was a healthy experience, and we had some comfort in the idea that he had to read all these papers. This he did with enthusiasm. A paper he would return would look the way library books ought not to look: ink and pencil marks all over, with lots of handwritten comments. Words would be underlined not once or twice, but three to five times. Of course, we students would, first of all, look for our grade. It was always written in longhand and ranged from "excellent" to something like "a little thin." There was a tough but healthy competition among the students from week to week. That competition was, however, among independent young scholars as they strove for maturity, not among epigones eager to echo their master's voice in misguided hopes of his approbation. Professor Mason left no doubt that he wanted to learn from his students as much as he wanted them to learn from him, that he would prefer a good argument, having students pit their minds against his, and develop independently their own way. His students heeded his advice. They can be found among conservatives no less than liberals, among behavioralists no less than institutionalists. This was the achievement of a classroom atmosphere characterized by freedom.

The idea of freedom, so characteristic of his teaching, is also the leading principle of his writing. One of Professor Mason's first books was entitled *Bureaucracy Convicts Itself.* The word "freedom" recurs again and again in the titles of his works. As a scholar, his assignment was no easy one when he was appointed as McCormick Professor of Jurisprudence, a chair that had previously been occupied by Edward S. Corwin and Woodrow Wilson. His predecessors are in good company. His writings are impressive from a quantitative as well as a qualitative point of view. His biography of Justice Brandeis remained on the best seller list for about five months and has sold well over 50,000 copies. *Harlan Fiske Stone, Pillar of the Law,* was called by a reviewer known for his reluctance to praise "one of the most important judicial biographies yet written," won the American Library Association's Liberty and Justice award of $5,000 for "the most distinguished book of 1956 in history and biography," and shared honors with George Kennan for the prestigious Francis Parkman prize in history.

In view of Professor Mason's drive and continuing productivity—he is now engaged in what may be the culmination of work he has undertaken for many years, a study on the office and powers of the Chief Justice— it would be premature to attempt an evaluation of his entire work. Aside from the Brandeis and Stone biographies, *The Brandeis Way, The Supreme Court: Palladium of Freedom,* and *The States Rights Debate: Antifederalism and the Constitution* perhaps stand out as the most significant works. And yet, it can already be said that his work was to a large degree influenced by three men who, as he once told me, "stand out like mountain peaks": Corwin, Brandeis, and Stone. For him, each exhibited qualities that may be described in terms of statesmanship: Corwin, the academic statesman; Brandeis, the social statesman; Stone, the judicial statesman. It would be hard to imagine that anyone living closely with these giants could help being influenced by them. But just as Professor Mason resented subordination by his students, he himself was never a mere epigone. Ingredients and influences derived from these men have been fused into something that is peculiarly his own. This is evident, for instance, in the last chapter of *The Supreme Court: Palladium of Freedom,* in which Madison's boast that ours is a political system without a model is developed along lines that depart significantly from Corwin; in the concluding chapters of *The Brandeis Way* which show Mr. Mason's own ideas and methods, inspired by Brandeis; in the last chapter of *The Supreme Court from Taft to Warren,* in which Stone's famous Carolene Products footnote provides the basis for an interpretation of judicial review as a liberalizing adjunct of popular government; in the last chapter of *The Supreme Court: Palladium of Freedom,* in which Alpheus Mason proposes the idea that defense of the political rights of minorities is the very foundation of majority rule, not its antithesis.

Professor Mason also likes to think of a young assistant professor he met at Princeton back in 1925, Walter Lincoln Whittlesey, a skeptic and iconoclast who questioned everything and shocked everybody and whose effect on young Mason's mind was "like a fresh breeze." Whittlesey spent countless hours at his colleague's side going over and re-writing poorly written manuscripts, and improving his writing.

In 1963, Alpheus T. Mason was elected to the American Academy of Arts and Sciences.

The familiar dichotomy, teaching vs. research, never presented itself as a problem to Alpheus T. Mason. Quite the contrary. For him, one has always been the helpmate of the other. Teaching he considers the natural auxiliary to research and writing, lectures as an opportunity to try out ideas that would later appear in print. In turn, his writing spreads the knowledge he gained through research and thus is a natural auxiliary to teaching. Mason is a professor in the genuine sense of the word, persistently clinging to a topic he wants to explore and generously imparting his knowledge to others. It is probably this belief in his academic calling, strengthened by his success as a scholar-teacher, that made him shun administrative duties.

In view of his absorption in his work, one wonders whether Professor Mason finds interest in anything that is not connected with his work. He does. Through the years one of his hobbies has been browsing around antique shops in the United States and abroad. At first he was primarily a collector of early American pieces, but with passage of years and travel to Europe and Japan his taste broadened, to include paintings, prints, porcelain figures, and icons. Interest in art objects has always been influenced by a delicate sense of composition. He wants things that he can visualize as part of an ensemble. He is not a collector *per se,* but buys things that fit in with the rest of his possessions, feeling that "everything has to compose." Interior decoration absorbs and delights him. He loves beauty in his surroundings, as his home attests.

His house is always open to former students. In its relaxed atmosphere, the visitor becomes most aware of Alpheus Thomas Mason, the man. He is not, as could be expected in view of his achievements, magisterial and detached. He is warm and friendly, and has a boyish capacity for enjoying the ludicrous side of life. Quick to see through "stuffed shirts" or "phonies," he has a Puckish sense of humor. His banter sometimes disconcerts literal-minded or very proper people who do not realize how often he is speaking with "tongue in cheek." His willingness to help and give advice on personal as well as professional matters make a visit to him a rewarding and delightful experience.

As his students, we pay tribute with this little volume to a great scholar and teacher. We hope he may find enough in it worthy of his teaching and example. May it bring him assurance that the values he instilled and imparted still live among those he has taught, and allow him delight in the gift without necessitating suspension of the critical judgment which he was wont to apply to us, his sometime students and lifelong friends.

G. D.

July 4, 1964

I

Founding Fathers

1

The Chasm that Separated
Thomas Jefferson
and John Marshall

Julian P. Boyd

"If American law were to be
represented by a single figure," declared Oliver Wendell Holmes in a
famous address, "sceptic and worshipper alike would agree without dispute that the figure could be one alone, and that one, John Marshall." So
qualified, the Olympian generalization could be applied with equal if not
superior force to Thomas Jefferson as an embodiment of the democratic
ideal. The appraisal testifies to the towering stature of the two men, for
law and democracy as two mutually indispensable elements of a free society could scarcely be symbolized by those not possessing qualities of
greatness.

But this pre-eminence of Jefferson and Marshall was not grounded in
either case upon that distinctive originality of thought by which sharp
breaks with the past are reached in the march of human affairs. The Declaration of Independence did for the first time in history declare certain
natural rights to be the basis of established political institutions, and the
obiter opinion in *Marbury* v. *Madison* did establish a landmark in the
development of American constitutional law. Yet in neither case, nor
elsewhere, did Marshall or Jefferson create distinctive or original concepts
of government. Their greatness in their respective spheres lay in the
felicitous combinations of character and dispositions that fitted them

superbly for their separate tasks. No surer hands had yet touched the executive and judicial powers when, in the opening days of the nineteenth century, these two hostile kinsmen were elevated to the offices for which nature had so amply qualified them and to which they gave new force and direction. If by some monumental perversity of fate their roles had been reversed, the consequences for American history would certainly have been different and very likely disastrous. Neither was fitted for role of the other.

Though the concepts of law and democracy which they symbolize are integral rather than opposed, the two men stood poles apart in their views of man and society. The unrelieved and implacable hostility existing between them as protagonists of differing theories of democratic government ran deep into the mysteries of personality, and it had a bearing on American institutions that could not have been possible theretofore when the executive and the judiciary spoke with harmonizing voices. Among the consequences were Marshall's resolute definition of the role of the judiciary in the federal system and, far more important, the first informed and extended public discussion of the nature of that role. These consequences, to be sure, were implicit in a government of checks and balances, though the time of their arrival depended upon the progress of events and the evolution of the political dialogue that had begun with the debate over the nature of the British imperial constitution and had led to the establishment of a new and distinctive form of federal government.

The first phase of that dialogue culminated in a confederated system in which all powers were vested in a single legislative body. The second, benefiting from the reaction to the inadequacies and dangers of such a government as well as from the "contest of principles of administration" between Hamilton and Jefferson that gave emphasis to the powers of the executive, ended in a corresponding reaction that was bound to moderate the tone if not the use of those powers. The beginning of the third phase with its shift of attention to the judiciary—a shift that might otherwise have been delayed much longer—was brought about by the election of 1800, by the political complexion and behavior of the existing judiciary, by the partisan effort of the outgoing administration to consolidate and expand its influence in that department, and, finally, by the act of John Adams in designating John Marshall as Chief Justice of the United States. Jefferson's muting of executive authority while making full use of executive power was predictable in the light of his own nature and of the tendency of preceding administrations to magnify the executive. But with the appointment of Marshall the beginning of this final phase in the seemingly natural sequence of the great dialogue on government was all but guaranteed. If nature, politics, and accident seem to have fitted the two men for their respective roles, the same forces benefited the American people in the task of shaping democratic institutions by bringing these men to the right posts at precisely the right time.

It was necessary as well as timely for the role of the judiciary to be examined. The discussions of the question in the Federal Convention of 1787, in the ratifying conventions, and in the accompanying pamphlet and newspaper debates had been anticipatory. These anticipations recognized that the role of a co-ordinate department of government not subject to electoral mandate or rebuke was made palatable under democratic theory by the paramount need of an independent judiciary. There was also an informed assumption that within its sphere the judiciary would function as the ultimate arbiter of the meaning of the Constitution. Neither a challenge to the idea of an independent judiciary nor a denial of the right of judicial review brought on the discussion, though both became endangered by the feelings that had been aroused. Not abstract concepts of the place of the courts in the federal system but political and other factors exacerbated those feelings. The establishment in the first place of a judiciary system too imposing and, so many thought, too costly for its task; the charges to grand juries invoking loyalty to government that shaded too easily into admonitions against disloyalty to administration; the confusing of the spheres of departmental jurisdiction in such matters as the giving of advice to the executive on vital questions of policy and, most objectionable of all, the acceptance of an executive diplomatic mission by the Chief Justice; the unquestioning enforcement of legislation of such dubious constitutionality as the Alien and Sedition Acts; and finally the flagrant displays of partisan prejudices on the bench in a climate of aroused political passions—all of this had the effect of inflaming the feelings of a large part of the nation against the federal judiciary. The result was a constitutional crisis that posed a grave threat to the distinctive federal system that had evolved in the latter quarter of the eighteenth century.

Jefferson and Marshall stood in the beginning on common ground, along with the generality of their countrymen. Their divergence in attitude in the immediate post-war years is apparent, though they did not meet until Jefferson became Secretary of State. Even then Marshall's position was so obscured by native caution or other factors that Jefferson, seeking as always to enlist young men of talent on the side of "the republican interest," but dubious of Marshall's convictions, achieved the distinction of being the first to recommend that he be made a judge. The divergence became fixed in the middle of Washington's second administration and was an inexorable gulf by the time Marshall administered the oath of office to the new president. The hostility between the two men achieved epic proportions in the ensuing years, being in no way diminished by the fact that Marshall, during the critical days of early 1801, looked on with less than judicial detachment at desperate Federalist efforts that some believed would place the executive power in his own hands.

Marshall regarded Jefferson as the personal embodiment of "the fatal philosophy of the day," as a man of vaulting ambition who had achieved power over the people by professions of democracy, who possessed a malignant, vindictive nature, and who was an enemy of every effort to thwart the popular impulses that were the source of his own power, being therefore hostile to the idea of an independent judiciary. Jefferson on his part regarded Marshall as the willing instrument of a discredited party that had consolidated itself in the stronghold of the judiciary whence it could loose its partisan bolts at the administration and yet remain beyond the reach of popular retaliation. He thought Marshall a man of strong political ambitions, capable of bending others to his will, determined to mobilize the power of the court by craftiness, by sophisticating the law to his own prepossessions, and by making its opinions those of a conclave which he would dominate. He attributed to Marshall also a quality of "mind of that gloomy malignity which will never let him forego the opportunity of satiating it on a victim." Neither Alexander Hamilton nor Patrick Henry aroused in Jefferson so enduring an animosity as Marshall evoked. It is difficult to believe that so profound and permanent a hostility was kept alive merely by partisan opposition or by the judicial tenure that insured for his foe an indefinite use of power long after he himself was required to lay down the reins. These were powerful factors, to be sure. But, believing that "the courts of justice exercise the sovereignty of this country in judiciary matters, are supreme in these, and liable neither to controul nor opposition from any other branch of the government"—believing, that is, both in judicial review and in an independent judiciary—Jefferson could scarcely look with detachment on a partisan use of power which, however inescapable and necessary in the hands of the executive, was for the judiciary unbecoming, incompatible, and indeed dangerous.

A key to the depth of the unending antagonism is to be found in Jefferson's famous letter to Mazzei that Marshall considered to be an impeachment of the morals of its author. What Marshall noticed in the letter was the charge of apostasy from republican principles and the identification of the executive, the judiciary, and a majority of the legislative branches with that charge. What he overlooked, both here and in the whole tenor of Jefferson's life, was the principles from which Jefferson had accused the government of apostatizing—"that noble love of liberty and republican government which carried us triumphantly thro' the war" to which he claimed the whole landed interest, a great mass of talents, and the main body of the citizens had remained true. The gravity of the charge and the manner in which it was made alienated Marshall forever from one who could level such an assertion at Washington, but the element of truth in the indictment rankled and the role in which this was revealed was that of Marshall the historian rather than Marshall the jurist. The analysis of parties in Marshall's *Washington* seemed to Jefferson to be a pre-emption for the Federalists of those principles of the Revolution which, by implying hostility toward such views on the part of the opposing party, misrepresented the nature of the political division. Jefferson believed this to be an artful, contrived analysis so far from reality as to be totally untrue to history, but the depth of his resentment on reading it could scarcely have been produced by mere party attachment. Partisanship was an armor that he wore lightly in any case, but Marshall's thrust was one that pierced far beneath the surface.

For by this definition of the opposing party Marshall impugned Jeffer-son's fidelity to republican principles. More than once Jefferson spoke of these principles of the Revolution as "the holy cause of liberty" and the almost religious nature of his attachment to that cause kept him alert to signs of apostasy in others and quick to measure these by the strength of his own zeal. If there was anything that could have aroused him more than a charge of his own defection, it was one making a like indictment of the national character and of the fidelity of his countrymen. Marshall had done both, and in Jefferson's mind this was almost equivalent to an accusation of treason against the nation. The true springs of his animus are revealed in the preface that he wrote to his *Anas* in 1818: "The partiality of this pen," he declared of Marshall's *Washington*, "is dis-played in lavishments of praise on certain military characters, who had done nothing military, but who afterwards, and before he wrote, had become heroes in party, altho' not in war; and in his reserve on the merits of others, who rendered signal services indeed, but did not earn his praise by apostatizing in peace from the republican principles for which they had fought in war. It shews itself too in the cold indifference with which a struggle for the most animating of human objects is narrated. No act of heroism ever kindles in the mind of this writer a single aspiration in favor of the holy cause which inspired the bosom, and nerved the arm of the patriot warrior. No gloom of events, no lowering of prospects ever ex-cites a fear for the issue of a contest which was to change the condition of man over the civilized globe. The sufferings inflicted on endeavors to vindicate the rights of humanity are related with all the frigid insensi-bility with which a monk would have contemplated the victims of an Auto da fé."

In delineating Marshall's detachment in the face of the most animating of human objects, Jefferson revealed how great and inextinguishable a flame that object had kindled in his own breast. In this dual portrait he thus transfixed the elements of Goethe's "two eternal spirits that contend for the government of all that men do or say: the spirit that creates and the spirit that denies, the hope that man can raise himself through the ages a little nearer God, and the mocking doubt that human nature can ever change its ways." For the essential nature of the gulf between Jefferson and Marshall was the diametrically opposed view each had of "the contest which was to change the condition of man over the civilized globe." Marshall was skeptical of the "fatal philosophy of the day," Jefferson deeply moved by the moral proposition set forth in the Declaration of Independence. The jurist was detached and dubious, the apostle of freedom burning with a zealot's devotion.

The cleavage, with its resultant impact upon their respective views of the Constitution and the nature of the union, can best be understood not by measuring its unbridgeable span after the two men came to power but by looking for its source along the common watershed. It was at that point that the true test came. Marshall's own testimony asserts that, on the first signs of boisterousness in the republican sea in the post-war years, he lost "the wild and enthusiastic democracy" with which he had been inspired at the beginning of the Revolution. Debts, inflation, opposition to taxes, commercial rivalries between the states, a temporary stagnation in business, the closing of the West Indies to trade, and, above all, the movement led by Daniel Shays caused him to gravitate toward the position of Washington and other men of substance who looked with anxiety upon the turbulence of popular government. In those years he found "every thing . . . afloat," sound principles of government "brought annually into doubt," and "no safe anchorage ground" to be discovered anywhere. These uncertainties in his estimate gave a high value to "that article in Constitution which imposes restrictions on the states." This statement in Marshall's autobiography has the tone of unmistakable accuracy. It is equally revealing. His nationalism was not that of a man wishing to strengthen and extend the domain of the democratic ideal. It was a shield for defense rather than a sun rising upon the promise of a new world. Its essential nature rested on emotions of fear and distrust of man's propensity for evil, not on an optimistic hope that he could conquer his licentious passions under a rule of reason. Thus at the first sign of storm, Marshall's enthusiasm for the great experiment waned and he looked for safe anchorage ground under a form of government that promised greater stability of law and order, valuing most that part which forbade the states to impair the obligation of contracts. For him the Articles of Confederation was not a constitution of government but an alliance of states, and it had served only to preserve the idea of union until a substantive law adequate to the exigencies of the nation could be formed.

Jefferson's concern was altogether different. He had anticipated that the voyage would be hazardous: it was a "bold and doubtful election" in 1776 that had committed the nation to the idea of government by consent. When the lowered prospects arrived in the form of Shays' Rebellion and other disturbances, he saw these as evidence that the people were awake and alert. There was no antagonism in his position either to the concept of law or to the rights of property, of course, but he looked for the safeguarding of both to a source that Marshall mistrusted or feared. Our government, Jefferson declared in 1801, was the strongest on earth because it was the only one in which every man would fly to the defense of the law as his own immediate concern. The source of that strength did not seem to him, as it did to Marshall, to be derived from the fabric of government devised in 1787. It antedated the Constitution and was indeed its bedrock. It gave strength and vitality even to the Articles of Confederation, which Jefferson like Adams regarded as "the first federal constitution." The strength of the cement of national union on which Jefferson founded his reliance was not to be measured by the extent of powers set forth in a document drawn up in 1787 or by those withheld from a document of 1781: it was to be found in the fidelity of the people to the proposition of 1776.

It was during this post-war period of disillusionment for Marshall that Jefferson proved the nature of his faith. As if demonstrating the validity of Bagehot's remark that the men of Massachusetts could work any constitution, Jefferson was confident the American people could make even the Articles of Confederation an effective instrument, provided only the "one People" who had asserted their nationality in 1776 retained the spirit of freedom: "when that is lost, all experience has shewn that no forms can keep them free against their own will." His nationalism was not grounded upon a form of government but upon a faith, and the highest expression of that faith as set forth in the Declaration of Independence was, as John Hancock declared in sending it forth to the various states, the ground and foundation of the government they were to erect for themselves, comprehending thereby whatever form it might become, whether that of an alliance of states which could be made effective by amendment or that of a more perfect union which would wholly dispossess its predecessor. It was therefore in Jefferson's view a profound misunderstanding of the nature of the American people and a narrowly legalistic conception of their union to insist that before 1787 their organic law was not in truth a constitution because it operated primarily upon states.

Yet, though that government was primarily a confederation of states, in Jefferson's conception it rested all its claims to power, in whatever degree of amplitude these existed, upon the ultimate foundation of the individual citizens, touching them in their most vital concerns and drawing its strength from their attachment. He was never likely to express himself in the dour words of William Maclay, who, goaded by Federalist declamation, ridiculed the description of the nation "under the old congress, as if neither wood grew nor water ran in America before the happy adoption of the new Constitution." Federalist rhetoric depended upon such an interpretation of history, and Beveridge made it the central theme in his analysis of Marshall. But what Jefferson had steadily in view was the nature of the journey on which the nation had embarked. He anticipated that forms of government would come and go, being changed as often and as drastically as changing circumstances required. The danger to be feared was not so much imperfection in the fabric as a failure in the people to discern the nature of the imperfection and to demand its remedy.

The post-war period is even yet occasionally characterized as one of such despotic democracy in the states as to threaten the continuation of the union. But Jefferson saw in these years no such fatal flaw as Marshall perceived. Hence there was no faltering in his faith as there was in the case of Marshall and many others. On the contrary, the evidences of turbulence and of protest were to him signs of a vigorous and alert people, and the only expression of disillusionment that escaped him was caused by the failure of the people to demand a bill of rights, an evidence of a degeneracy of spirit to which he had allowed four centuries instead of four years. His own acts in that period revealed the same optimistic confidence in the essential power of the national government, whatever its form, and in performing them he stretched to the limit Marshall's own later doctrine that the means are available when the end is legitimate.

In preparing the report on a money unit based on decimal notation, for example, he would have extended the same principle to measures, weights, and even to time had the disposition of others matched his own. His objective was dual, and consciously so. By committing the nation to a single and symmetrical system universally applicable to daily transactions, he would have reduced diversity to simplicity and at the same time this would have multiplied the bonds of union. In carrying out the new American diplomacy whose principles he had helped to formulate, he even went beyond the permissible bounds of delegated authority by proposing a treaty to make reciprocal all rights of citizenship of every sort whatsoever enjoyed by the nationals of the contracting states—a use of delegated powers that he conceded to be well beyond his own powers and even beyond those of the national government, but one on which he was willing to risk himself. The idea, prompted by a zeal to extend the sway of those principles of equality and justice to which the republic was committed, was beyond all hope of realization by his own or by other nations, though it was prophetic of the direction in which Europe would one day seem to move. But in the general and more practicable uses of the treaty power his intent and policy was to stretch that delegated authority to cover the deficiency of powers not granted, in so far as it could do so. "I own to you," he declared to John Adams in 1785, "that my wish to enter into treaties with the other powers of Europe arises more from a desire of bringing all our commerce under the jurisdiction of Congress, than from any other views." In closing his remarkably fruitful legislative career in 1784, Jefferson reported with simple accuracy that he had made Virginia's "just rights . . . and the cement of that union in which her happiness and security is bound up" the leading objects of his conduct.

In no particular is the validity of such an appraisal of Jefferson's aim made more explicit than in the most constructive single achievement of government under the Articles of Confederation—the creation of the national domain. For here, through his insistent effort to induce Virginia to surrender her vast western claim, Jefferson sought to employ the power of a state as he did in 1798 and at other times primarily to achieve a national purpose. No issue in the early period of American history sustains so clearly as this does the divergences between Marshall and Jefferson. Next to the people themselves and the spirit which animated them, land was the great resource on which all else pivoted, affecting with powerful immediacy the attitudes and indeed the livelihood of every citizen. It influenced directly or indirectly almost all of the great matters of policy that came before the government. The fundamental question, once the claims of individual states had been relinquished, was the manner in which this resource would be employed. The national domain contained immense potentialities for the union both disruptive and cohesive, and the choice depended in large measure upon the degree to which one's private interests were submerged in those of the public. On this issue Jefferson determined at the outset of his public career never to join those who engaged in speculative ventures to engross large tracts of land lest his private interests influence or impede his performance of public duty. This was an abnegation for the sake of an elevated concept of the role of legislator that was neither required by the political ethics of the day nor duplicated by any other of the leading figures of the nation. Though its relevance for a jurist was at least as great as for a legislator, Marshall found himself both as an individual and as an expounder of the law most often allied with those interests on which Jefferson had turned his back. The correctness of either course in a legal sense must be admitted. But by his deliberate rejection of the possibility of private gain because of his concern for a paramount public interest, Jefferson provided another measure of an attachment to the nation that transcended mere legality.

The disruptive forces springing out of this great resource existed in the removal of barriers to westward expansion, the devaluation of soldiers' land certificates, depleted state treasuries, the presence of a small number of men ready to take advantage of these facts by virtue of credit or ready capital accumulated in good part by profits on war contracts, the revival of the claims of such land companies as Vandalia, Illinois-Wabash, and Indiana to many millions of acres of land, and the newer combines of adventurers who wished to set up for themselves independent common-wealths along the great arc of the frontier extending from New Hampshire to Georgia. These and other factors produced a tangled web of politics in state and nation, thus making an interest in western lands induce some men to look to the national government for support, others to turn to state legislatures for realization of their hopes, and still others to seek the creation of their own separate sovereignties. The threat to the union was complicated by the fact that two states had actually been engaged in armed conflict over their territorial claims and similar outbreaks threatened in the case of others.

The cohesive force arising out of the western wastes exerted its strength most powerfully upon those who were still under the spell of revolutionary impulses. "The western world opens an amazing prospect as a national fund . . . equal to our debt," declared a Rhode Island nationalist. "As a source of future population and strength, it is a guarantee to our inde-pendence. As its inhabitants will be mostly cultivators of the soil, republi-canism looks to them as its guardians. When the states on the eastern shores . . . shall have become populous, rich and luxurious, and ready to yield their liberties into the hands of a tyrant, the gods of the mountains will save us." This was an echo of the spirit that inspired Jefferson's plan for the government of the national domain. As early as 1776 he had en-deavored to amend the proposed Articles of Confederation so that western lands could be "given freely to those who may be permitted to seat them" but that hope—not to be realized for a century—failed as his similar policy in 1784 was bound to fail, not because the need to meet the national debt was not pressing, or because there were no settlers eager to make the option, but because the need to make compromises with the land-specu-lating interests was more insistent.

The proponents of new republics on the western waters may have been inspired by dreams of great suzerainties for themselves and their families, but in support of their aims they employed the rhetoric and the justify-ing principles of the Declaration of Independence itself. Were these new sovereignties to be encouraged to set up such forms of government as would "seem most likely to effect their safety and happiness"? Much could be said for this on the score of both principle and expediency, and for a time Jefferson himself entertained the idea without being involved in the economic base out of which it arose. Or, since these areas lay within the territory ceded to the United States by the Treaty of Paris and were thus acquired by the common effort, were they to be regarded as colonial dependencies of the old confederation? This was by no means a new dilemma, for it lay at the center of the debate before the Revolution on the nature of the British empire. Neither extreme was desirable, and so realistic a statesman as Madison thought there was no middle ground between the two. Yet in this age of political experimentation Jefferson and his legislative colleagues proceeded to adopt such a middle doctrine. The new governments would be neither colonial dependencies nor independent sovereignties, but would progress from a temporary status of self-government to organic statehood and finally to full admission to the union on a plane of equality. This great legislative achievement of 1784 which gave to American federalism its distinctive cast, enabling it to expand westward across the continent and indeed into an indefinite future, was a formulation of policy for which no delegated authority could be found in the Articles of Confederation. "Congress," declared Madison in *The Federalist*, "have undertaken . . . to form new States, to erect temporary governments, to appoint officers for them, and to prescribe the conditions on which such States shall be admitted into the Confederacy. All this has been done . . . without the least color of constitutional authority. . . . The public interest, the necessity of the case, imposed upon them the task of overleaping their constitutional limits."

While this federative principle for an expanding domain of law and democracy became permanently imbedded in the Constitution, the sale of vast tracts of public lands to organized speculators and the substitution of territorial government administered by Congress for local self-government soon reversed two cardinal points in Jefferson's policy. "It seemed necessary," one delegate from Virginia wrote to Washington in explaining the Ordinance of 1787, "for the security of property among uninformed, and perhaps licentious people, as the greater part of those who go there are, that a strong-toned government should exist, and the rights of property be clearly defined." Thus, retaining for its own committees the right to appoint territorial officers and negotiating with the powerful land group that wished to acquire an extensive tract of public land, Congress for the first time placed in national legislation a prohibition against local statutes that would, "in any manner whatever, interfere with or affect private contracts, or engagements *bona fide*, and without fraud previously formed." Marshall and Washington were by no means alone in making *bona fide* engagements for the purchase of land claims of impecunious soldiers that would thus be protected against legislative whims by the guarantees of a strong-toned government. The substance of this guarantee was repeated a few weeks later in the Constitution, and in abbreviated language that allowed wide latitude for judicial construction. Thus the article that had so strong an appeal for Marshall and provided so powerful an instrument for the protection of corporate interests against state regulatory legislation of the nineteenth century traces its lineage from a policy for the national domain that was the exact reverse of Jefferson's. In that lineage is the opinion of Alexander Hamilton in 1796 which asserted that the act of the Georgia legislature revoking the Yazoo grants was "a contravention of the first principles of natural justice and social policy." Its full flowering came in the decision in *Fletcher* v. *Peck* in 1810. In that case Marshall, employing the legal fiction of an implied contract and the concept of property as a natural right, invalidated a state law as impairing the obligation of contracts even though the entire nation knew that the grant of land annulled by that law was based on fraud. But the interpretation of national policy on which this doctrine was grounded stems from forces creating the Ordinance of 1787, not from the opposing democratic spirit that Jefferson gave to that of 1784.

Thus in these formative years of the young nation and of his own career, Marshall took the path that led him to prefer order, stability, and a narrow application of those "principles of natural justice and social policy" in defense of property and contractual rights. Such a legalistic position involved no necessary antagonism to democratic policies, but the fact is that at the summit of his career Marshall came to fear the unsettling tendencies of the popular mind far more than he had in the beginning. This was not merely because nature and experience had prepared him for such apprehensions but also because he came more and more to associate republicanism in America with revolutionary excesses in France, to identify the spirit of change and innovation with "the fatal philosophy of the day," and to personify these in the figure of one he spoke of derisively as "the great Lama of the Mountain." Toward the end he felt that the nation could scarcely survive such tendencies. "The union has been prolonged thus far by miracles," he wrote to Joseph Story in 1832. "I fear they cannot continue."

Jefferson entertained no such fears. He steadily maintained the path of nationalism on which he had set out in the beginning, regarding this as being along the common highway that belonged not to this nation alone but to all men. The contest for the improvement of the condition of man was to him not merely an acceptance of the idea of change but also a commitment to the task of bringing change about. His was a realistic and a pragmatic experimentalism, and he saw with Bacon that improvement in the condition of society presupposed improvement in the mind of man. "To be really useful," he wrote in 1807, "we must keep pace with the state of society, and not dishearten it by attempts at what it's population, means, or occupations will fail in attempting." But nothing in the spirit of the American people gave him greater confidence in the vitality of the nation and the stability of its institutions than the spirit of innovation. When in 1784 he drafted a report sustaining the authority of the national government as final and conclusive in the most difficult role a federative body could perform—that of acting as arbiter between two states of the union in a matter of vital importance to both—it was quite characteristic that he should see the example as one of universal applicability. "Perhaps," he declared for the benefit of a European audience, "history cannot produce such another proof of the empire of reason and right in any part of the world as these new states now exhibit. Other nations have only been able to submit private contests to judiciary determination; but these new states have gone further. They have . . . by wise and just arrangements submitted the causes of Nations to be weighed in the scales of justice by a tribunal so constituted as to ensure the confidence of all parties and so supported by the rest of the Union as to secure the execution of it's decisions." The acquiescence in the federal determination of the jurisdictional claims of two states was by no means so submissive as Jefferson indicated, but even the exaggeration suggests that what he valued most was the innovative example in government set by the new world before the eyes of the old. This to him was evidence of a spirit in the people that had enabled them to achieve unprecedented heights in the development of their political institutions. The new federal constitution was a great new summit in this progressive experimentation, and Jefferson's own commitment to the revolutionary innovation it represented was reflected in the remarkable summation of American political inventiveness that an obscure New England merchant addressed to him in the autumn of 1789: "Our country," wrote John Brown Cutting, "has already credit among the enlighten'd for the first establishment of religious liberty, the first complete seperation of constitutional from legislative power, the creation of the first national judiciary that was ever impowered to decide not only doubtful points of *jurisprudence* but constitutional law, and likewise the first legitimate provision for amending the Constitution itself."

But it was not pride in American primacy in political experimentation that mattered. The significant meaning for Jefferson was that the merchant's observations came in the context of an inquiry concerning "the improvements that ought to be aimed at . . . in the manner of exercising elections." Should this be by voice or by ballot? Should any property be requisite for suffrage, and if so what kind and quantity? What number of electors could be safely allowed to gather on the same spot? Should feasts or refreshments given by candidates be allowed or prohibited? How induce "an universal attention of the electors at the time and place of election?" How constitute the best judiciary for determining that time and place? The inquiries, their author thought, might provide a "germ of reformation" much needed by the United States and be of great value thereafter to "the whole civiliz'd world." For Jefferson these acute observations and inquiries provided a profoundly reassuring evidence of the vitality of "the empire of reason and right" among the American people. The germ of reformation was to be nourished and fostered, for on this rested the best hope for the ultimate outcome of the contest.

The impulse toward reform and innovation was abhorrent to Marshall, but it was by no means original with Jefferson. "If men are not oblig'd to live in Caves and hollow trees, to eat Acorns, and go naked," asked Algernon Sidney in the seventeenth century, "why should they be forever oblig'd to continue under the same form of Government that their ancestors happen'd to set up in the time of their ignorance?" "We might as well require a man," echoed Jefferson in the nineteenth century, "to wear still the coat which fitted him when a boy as civilized society to remain forever under the regimen of their barbarous ancestors." But acceptance of change and unending effort to bring it about, disturbing as this was to Marshall, was far less reprehensible in his eyes than that concept which, late in life, he named first among the distinctive Jeffersonian principles. This was the political relativism that was as antipodal to the "fundamental principles of natural justice and social policy" to which Marshall gave allegiance as any political belief could possibly have been. It was, in his view, a substitution of the quicksand of a visionary philosophy for the bedrock of law.

This was the one political theory that Marshall, always ready to identify Jefferson's ideas with French revolutionary philosophy, could justifiably have labelled as derivative. Although his fundamental principles were fully matured long before he arrived in France, Jefferson did acquire there a doctrine of profoundly revolutionary potentialities, one capable in its logical extension not merely of unsettling the law of contracts but also of putting an end to every sort of social institution, including the state itself. The concept was suggested to him only a few weeks before he received the inquiries of the New England merchant, and he expounded it in what has been generally accepted as being in fact, as it was in form, only another letter in the unparalleled correspondence that he carried on with James Madison for nearly half a century. "The question whether one generation of men has a right to bind another," Jefferson wrote from Paris in 1789, ". . . is a question of such consequences as not only to merit decision, but place also among the fundamental principles of government. The course of reflection in which we are immersed here on the elementary principles of society has presented this question to my mind; and that no such obligation can be so transmitted I think very capable of proof. I set out on this ground, which I suppose to be self-evident, *that the earth belongs in usufruct to the living*: that the dead have neither powers nor rights over it. The portion occupied by any individual ceases to be his when himself ceases to be, and reverts to the society." Jefferson then developed his proof of the self-evident proposition and applied the principle first to the question of the massive national debt under which France labored. Would it not be wise and just, he asked, for that nation "to declare in the constitution they are forming, that neither the legislature, nor the nation itself, can validly contract more debt than they may pay within their own age," or within the limit of a single generation? This he thought would reduce the faculty of borrowing within its natural limits and would tend thereby to bridle the spirit of war. On similar ground he concluded that "no society can make a perpetual constitution, or even a perpetual law. The earth belongs always to the living generation. They may manage it, then, and what proceeds from it, as they please, during their usufruct."

In order that the point might not be lost, Jefferson spelled out the application. "This principle . . . is of very extensive application and consequences, in every country," he declared, "and most especially in France. It enters into the resolution of the questions whether the nation may change the descent of lands given antiently to the church, to hospitals, colleges, orders of chivalry, and otherwise in perpetuity? Whether they may abolish the charges and privileges attached on lands, including the whole catalogue ecclesiastical and feudal? It goes to hereditary offices, authorities and jurisdictions; to hereditary orders, distinctions and appellations; to perpetual monopolies in commerce, the arts and sciences; with a long train of et ceteras: and it renders the question of reimbursement a question of generosity and not of right." In sum, property rights were rights created by society, not rights falling under the protection of an indefinable natural justice. Property, as Sidney would have put it, was an appendage of liberty.

In one sense this disquisition was wholly uncharacteristic. Never before nor afterwards did Jefferson discourse at length and systematically upon an abstraction. The whole tenor of his vast correspondence, particularly that with Madison, is concerned with immediate realities in a world of practical politics. While the distinctive cast of his mind was such that he perceived universals in every situation great or small, his letters were almost always addressed to existing realities. The incongruity in this instance is explicable only on the assumption that, while in form directed to Madison, in substance the letter was addressed to those leaders of the National Assembly of France with whom Jefferson was in constant association. The disguised aim was necessary for a diplomat engaged in political consultations with leaders of the nation to which he was accredited. If the assumption is correct, the ostensible letter to Madison became a theory for liquidating the inherited burdens under which the French people found themselves encumbered in their struggle for freedom.

But in another and more important sense the concept was wholly in accord with the Jeffersonian position. It was one to which he recurred again and again throughout life, though he could anticipate Madison's observation that the philosophical truth was one that would take long to become "visible to the naked eye of the ordinary politician." He was prepared, too, to anticipate the obvious proposition that a tacit acquiescence in established constitutions and laws must "be inferred from the omission of an express revocation," otherwise organized society could scarcely continue to exist. Yet the need for a theory that would justify an assertion of sovereign right over any unjust legacy from the past—including such an improvident and fraudulent granting away of the public domain as Marshall was able to justify in *Fletcher* v. *Peck*—caused Jefferson to hold fast to the concept, though never again did he propose that it be incorporated in either fundamental or statute law. So modified in his own thinking and practice, the theory became only an extension, though a radical one, of his unending insistence upon the need for improvement and reformation in the condition of man. It was a generous, humane view of the rights of succeeding generations and it prepared Jefferson to anticipate with serenity, as few in his generation could have, the vast technological and scientific changes that lay in the future and the even more unsettling relativism in all domains of thought that came with these changes—including, of course, the shifting uncertainties in the realm of law. This was a philosophy that Marshall could never accept.

Marshall and Jefferson—kinsmen, products of the Virginia Piedmont, students of the law under George Wythe—became inexorable protagonists of two opposed views of man and society. Perhaps because of this similarity of background, each mistook the aim of the other. Marshall mistakenly thought Jefferson hostile to the idea of an independent judiciary, and believed this hostility to be in fact part of "a deep design to convert our government into a mere league of states." Jefferson thought that under Marshall the judiciary was "ever acting with noiseless foot and unalarming advance, gaining ground step by step, and . . . engulfing insidiously the special governments into the jaws of that which feeds them." These fears found reflection in words and in official acts, each man expressing his natural preference for the concerns that to him seemed most vital. Those dominant in the attitude of Marshall clustered about the rights of property and those that Jefferson placed first involved the rights of man. The dual portrait that Beveridge drew so eloquently and in such contrasting colors of a courageous nationalist defending the purity of the judiciary and the right of judicial review against a cunning and vindictive executive seeking to subvert the Constitution and return to the days of the Articles of Confederation should long ago have been discarded as a simple and inaccurate caricature. The image of Jefferson as a nationalist profoundly animated by the promises and professions of the new republic and as one who cherished the independence of the judiciary and its right of review has become clearly defined as a result of the work of modern scholars. The portrait of Marshall needs to be subjected to the same searching scrutiny, but the process has scarcely begun.

In his greatest decision Marshall voiced the view that the Constitution was intended to endure for ages to come and to be adaptable to the various crises of human affairs. But the whole tenor of his judicial thought was at variance with the philosophy thus expressed in his most viable and most enduring decision. Nothing is more surely demonstrable in the entire range of his decisions than his steady opposition to reformation, his intransigence in setting himself against the aspirations and needs of a growing people, his narrow interpretations of the broad grants of constitutional power in support of the confined interests of a special class. Imprisoned in his own allegiance to the Hamiltonian philosophy of government, Marshall thus becomes in the final analysis the strict constructionist, bound to the concepts of his own era. The rivets he employed to fasten in place what he regarded as the permanent elements of American constitutional law have in large part been replaced, and those he used to fix the role of the judiciary in the federal system would indubitably have been driven at their appointed time in any event. The partisan use of the judiciary that he feared under Jefferson was indeed an approximation of what had actually occurred under the first Federalist administrations. The glint of partisan prejudice was by no means absent from the Marshall court itself.

Jefferson's role thus becomes the opposite of that so long assigned him. Marshall's absolutes, including the concept of property as a natural right, have become less tenable and his figure has receded into the background. Jefferson's relativism, which embraced that feature of his thought that Marshall found most abhorrent, makes him seem at home in a wholly different age. But it was not Jefferson's conception of the changeableness of all laws and constitutions or even his persistent effort to promote conditions congenial to reformation that makes him enduringly relevant. It was rather the steadfast devotion with which he clung to his one absolute and gave it precedence over all others. "Nothing, then," he declared toward the end, "is unchangeable but the inherent and unalienable rights of man."

The significance of the implacable hostility between Marshall and Jefferson lies in the fact that, when one was Chief Justice and the other President, there came about the first elevated, informed discussion of the role of the judiciary. Marshall did not generate the profound and widespread resentment against partisan uses of the courts but neither did his decisions or his political attitudes tend to alleviate fears. The inflamed feeling that the judiciary should be brought to account for flagrant acts of partisanship might well have gone much further than it did. Amendments to the Constitution were proposed that would have altered the role of the judiciary permanently, and with it the nature of the federal government. That this first outburst did not so result speaks eloquently of a citizenry that could carry on a great public debate in the informed and responsible manner that befitted so vital an issue. It speaks quite as eloquently of restraint in the use of executive power—indeed of more than mere restraint. To Jefferson the most cherished element of the Constitution was the Bill of Rights. This had been flagrantly violated by the Alien and Sedition Acts, with the tame and at times eager acquiescence of the judiciary. This overarching threat to a free press and to the right of the opposition to be heard had in fact been largely responsible for bringing Jefferson from retirement to a position of power. Under his leadership the nation had been unified and the opposition had been given a mortal wound. His party was not merely triumphant but was clamoring for curbs to put an end to judicial partisanship. Another Chief Magistrate in such circumstances, under the influence of a monumental enmity existing between him and the Chief Justice, might well have reached for one of the weapons that Marshall thought Jefferson intended to use. But respect for the independence of the judiciary and an understanding of its importance in a government of checks and balances—these enduring convictions rather than personal animus guided Jefferson's hand in this first great crisis over the judiciary. But to the end of his days Marshall saw only the hand and purpose of malignity.

II

Free Government

2

Representative Equality:

"Political Thicket" or Voting Right?

Gordon E. Baker

There is not under our Constitution a judicial remedy for every politi-cal mischief, for every undesirable exercise of legislative power. The Framers carefully and with deliberate forethought refused so to enthrone the judiciary. In this situation, as in others of like nature, appeal for re-lief does not belong here. Appeal must be to an informed, civically mili-tant electorate. In a democratic society like ours, relief must come through an aroused popular conscience that sears the conscience of the people's representatives.

—Justice Felix Frankfurter *

It is ludicrous to preclude judicial relief when a mainspring of representa-tive government is impaired. Legislators have no immunity from the Constitution. The legislatures of our land should be made as responsive to the Constitution of the United States as are the citizens who elect the legislators.

—Federal District Judge J. Frank McLaughlin **

When the United States Supreme Court announced on March 26, 1962, its landmark decision in the apportionment case of *Baker* v. *Carr*,[1] it culminated a marked shift in American jurisprudence from the doctrine of judicial nonintervention argued by Mr. Justice Felix Frankfurter only sixteen years earlier in *Colegrove* v. *Green*.[2]

---

* Dissenting in *Baker* v. *Carr*, 369 U.S. 186, 270 (1962).
** *Dyer* v. *Kazuhisa Abe*, 138 F. Supp. 220, 224 (1956).
[1] 369 U.S. 186 (1962).
[2] 328 U.S. 549 (1946).

Termed by one scholar as probably the supreme tribunal's "most important decision since *Marbury* v. *Madison*," [3] the *Baker* case soon triggered a land-office business for state and federal courts in apportionment suits. Charles Rhyne, successful counsel for the urban plaintiffs in Tennessee, declared that "*Baker* v. *Carr* has had an impact like an earthquake. An impact far beyond even [our] most optimistic dreams. . . ." Summarizing the major events in a period of only five months after the Supreme Court's decision, Rhyne elaborated as follows:

1. Courts have directly or indirectly invalidated state law or constitutional apportionments of legislatures in whole or in part in 16 states. . . .
2. There are over 50 cases pending in 32 states with new cases being reported constantly.
3. Over 40 opinions have been rendered and many more orders have been signed by courts.
4. Eight legislatures have held special sessions to adopt new laws or proposed constitutional amendments.[4]

This is a remarkable list of consequences indeed for a ruling which cautiously avoided deciding on the merits and left many questions unanswered. What the Court actually held in *Baker* v. *Carr* was that the apportionment of seats in a state legislature is subject to the constitutional scrutiny of federal courts. In accepting jurisdiction of such cases, the high tribunal declared that allegations of a denial of equal protection must be determined by trial courts and that the right to such a proceeding "is within the reach of judicial protection under the Fourteenth Amendment." [5]

The obvious importance of the Supreme Court's decision, plus the unanswered questions it raised, stimulated an unusual amount of commentary.[6] Most of the serious analyses have concerned the consequences

---

[3] Ruth C. Silva, "Apportionment in New York, Part One: The Legal Aspects of Reapportionment and Redistricting: *Baker* v. *Carr*," 30 *Fordham Law Review* 581 (1962). Professor Silva explained that "While *Dred Scott*, the *Slaughter-House Cases*, and the segregation cases affected social relations, *Baker* v. *Carr* will affect the governmental power structure by shifting the balance of state legislative power from rural conservatives to city and suburban voters who tend to be sympathetic toward social change and governmental intervention."

[4] "An End to Government by Minority: The Reapportionment Results of *Baker* v. *Carr*," address before joint meeting of American Political Science Association and the National Municipal League, September 8, 1962, Washington, D.C. (mimeographed), 1, 4. Keeping abreast of the plethora of federal and state court decisions on apportionment following *Baker* v. *Carr* has been greatly facilitated by the National Municipal League, which undertook to reproduce by photo-offset all such opinions available. By the summer of 1963, only 15 months after the *Baker* ruling, five volumes of 66 court decisions had been released.

[5] 369 U.S. 186, 237 (1962).

[6] "The alarums and excursions that ensued in the legal-political world exceeded anything evoked by a Supreme Court decision since 1954, and memory would have to

and implications of the decision for future political development. As the outlines of judicial determination on apportionment cases emerge more clearly, the resulting analyses will inevitably focus on the political and legal ramifications involved. It is the purpose of this paper to go back of the apportionment decision of 1962 and try to explain the major developments which underlay it and account for the dramatic acceptance by the Supreme Court of a role which it had previously shunned.

THE CONCEPT OF REPRESENTATIVE EQUALITY

When this country was first settled, the apportionment of legislative seats was hardly a theory at all but rather a response to a practical situation. Representation in colonial America was originally based on localities regardless of their size or importance, a natural reflection of isolated, highly autonomous communities. Representation, initially regarded not as a right but as a duty, was often fulfilled with reluctance. By the time of separation from Great Britain, however, the basis of representation was shifting to population. As early as 1776 the right of every town to be represented was vigorously challenged in Massachusetts, where a constitutional convention brought forth the following pronouncement from the Essex county delegation:

> The rights of representation should be so equally and impartially distributed that the representatives should have the same views and interests with the people at large. They should think, feel, and act like them, and, in fine, should be an exact miniature of their constituents. They should be, if we may use the expression, the whole body-politic, with all its property, rights, and privileges, reduced to a smaller scale, every part being diminished in just proportion. . . . Let the representatives be apportioned among the respective counties, in proportion to their number of freemen.[7]

Similar protests arose in the other new states. Indicative of the growing democratic theory were the views of Thomas Jefferson, whose intense interest in the composition of state legislatures might well be ascribed to his unhappy experiences as Virginia's governor for a brief term during the Revolution. Writing in his *Notes on Virginia*, Jefferson specifically criticized the unequal apportionment of legislative seats: "Among those who share the representation, the shares are very unequal. Thus the county

---

reach back a good many years more to find another adequate comparison."—Robert G. McCloskey, "The Supreme Court, 1961 Term, Foreword: The Reapportionment Case," 76 *Harvard Law Review* 54–74 (1962). For other commentaries see, e.g., Paul T. David and Ralph Eisenberg, *State Legislative Redistricting: Major Issues in the Wake of Judicial Decision* (1962); "The Problem of Malapportionment: A Symposium on *Baker* v. *Carr*," 72 *Yale Law Journal* 7 (1962); Alpheus Thomas Mason, "Myth and Reality in Supreme Court Decisions," 48 *Virginia Law Review* 1385 (1962).

7 Quoted in Robert Luce, *Legislative Principles* (1930), p. 344.

of Warwick, with one-hundred fighting men, has an equal representation with the county of Loudon, which has one thousand seven hundred and forty-six. So that every man in Warwick has as much influence in the government as seventeen in Loudon." [8] Jefferson proposed a model constitution, with legislative representation in both houses based on the number of qualified electors.

That these views indicated a widespread consensus during the nation's formative years is revealed by the Northwest Ordinance of 1787, setting forth the framework for the future organization of state governments in the vast region beyond the Appalachian Mountains. The ordinance provided among its basic guarantees that the inhabitants of the new territory should always be entitled to "a proportionate representation of the people in the legislature." [9] Moreover, as the nation moved westward during the nineteenth century, Congressional statutes establishing new territories usually contained similar provisos of equal representation.

As new states were formed and the constitutions of older ones revised, legislative apportionment on a general population standard became widespread. In his dissenting opinion in *Baker* v. *Carr*, Justice Frankfurter insisted that representation proportionate to population "has never been generally practiced, today or in the past." [10] The best that can be said of this observation is that it is a gross exaggeration and oversimplification. It ignores the fact that most of the deviations in the nineteenth century were casual consequences rather than purposeful discrimination. It is true that some states, especially those with large areas and few inhabitants, took account of territory as well as people, but the inclusion of territorial units such as towns and counties often made little practical difference. Frontier conditions of isolation and poor communications furnished a rationale for representing each political unit. Also, counties were often given a minimum representation in the legislature, but such situations were typically more a matter of convenience and simplicity than of political philosophy. In any case, the deviations from population that did occur seemed to do little violence to the principle of representative equality when the distribution of a state's inhabitants was fairly equal and the number of counties comparatively few.

On the national level, the problem of representation caused the central debate at the federal convention of 1787 in Philadelphia. While James

---

[8] *The Writings of Thomas Jefferson* (Library Edition, 1903), II, 160–161. For a discussion of the role played by the issues of suffrage and representation in state constitutional reform in the latter eighteenth and early nineteenth centuries, see Alpheus Thomas Mason and Richard H. Leach, *In Quest of Freedom: American Political Thought and Practice* (1959), Chap. 9.

[9] 1 Stat. 50–2 (1787): *An Act to Provide for the Government of the Territory Northwest of the River Ohio.*

[10] 369 U.S. 186, 310 (1962).

Madison, James Wilson, Edmund Randolph, and others, vigorously asserted that representation in accordance with numbers was the only truly republican principle, and while such a proposal for both houses of Congress actually received a favorable vote at one point, adamant opposition from the smaller states forced the famous compromise. In Number 62 of *The Federalist*, Madison emphasized that the arrangement was a result of concession and necessity rather than theory, and added almost apologetically:

A government founded on principles more consonant to the wishes of the larger States, is not likely to be obtained from the smaller States. The only option, then, for the former, lies between the proposed government and a government still more objectionable. Under this alternative, the advice of prudence must be to embrace the lesser evil.[11]

At the same time, the convention took several steps, including provisions for a federal census and for ultimate federal regulation of Congressional elections, to insure that the House of Representatives be, in George Mason's words "the grand depository of the democratic principle of the government." [12]

Throughout the nineteenth century the general trend of political thought continued in the direction of political equality. While the practice—both in Congressional and state legislative districts—frequently fell short of the prevailing ideal, most of the significant inequalities were random and accidental rather than calculated. Also, while the young nation was growing westward, with an ever mobile population, both the Congress and state legislatures could circumvent major political frictions by simply adding more legislative seats to accommodate increasing population and land area. This usually avoided the necessity of disturbing incumbents by taking representation away from older, declining districts.

By the beginning of the twentieth century, however, a distrust of growing cities led to restrictions on urban power in many states—often in the form of constitutional modifications. Moreover, many legislative bodies had reached their maximum or optimum sizes, so that any redistricting to reflect population changes would involve internal redistributions of strength directly affecting numerous lawmakers as well as communities of interest. As a consequence, legislatures became increasingly reluctant to carry out periodic reapportionment. Thus the political crisis over the doctrine of representative equality has developed in large part during the twentieth century. Each successive decade has ushered in new population configurations, particularly the accelerating growth of urbanism and the

[11] As quoted and discussed by Robert B. McKay, *Reapportionment and the Federal Analogy* (1962), pp. 5–6.

[12] Quoted in Joel Francis Paschal, "The House of Representatives: 'Grand Depository of the Democratic Principle'?," 17 *Law and Contemporary Problems* 277 (1952).

resulting metropolitan problems which seemed increasingly less adaptable to the traditional pattern of politics carried over from a different era.[13]

THE DOCTRINE OF JUDICIAL NONINTERVENTION

In view of America's tradition of written constitutions and judicial review, it is not surprising that attempts to implement more equitable representation have frequently taken the form of appeals to the judiciary. At the state level, courts have long exercised jurisdiction to pass upon the validity of reapportionment acts of legislatures. Such suits have frequently produced eloquent assertions of democratic ideals. For example, in 1907 the Kentucky supreme court proclaimed:

> Equality of representation is a vital principle of democracy. . . . Without equality, Republican institutions are impossible. Inequality of representation is a tyranny to which no people worthy of Freedom will tamely submit. To say that a man in Spencer County shall have seven times as much influence in the government of the state as a man in Ohio, Butler, or Edmonson, is to say that six men out of every seven in those counties are not represented in the government at all. They are required to submit to taxation without representation.[14]

In spite of such stirring declarations, state courts limited themselves to striking down only the grosser malapportionments, but this merely perpetuated the prior (and usually even less equitable) districting pattern.[15] State courts uniformly interpreted the doctrine of separation of powers as prohibiting any attempt by the judiciary to prod legislatures into positive action. Even when holding reapportionment to be a clear and mandatory legislative duty, state tribunals typically concluded with the futile suggestion that "the people have no remedy save to elect a General Assembly which will perform that duty." [16] Judges did not explain how an underrepresented majority of the electorate could hold a recalcitrant legislature accountable. Since representative inequality generally stemmed from either legislative inaction or constitutional formulas, the negative judicial role was of little avail.

Failing state remedies, some underrepresented interests turned to the federal courts by asserting rights under the United States Constitution. For example, in 1931 a federal appeals court denied the claim of a Chicago resident that the United States government had failed to guarantee a republican (*i.e.*, representative) form of government in Illinois.[17]

[13] See E. E. Schattschneider, "Urbanization and Reapportionment," 72 *Yale Law Journal* 7 (1962).
[14] Quoted in James E. Larson, *Reapportionment and the Courts* (1962), 13.
[15] See V. O. Key, Jr., "Procedures in State Legislative Apportionment," 26 *American Political Science Review* 1050–1058 (1932).
[16] *Fergus* v. *Kinney*, 333 Illinois 437 (1928).
[17] *Keogh* v. *Neeley*, 20 Fed. (2d) 685 (1931).

At the Congressional level, representation was redistributed among the states by Congress after each census during the nineteenth century, with the more vexing problems of shifting power from some states largely avoided by periodically increasing the size of the House of Representatives.[18] The first and only time Congress failed to reallocate its own seats occurred after the census of 1920, by which time the maximum size of 435 for the House had been fixed. No attempt was made to challenge in federal courts this Congressional failure to carry out its expected duty of reapportionment.[19] However, the increasing political conflicts over Congressional power in the twentieth century did result in several suits challenging the *districting* for the House of Representatives by the state legislatures, with jurisdiction accepted by federal courts.[20]

The major source of representative inequality for the lower house of Congress, however, was not state action in creating districts of disparate size. Rather, it stemmed from the lengthy failure of some state legislatures to revise district lines in accordance with population shifts, thus permitting the growth of "silent gerrymanders." This issue finally arrived in a judicial forum when Professor Kenneth Colegrove, a political scientist at Northwestern University, and other urban residents of Illinois, sued their governor, Dwight Green. This state's Congressional districts had remained unchanged since 1901. The appellants resided in districts which contained populations as large as 914,053, as of the 1940 census, compared with the least populous district (downstate) of only 112,116. Colegrove contended that his vote was diluted by sharing it with so many others and was worth proportionately far less than that of a voter in the less populous districts. He and his fellow petitioners sought relief in federal courts by invoking various acts of Congress, the requirements of Article I, Section 2 of the United States Constitution, plus the Fourteenth Amendment's guarantees of due process and equal protection of the laws. Plaintiffs asked the courts to declare existing districts invalid and to bar their use by state officials. The result of the injunction sought would have been an at-large election of the 26 Congressmen from Illinois until the state legislature enacted a constitutional apportionment act.

After hearing arguments in this case—*Colegrove* v. *Green*—the Supreme Court announced its decision on June 10, 1946. The Court was not only closely divided, but not at full strength. (Chief Justice Harlan F. Stone had died between the argument and decision day, and Justice Robert

---

[18] Emanuel Celler, "Congressional Apportionment—Past, Present, and Future," 17 *Law and Contemporary Problems* 270–271 (1952).

[19] "It never occurred to anyone that this Court could issue mandamus to compel Congress to perform its mandatory duty to apportion."—Justice Frankfurter, in *Colegrove* v. *Green*, 328 U.S. 549, 555 (1946).

[20] E.g., *Ohio ex rel. Davis* v. *Hildebrant*, 241 U.S. 565 (1916); *Carroll* v. *Becker*, 285 U.S. 380 (1932); *Smiley* v. *Holm*, 285 U.S. 355 (1932).

H. Jackson was representing the United States at the Nuremberg war trials.) Justice Frankfurter wrote the prevailing opinion, joined by Justices Stanley F. Reed and Harold H. Burton, denying the relief sought. Declaring that the situation presented was not a matter for judicial determination, Frankfurter asserted that "the remedy for unfairness in districting is to secure State legislatures that will apportion properly, or to invoke the ample powers of Congress." [21] In Frankfurter's view, the case was of a "peculiarly political nature" and it would be "hostile to a democratic system to involve the judiciary in the politics of the people." [22] Finally, in a much-quoted phrase, Frankfurter warned that "Courts ought not to enter this political thicket." [23]

Balancing this three-justice view expressed by Frankfurter was a dissenting opinion written by Mr. Justice Hugo Black for himself and Justices William O. Douglas and Frank Murphy. The dissent insisted that the Fourteenth Amendment's equal protection clause, plus Article I of the Constitution, forbad states from the kind of discrimination in political weight found in Illinois' Congressional districts. "What is involved here is the right to vote . . .," [24] Black insisted. A state, he added, would not be permitted to select one group of citizens and deny them the vote altogether, or to allot expressly a half-vote to some citizens and a full vote to others. Yet grossly unequal apportionments have the same effect. It was a mere "play upon words," the dissenters continued, to term such a controversy "political" in the sense that "courts have nothing to do with protecting and vindicating the right of a voter to cast an effective ballot." [25]

The deciding vote in the *Colegrove* case was cast by Mr. Justice Wiley Rutledge, who felt the issues were judiciable according to precedent, but who would dismiss the suit for want of equity. Expressing no opinion on the merits of the constitutional issue, Rutledge wished the Court to decline an exercise of its jurisdiction due to: the proximity of the forthcoming Congressional election; the undesirability of at-large elections; and the delicate relationships with Congress and the states which might stem from the Court's intervening at that time.

It is remarkable that a case evoking such a variety of opinions from a closely divided and undermanned Supreme Court so readily assumed the role of precedent for the doctrine of judicial nonintervention in legislative apportionment. In a number of one-line *per curiam* decisions after *Colegrove* v. *Green*, the Court refused to review other attacks on un-

---

[21] 328 U.S. 549, 556 (1946).
[22] *Ibid.*, pp. 553–554.
[23] *Ibid.*, p. 556.
[24] *Ibid.*, p. 574.
[25] *Ibid.*, p. 573.

representative legislatures, with *Colegrove* as the leading authority cited.[26]
Two subsequent cases on separate but closely related issues are also of
interest. In 1948 the Court, in a *per curiam* opinion, affirmed dismissal
of a suit by the Progressive Party, which contended that it had been denied a place on the Illinois general election ballot through state laws so
stringent and discriminatory as to violate the Fourteenth Amendment.
The party had gathered 75,000 signatures on petitions, three times the
number needed to qualify, but had failed to obtain at least 200 in each
of 50 counties. The Court's opinion did not hesitate as to judiciability
and went to the merits: "To assume that political power is a function
exclusively of numbers is to disregard the practicalities of government." [27]
Citing *Colegrove* v. *Green,* the Court's majority insisted that a state
could constitutionally "assure a proper diffusion of political initiative as
between its thinly populated counties and those having concentrated
masses, in view of the fact that the latter have practical opportunities
for exerting their political weight at the polls not available to the
former." [28]

This statement of judicial philosophy reveals a clear-cut value preference
and an amazing turnabout from the Court's earlier professed reluctance
to discuss the merits of weighing geographic interests versus population
equality. Two years later, another rebuff to advocates of representative
equality ocurred when *South* v. *Peters* sustained the Georgia county unit
system, which carried over inequalities in the legislature to the statewide
and Congressional primary elections. With citations to both the *Colegrove*
and *MacDougall* cases, the Supreme Court refused to exercise its equity
powers in a case "posing political issues arising from a state's geographic
distribution of electoral strength among its political sub-divisions." [29]

By the early 1950's, then, the doctrine of judicial noninvolvement in
questions concerning the representative character of political institutions
seemed established. The precedent was far from clear-cut, for there was
a lack of consistency by the high Court on questions of judiciability and
merits, while on the constitutional issues the justices remained divided,

[26] For a good summary and discussion of these cases, see Stanley Friedelbaum, *"Baker
v. Carr:* The New Doctrine of Judicial Intervention and Its Implications for American
Federalism," 29 *University of Chicago Law Review* 680–684 (1962).

[27] *MacDougall* v. *Green,* 335 U.S. 281, 283 (1948). The five-man majority elaborated: "thus the Constitution protects the interests of the smaller against the greater
by giving in the Senate entirely unequal representation to population." This "Federal
analogy" met objection by Douglas in a dissent (joined by Black and Murphy) which
cited Federalist Number 62 as to the reasons for the composition of the Senate and
their inapplicability to other levels.—*Ibid.* pp. 289–290. Rutledge concurred because
of the immediacy of the election (only 12 days away) but expressed no opinion as to
the substantive issues.

[28] *Ibid.,* p. 284.

[29] *South* v. *Peters,* 339 U.S. 276, 277 (1950). Douglas and Black dissented. This
decision was reversed *sub silentio* in the Spring of 1963. See note 58 below.

with enough dissenting and concurring opinions on the record to furnish ammunition for any future change of direction. But such an eventuality seemed either unlikely or very distant. Yet by 1962 the *Baker* case revealed a clear-cut shift to a role of judicial activism. What accounts for such a reversal? The significant landmarks that offer some explanation are discussed in the next section.

THE PATH LEADING TO BAKER v. CARR

Any attempt to trace the Supreme Court's willingness to enter the "political thicket" of legislative representation can conveniently begin with a judicial decision on quite a different subject matter—the school segregation decisions of May 17, 1954.[30] While there was hardly even an indirect relationship between this issue and that of representative equality [31] the 1954 segregation decisions signalled a willingness by the supreme tribunal to take a more positive role in the American governmental system. Within a few years the Court's new boldness had manifested itself in several areas, as the justices made it clear that they were willing to take a fresh look at matters that they had previously avoided with caution.[32] "The most ambitious assertions of judicial power," one astute scholar recounted in 1962, "came over the past half-decade and were strengthened by the assumption that the precedential value of *Colegrove*, never firmly rooted, was being undermined sub silentio by the Court itself in a continuing re-definition of equal protection." [33]

If this judicial expansion of equal protection continued, could it for long avoid a re-examination of unequal voting power via representative institutions? The answer was not long in coming. Only two years after the segregation decisions of 1954 a federal district court in Hawaii took the first step away from the doctrine of judicial noninvolvement. There, some residents of Oahu brought a suit contending that the failure of Hawaii's territorial legislature to reapportion since 1901, despite provisions of the Organic Act, deprived them of the equal protection of the laws guaranteed by the Act, and of due process of law guaranteed by the federal

[30] See, e.g., *Brown v. Board of Education*, 347 U.S. 483 (1954); *Bolling v. Sharpe*, 347 U.S. 497 (1954).

[31] However, Justices Black and Douglas had already drawn occasional though general parallels to the race issue. In his *Colegrove* dissent, Black made some analogies between diluted representation and prior Negro voting cases. See 328 U.S. 549, 572–574 (1946). And in *South v. Peters*, Douglas' dissent asserted that Georgia's county unit system resulted in a special discrimination against Negroes, since they had achieved a greater degree of suffrage in the populous counties with less political weight. See 339 U.S. 276, 278 (1950).

[32] See Alpheus Thomas Mason, *The Supreme Court from Taft to Warren* (1958), pp. 3–4.

[33] Friedelbaum, *loc. cit.*, p. 684.

Fifth Amendment. Petitioners sought an injunction to require an election of legislators at large until a proper reapportionment took place.

While recognizing that the judiciary had uniformly refused effective redress to voters because of reluctance to interfere with the legislature, the district court in Hawaii insisted that "this is merely an easy way out of a difficult problem." [34] The court denied a motion to dismiss the complaint, and called for a broader ground as a basis for its action than the special nature of territorial-federal relations. Stressing the recent segregation decisions, District Court Judge J. Frank McLaughlin asserted: "A classification which discriminates geographically has the same result. It deprives a citizen of his constitutional rights. Reasons of delicacy should no longer stay the judicial hand. . . . Any distinction between racial and geographic discrimination is artificial and unrealistic; both should be abolished." [35] Finally, the opinion concluded with a stirring plea for judicial activism:

> The time has come, and the Supreme Court has marked the way, when serious consideration should be given to a reversal of the traditional reluctance of judicial intervention in legislative reapportionment. The whole thrust of today's legal climate is to end unconstitutional discrimination.[36]

As for the decision itself, the threatened at-large election for the territory of Hawaii was circumvented when Congress passed an amendment to the Organic Act, specifying new districts, shifting the duty of reapportionment to the governor, and providing for court enforcement.

While the Hawaii case was remarkable for both its decision and its *obiter dicta*, and possibly indicated a shift in judicial thinking, its value as a precedent for state and Congressional districting was less clear. Late in 1956 a Federal District Court in Alabama held *Dyer* v. *Kazuhisa Abe* inapplicable to state legislative apportionment, since that case had involved the application of a Congressional law (Organic Act) to a territorial government. No comparable federal statute applies to state legislatures.[37] This meant that such suits would inevitably have to rest on the Fourteenth Amendment's equal protection clause, not relevant in the Hawaii case.

By this time, groups in several states were organizing legal attacks on legislative malapportionment on both state and federal grounds. Of these, the first promising result occurred in Minnesota, where several voters challenged their legislature's refusal to reapportion since 1913. Contending that their federally-guaranteed rights had been violated, petitioners asked a federal district court to require at-large elections for state legislators in

---

34 *Dyer* v. *Kazuhisa Abe*, 138 F. Supp. 220, 224 (1956).
35 *Ibid.*, p. 236.
36 *Ibid.*
37 See Larson, *Reapportionment and the Courts*, p. 23.

the primary and general elections of 1958. Here as elsewhere, plaintiffs called attention to the recent school desegregation decisions for indirect support. At least as important as equality of education, went the argument, is an equal share of legislative representation. The brief for the plaintiffs insisted that a basic civil right was involved, for "free and equal elections are the very cornerstone of our democratic society from which all other benefits flow, one of which is public education." [38]

The District Court in Minnesota accepted jurisdiction, and in denying motions to dismiss, cited a lengthy excerpt from the recent Hawaii opinion. Moreover, the court acknowledged the factual data documenting the growth of representative inequality over a period of 45 years of failure by the Minnesota legislature to reapportion. But in a bold and imaginative stroke, the federal court postponed a decision on the merits until the legislature had one more opportunity to deal with the problem and fulfill its "unmistakable duty." While thus professing restraint where recourse to state action was possible, the potential threat of an order for at-large elections remained:

> Early in January 1959 the 61st session of the Minnesota legislature will convene, all of the members of which will be newly elected on November 4th of this year. The facts which have been presented to us will be available to them. It is not to be presumed that the legislature will refuse to take such action as is necessary to comply with its duty under the state constitution. We defer decision on all the issues presented (including that of the power of this court to grant relief) in order to afford the legislature full opportunity to "heed the constitutional mandate to redistrict." [39]

The court added that any judicial disruption of the current apportionment or election machinery should be avoided "unless and until it can be shown that the legislature . . . has advisedly and deliberately failed and refused to perform its constitutional duty to redistrict the state." [40]

Since the Federal District Court retained jurisdiction, the Minnesota legislature could hardly escape serious concern about the consequences of any further failure to reapportion. The lawmakers struggled with the issue for nearly four months of the regular 1959 session and another seven weeks in special session before finally passing Minnesota's first redistricting of the state legislature in 46 years. Though many of the new districts still fell short of the population basis stipulated by the state constitution, the new pattern was a substantial improvement over the former one. The populous five-county Twin City metropolitan area won twelve new house and five new senate seats, plus fractions of another in each house.[41]

[38] Quoted in *ibid.*, p. 25.
[39] *Magraw* v. *Donovan*, 163 F. Supp. 181, 187 (1958) [quoting *Smith* v. *Holm*, 220 Minn. 486 (1945)].
[40] *Ibid.*
[41] See Gordon E. Baker, *State Constitutions: Reapportionment* (1960) pp. 54–55.

The Minnesota case gave immediate hope and encouragement to groups seeking more representative legislatures in other states, though other federal courts did not at once follow this example. Late in 1959, a three-judge federal district court in Tennessee dismissed a similar suit, relying heavily on *Colegrove* v. *Green,* and concluding that "federal courts, whether from a lack of jurisdiction or from inappropriateness of the subject matter for judicial consideration, will not intervene in cases of this type to compel legislative apportionment." [42] This case—*Baker* v. *Carr*—was then appealed to the United States Supreme Court and in March of 1962 made judicial history.

There are interesting similarities in the situations in the Minnesota and Tennessee reapportionment suits which made them both choice prospects for continuing the judicial break-through. The state constitutions required a population basis for both legislative houses (only slightly modified in Tennessee). Both states operated under extremely dated apportionments (1901 and 1913) reflecting totally different political ecologies from the late 1950's. In each case state courts had denied relief, while condemning the legislature's failure to conform to its constitutional mandate.[43] No alternative sources of change, such as the initiative process, were available. Consequently, in the words of a Tennessee district court judge, "if there is no judicial remedy there would appear to be no remedy at all." [44] Had the Federal district court in Minnesota denied any relief instead of prodding the state legislature into action, the course of subsequent judicial development would probably have differed in one interesting respect. Since an appeal would presumably have reached the United States Supreme Court before the Tennessee case, the "landmark apportionment decision" would have been the Minnesota case of *Magraw* v. *Donovan* instead of *Baker* v. *Carr.*

There remains one final turning point on the path to the Court's announcement in the *Baker* case. As has been indicated so far, the segregation decisions of 1954 played an indirect role in the willingness of courts to re-examine the doctrine of judicial noninvolvement in legislative apportionment suits. The opinion in the Hawaii case questioned any distinction between racial and geographic discrimination. Then, in 1960, the United States Supreme Court heard a case which combined both racial discrimination *and* a geographic gerrymander. *Gomillion* v. *Lightfoot* challenged an action by the Alabama legislature in redrawing the city boundaries for Tuskegee, where Negro voting potential was growing sufficiently strong to perturb the ruling white minority. The result was a strangely irregular 28-sided figure which removed from the former city all

---

[42] *Baker* v. *Carr,* 179 F. Supp. 824, 826 (1959).
[43] See, e.g., *Kidd* v. *McCanless,* 200 Tenn. 273 (1956); *Smith* v. *Holm,* 220 Minn. 486 (1945).
[44] Quoted in Larson, *Reapportionment and the Courts,* p. 30.

but four or five of the 400 Negro voters, while not disturbing a single white voter or resident. Lower courts had upheld the state's action on the basis of long-established precedents allowing state governments to change boundaries of its political subdivisions without consent of the inhabitants or judicial inquiry into legislative motives.

In October of 1960 the United States Supreme Court heard oral arguments on the *Gomillion* case. It was already clear that the possible application of *Colegrove* v. *Green* would arise. A perceptive observer in the Court's chambers reported the following scene:

> Justice Black set the stage with a couple of soft-spoken, easygoing queries. . . . Then his demeanor changed as he leaned forward and demanded, "Well, what do you do about Colegrove? Are you asking us to overrule Colegrove?" A thin smile appeared on Justice Douglas's lips. Down the bench, Justice Frankfurter put his hands over his eyes, as if suddenly weary.[45]

"In his endeavor to tiptoe past Colegrove," continued this commentator, the plaintiff's attorney "was suavely assisted by Justice Frankfurter, who, it had begun to appear, was also concerned with keeping the two issues separate. One had the sense that complicated strategies were involved—for the justices as well as for the attorneys." [46]

For a variety of reasons, it was unlikely from the outset that the Supreme Court would uphold so obvious a racial discrimination as the Tuskegee gerrymander. The consequences of doing so would have been a set-back in the general judicial stand against segregation. Moreover, allowing a state the freedom to gerrymander city boundaries would doubtless encourage some southern states to avoid school integration by gerrymandering school districts along racial lines.[47]

A unanimous Supreme Court reversed the lower courts and thus killed the Tuskegee gerrymander. The Court's opinion was written by Justice Frankfurter, who took great pains to distinguish the case from the *Colegrove* decision: "While in form this is merely an act redefining metes and bounds, if the allegations are established, the inescapable human effect of this essay in geometry and geography is to despoil colored citizens, and only colored citizens, of their theretofore enjoyed voting rights. That was not *Colegrove* v. *Green*." [48] While the Court elaborated distinctions between the racial gerrymander at hand and earlier districting cases, it

---

[45] Bernard Taper, *Gomillion* v. *Lightfoot* (1962), p. 92. This author also reports later speculation by an Assistant Solicitor General that Black and Douglas "by their sharp questioning had been attempting to broaden the issue beyond the racial question, so as to use the case as a wedge for breaching the entire judicial blockade against discussion of gerrymanders."—*Ibid.*, p. 108.

[46] *Ibid.*, p. 93.

[47] See Jo Desha Lucas, "Dragon in the Thicket: A Perusal of *Gomillion* v. *Lightfoot*," *The Supreme Court Review*, 1961 (1961), p. 242.

[48] *Gomillion* v. *Lightfoot*, 364 U.S. 339, 347 (1960).

did little to clarify some of the unresolved questions posed by the past cases. Instead, as Professor Jo Desha Lucas has pointed out, "the Court proceeded to make unintelligible that which had been merely obscure." [49]

The attempt to distinguish *Gomillion* from any prospective challenge to geographic malapportionment may help explain Frankfurter's use of the Fifteenth rather than the Fourteenth Amendment in striking down the Tuskegee gerrymander. This neatly confined the issue to racial restrictions on the right to vote. Yet this poses obvious problems. While the Court referred to "the right to vote in municipal elections," [50] what does this mean? What right does a citizen have to be included in any particular governmental subdivision? Negro voters excluded from Tuskegee still retained their franchise in county, state and national elections. Frankfurter's reasoning adds up to what Professor Lucas has termed the "vested" vote concept—"Petitioners were entitled to four votes; now they are entitled to three. Four minus three equals one. They have lost a vote." [51] This kind of problem was avoided by Justice Charles E. Whittaker, whose concurrence would base the Court's decision on the Fourteenth Amendment's equal protection clause, on the grounds that Alabama's action in "fencing Negroes out" of Tuskegee was an unlawful segregation of races; but he felt it was not a violation of the Fifteenth Amendment so long as the Negro voters enjoyed the same voting privileges as all other citizens in whatever geographic subdivision they found themselves. Whittaker added that this basis would still not involve the *Colegrove* problem.[52]

While Justice Frankfurter carefully tried to avoid any possible extension of the Tuskegee decision to other types of gerrymanders, the attention he paid to *Colegrove*, plus the pointed questions by members of the Court during the arguments on *Gomillion*, indicated that the issue was a difficult one to submerge. Moreover, only three members of the Court—Frankfurter, Black, and Douglas—had participated in *Colegrove* and subsequent cases concerned with representative equality. By this time, all nine justices were undoubtedly aware of the increasing frequency of apportionment cases in the lower courts, not to mention the diversity of their disposition. Only a week after deciding *Gomillion* v. *Lightfoot*, the supreme tribunal agreed to review the Federal district court decision in *Baker* v. *Carr*.[53]

This brief survey has suggested the main judicial landmarks charting

[49] Lucas, *loc. cit.*, pp. 232 ff. for elaboration.
[50] 364 U.S. 339, 341 (1960).
[51] Lucas, *loc. cit.*, p. 210.
[52] 364 U.S. 339, 349 (1960). Douglas also concurred separately with the Court's opinion, but recorded his adherence to former dissents in *Colegrove* v. *Green* and *South* v. *Peters*.
[53] 364 U.S. 898 (1960).

the path from the *Colegrove* doctrine of judicial noninvolvement to the more active role for the courts ushered in by *Baker* v. *Carr*. The handful of decisions mentioned in no sense comprises a direct line of precedent, but rather indicates a subtle shift in judicial mood. This reappraisal in turn rested upon a more general ferment in society. The period between the *Colegrove* and *Baker* cases—1946 to 1962—was one of monumental population change. The older patterns of rural-urban America disappeared and new configurations took their place. In particular, the mushrooming spread of suburbia introduced a fresh ecological development, and the swift rise of a new geographic minority to feel the impact of legislative malapportionment.[54] Moreover, the changing needs of public policy focused greater attention on those institutions of government responsible for decisions. In the words of one astute writer:

> The effects of malapportionment are much graver today than they were a century ago. In a day when the federal government subsisted primarily on tariff revenues, unequal representation could be regarded as an insignificant evil; government itself had a less significant impact on society. But when the federal and state governments spend a third of the national income, when they are relied upon to regulate every aspect of a complex industrial civilization, the consequences of unequal representation are correspondingly more severe. The rapid growth of our population and change in its character make even more urgent the need for regular, equitable adjustment of representation.[55]

Finally, representative inequality had become progressively greater in most states, with little prospect of improvement by so-called political channels. In 1961, while the Tennessee apportionment suit was under review by the United States Supreme Court, Professors Paul T. David and Ralph Eisenberg published a comprehensive statistical study on the changes during the twentieth century in the relative representative power patterns within all states. They found that while the inequities a half century earlier were relatively modest, they had become increasingly severe with the passage of time. By 1960, residents of small counties (under 25,000) had—on a national average—well over double the weight of voters in the medium-sized and largest urban and suburban counties.[56]

[54] See, e.g., Andrew Hacker, *Congressional Districting: The Issue of Equal Representation* (1963), pp. 105–112.

[55] Anthony Lewis, "Legislative Apportionment and the Federal Courts," 71 *Harvard Law Review* 1095–1096 (1958). Lewis, *New York Times* writer who won a Pulitzer Prize in 1963 for his coverage of the Supreme Court, wrote this article while a Nieman Fellow at Harvard University. He makes a complete survey of both the general literature and judicial precedents on legislative apportionment and argues persuasively for judicial intervention as the only realistic remedy for inequitable representation. It is not unlikely that this article in itself played a role in judicial reappraisal, as it was cited in several opinions, including *Baker* v. *Carr*.

[56] Paul T. David and Ralph Eisenberg, *Devaluation of the Urban and Suburban Vote* (1961), pp. 7–10.

These findings were made available to counsel for plaintiffs while the *Baker* case was on appeal, and, at its request, to the library of the United States Supreme Court.[57]

All of these considerations furnish a contextual background for the judicial willingness to hear challenges to alleged malapportionments. The Supreme Court's own membership had changed markedly in the period discussed above. At the same time, the supreme tribunal's conception of its own role in the governmental system had undergone a pronounced shift since the halcyon quiescense which, in the late 1940's and early 1950's had characterized the Vinson Court.

CONCLUSIONS

The decision of the Supreme Court in *Baker* v. *Carr* did not end the debate over the principle of representative equality. In focusing on matters of judiciability and jurisdiction, the Court left many questions for future developments to resolve. During the following term, the justices decided only one case as a direct consequence of the 1962 decision. By an eight to one vote, the Court on March 18, 1963, struck down the Georgia county unit system (with no mention, incidentally, of *South* v. *Peters!*).[58] A few months later, prior to summer adjournment, the Court agreed to hear arguments during the next term on several cases, some involving Congressional districting, others on state cases resolved by lower courts in different ways. On February 17, 1964, the high tribunal disposed of the Congressional cases. In a decision (*Wesberry* v. *Sanders*) certain to have a major impact on the future make-up of the House of Representatives, the Supreme Court, dividing six to three, held that "as nearly as is practicable one man's vote in a Congressional election must be worth as much as another's." [59] Population disparities of over three to one among Georgia's districts were held to violate Article I of the Constitution. But in another case decided the same day, the Court refused to enter the real "political thicket" posed by a charge of partisan and ethnic gerrymandering in New York City's Congressional districts, which were reasonably equal in population. It seemed likely that state and federal courts could be involved in apportionment litigation for many years.

While it is difficult to predict the precise future direction of judicial action on various questions of representation and apportionment, one conclusion does seem clear. The doctrine of judicial noninvolvement expounded so eloquently by Justice Frankfurter is not likely to be revived. Frankfurter's lengthy and elaborate dissent in *Baker* v. *Carr* might well

[57] Letter to author from Paul T. David.
[58] *Gray* v. *Sanders*, 9 L. ed. 2nd. 821 (March 18, 1963).
[59] Quoted in *The New York Times*, February 18, 1964, p. 31.

be considered as his valedictory from the Court, with illness only a few weeks later removing him from participation and causing his retirement prior to the 1962 term. As in his earlier *Colegrove* opinion, Frankfurter's dissent in 1962 espoused judicial noninvolvement by arguing that the remedy for malapportionment lies in "an informed, civically militant electorate," and that any relief must come "through an aroused popular conscience that sears the conscience of the people's representatives." [60] But even assuming that legislators have a collective conscience (and the evidence of this on matters of apportionment is slight) how can this conscience be "seared" when it is not accountable to a majority of the electorate? The same philosophy of judicial self-restraint expressed by Frankfurter in the *Colegrove* case brought this perceptive commentary from Professor Alpheus T. Mason: "Such deference to the legislature illustrates the logical inconsistency of the application of judicial self-restraint in cases affecting political rights. To say that the only remedy lies with the body that perpetuates the abuse is to admit that there is no remedy." [61]

Indeed, Justice Frankfurter seemed involved in an internal contradiction which he has never satisfactorily resolved. His warning that courts should not enter the "political thicket" of malapportionment is posited on democratic assumptions. Courts are not elected, they are thus not directly representative of or responsible to the people. They should therefore not interfere with the wishes of the people or their representatives on matters of public policy. Yet this assertion *depends* in turn upon policy-making bodies—whether state legislatures, Congress, or executives—which *are* in fact representative of the people and which can be held accountable to them. If courts uphold principles of representative equality they are not necessarily entering a forbidden "political thicket." They do not tamper with the legislative *product* on substantive policy. They can better be understood as keeping open the channels of communication and responsibility between the people and their representatives, so that popular sovereignty is a reality and not a myth. Shortly before his appointment to the United States Supreme Court, Robert H. Jackson put the matter in these words:

> When the channels of opinion and of peaceful persuasion are corrupted or clogged, these political correctives can no longer be relied on, and the democratic system is threatened at its most vital point. In that event the Court, by intervening, restores the processes of democratic government; it does not disrupt them. . . .[62]

[60] 369 U.S. 186, 270 (1962).
[61] Mason, *The Supreme Court from Taft to Warren*, p. 178.
[62] Robert H. Jackson, *The Struggle for Judicial Supremacy*, quoted in Lewis, *loc. cit.*, p. 1096.

The school of thought which urges judicial self-restraint on matters of unequal political apportionment views the issue as one of governmental structure and insists that the judiciary should not tamper with the make-up of either a coordinate branch or with the prerogatives of the states regarding their own institutions. On the other hand, those who feel that the situation requires a judicial remedy begin at a different point in the political process—the individual. In this sense, representative equality is regarded as a voting right, as worthy of vindication as those protections for minorities which fall under the broader rubric of civil rights. Hence, any substantial distortion in the representative picture means a dilution or devaluation of some votes—in effect, a restriction on suffrage. While the attempt to translate this principle into some viable form of judicial action is recent, and while progress toward its realization may be neither swift nor easy, the ideal itself is hardly new. It had already won widespread allegiance when Thomas Jefferson gave it eloquent expression nearly a century and a half ago: "Equal representation is so fundamental a principle in a true republic that no prejudices can justify its violation because the prejudices themselves cannot be justified." [63]

[63] Jefferson to William King (November 19, 1819), Jefferson Papers, Library of Congress, Vol. 216, p. 38616.

3

Imperium in Imperio Revisited

Andrew Hacker

DEMOCRATIC POLITICS AND CORPORATE ECONOMICS

"The New Imperium in Imperio" was the sobriquet that Alpheus T. Mason gave to the emerging power of large corporations in American life.[1] Antedating by several years the studies by Adolph Berle, Walton Hamilton, C. Wright Mills, and Floyd Hunter, Mason expressed concern over the ways in which corporations were influencing public policy and shaping the contours of postwar society.[2] He asked whether power of this order could be reconciled with the principles of political equality and the institutions of self-government. What he saw was "the obstinate determination of big business to . . . replace government with a power system of its own." [3] This development was taking two forms. The first was the assumption by corporations, under a new and sophisticated form of paternalism, of welfare functions that are rightly the province of government. The second was the attempt of corporations to so influence the makers of public policy that government would capitulate and settle for a subordinate role in a society dominated by large business institutions. In the dozen years since Mason's study appeared the corporation has become a major interest of students of American society. Yet few of the discussions that

[1] Alpheus T. Mason, "Business Organized as Power: The New Imperium in Imperio," 44 *American Political Science Review* 323–342 (1950).
[2] A. A. Berle, *The Twentieth Century Capitalist Revolution* (1954) and *Power Without Property* (1959); Walton Hamilton, *The Politics of Industry* (1957); C. Wright Mills, *The Power Elite* (1956); Floyd Hunter, *Top Leadership* U.S.A. (1959).
[3] Mason, *op. cit.*, p. 342.

are heard are informed by the understanding of history and political theory that Mason brought to his analysis of the subject. For conventional notions of private property, of the relations between the political and economic spheres in society, must be re-evaluated in the light of the rise of the corporation.

It is no surprise that the large industrial corporation is a tantalizing conversation piece for contemporary social scientists. Everyone knows something about it and feels obliged to make some comment. But few are quite clear on just what it is they should be saying. The corporation, all agree, is both significant and powerful. It is, all concur, both secretive and public. It is, all acknowledge, both social and political. Nevertheless there soon comes a lull in the conversation. For while the major outlines of corporate structure and behavior are known it is extremely difficult to make evaluations. The problem that confronts the student of the corporation is more ideological than anything else. For the corporation is a capitalist institution: it is, at heart, private property. Social scientists no less than other Americans eschew socialist doctrine and they have avoided any serious flirtation with the notion of public ownership. While this stance may win praise for its realism, it can be debilitating from an intellectual standpoint. For how is corporate behavior to be evaluated if the commentator himself has no stand, no place on which to stand? Lilliputian darts are hurled at Gulliver—"advertising encourages materialism," "organizations promote conformity," "rhetoric about competition is hypo-critical," "the profit motive neglects human values"— but they are cast half-heartedly because the critics themselves sense that they cannot or will not say anything that amounts to real criticism.[4] We live in a time of affirmation, in a period when criticism must be constructive, and it is considered bad form to attack institutions without offering some alternative. Ideologically committed to capitalism, we are committed to the corporation. Consenting to private ownership, we consent to the power and the dominant values of business.

That is why the conversation meanders. Still and all, social scientists are men of reason. Deep in their hearts they wish to see America transformed into a more rational society. While his conception of that society is both vague and unstated, the sociologist or economist or political scientist is more often than not a person of liberal temper. This liberalism, while not doctrinaire, quests after the principle of equality: it embraces not only the redistribution of wealth but also the redistribution of power. Even as the contrasts between poverty and opulence are lessened, the growth of great corporate institutions suggests that power is as con-

---

[4] See, for example, the essays in Edward Mason, ed., *The Corporation in Modern Society* (1960).

centrated now as it ever was in the past. The liberal instincts of the social scientist demand that all men be free to shape their own lives and to contribute to the development of society. Yet anything approaching an equal distribution of power is impossible so long as corporations dominate the social scene. In politics, in particular, the influence of corporations in the making of public policy dwarfs the small and often unheard voice of the ordinary citizen. Here, indeed, is the crossroads where corporate capitalism and political democracy meet. Is it right that General Motors and General Electric be weighed in the same balance with John Smith and Robert Jones? If corporations and individuals both have legitimate status as political constituents, then the system itself takes on a curious asymmetry. The student of society, adhering to the tenets of rational liberalism and equalitarian democracy, frequently suspects that corporate power is not rightful power. But if there are objections it is not at all clear how they should be phrased. In sensing that the arrangements that constitute the status quo have not been sufficiently justified, he is faced with a serious problem. For sensations are no substitute for a theory. And a theory of corporate institutions, as has been remarked, will only emerge from those who are willing to pick a ground on which to stand. Most of us, at this point, are trying to find our feet.

THE VARIETIES OF POLITICAL ACTIVITY

The political activities of corporations may be summarized under two headings: partisan and legislative. The former comprise efforts, by means of campaign contributions or personal participation, to elect favored candidates to public office. The latter comprise attempts, through lobbying or public relations, to influence individuals already in office.

Partisan activities: campaign contributions.

With the detailed breakdowns and cross-referencing of campaign contributions in recent years we have a working knowledge of the ways in which large firms provide aid and comfort to their partisan friends. In the 1956 elections, for example, executives and directors of the 225 largest corporations reported that they gave, in gifts of $500 or more, a total of $1,936,847 to various campaign committees—94 per cent of this sum going to Republican groups.[5] Among the more generous companies were: Pan-American Airways (five officials giving a total of $24,500), Gulf Oil (seven giving $87,550), Sun Oil (five giving $104,650), du Pont (seventeen giving $138,745), Ford (eight giving $35,399), General Electric (sixteen giving $68,349), General Motors (thirty-seven giving $163,250),

---

[5] Alexander Heard, *The Costs of Democracy* (1960), p. 115.

International Business Machines (seven giving $33,500), Olin-Mathieson (nine giving $100,250), and Westinghouse (twenty-two giving $41,750).[6]

Was this "corporation money"? The straightforward answer must be that it was. Section 610 of the Criminal Code of course forbids corporations to give money to candidates or campaign committees and all existing evidence suggests that the large companies adhere to the letter of this law.[7] At the same time it must be acknowledged that the "personal" contributions of executives and directors came out of the high salaries and bountiful dividends that corporations pay to their top men. In the case of these men, their corporate positions are quite understandably the dominant roles in their lives. In many companies no reminders are needed that campaign contributions are expected from those holding well-paid executive positions. Checks are of course written from personal accounts, but even in such instances a line cannot easily be drawn between the donor's role as an executive and his personal capacity. A Westinghouse vice president who gives $1000 to the Republican party *seems* to be giving on behalf of his company as well as himself. A Yale professor who donates $25 to the Democrats, in contrast, does not give the appearance of contributing at the suggestion of his university nor is there much reason to believe that such a gift will serve to promote the university's interests.

Partisan activities: personal participation

With the Congressional sweep by the Democrats in 1958, corporation executives throughout the country foresaw two or more years of undisputed rule by labor unions and liberal ideologues. Perhaps not all were so gloomy as Archie Gray, Senior Vice President of Gulf Oil, who anticipated the hegemony of "labor gangsters and socialist politicians," but enough were aroused so that action was the order of the day.[8] Thus was born the "businessman in politics" movement. The rationale was quite simple. Labor unions had mobilized their members not only into active voters but also as party workers. While it was never clear how many of

[6] *Congressional Record*, August 19, 1958, pp. 18411–18421. There is some overlapping in these figures, but not much. For example, Henry Ford II's contribution of $18,899 to the Republicans is counted twice: once for the Ford Motor Company, of which he is an executive, and once for General Electric, of which he is a director. Another instance is Henry du Pont, whose $6100 gift is listed with both du Pont and General Motors.

[7] Section 610 reads: "It is unlawful for any . . . corporation organized by authority of any law of Congress, to make a contribution or expenditure in connection with any election to any political office." Some corporate violations of the law are mentioned in Duncan Norton-Taylor, "How to Give Money to Politicians," *Fortune* (May 1956), p. 238.

[8] Gray's remark is quoted in the *Washington Post and Times-Herald*, September 23, 1958, p. 26.

the fifteen million AFL-CIO members were induced by COPE to contribute their time and money to partisan activity, many executives believed that labor politicians were instrumental in deciding who were to be the nominees of the Northern wing of the Democratic Party and that the labor vote was turned out to elect that party's candidates.[9] If this force was to be countered, a new group of citizens would have to enter the partisan arena in an organized and purposeful way. Prior to 1945 such a constituency probably did not exist. However since the end of World War II, America's large corporations had been augmenting their white-collar labor force in an unprecedented way. While technological developments slackened the need for production employees, millions of new jobs were created for clerical, professional, and managerial people. These individuals were on salaries rather than wages, they came to work at 9:00 A.M. rather than 8:00 A.M., they thought of themselves as middle-class. They were impervious to unionization and not a few thought of themselves as businessmen—albeit of the managerial rather than the entrepreneurial variety. If these citizens, hitherto indifferent to politics, could be drawn into the parties then a mighty conservative influence would be brought to bear.[10]

The central theme of the "businessmen in politics" program was to motivate middle-management employees to become part-time politicians. Corporations offered classes, seminars, and workshops which imparted fundamental political lore: the most important fact being that parties are local in their base. To become influential within a party an individual must gain power at the level of the ward or precinct. Students in the corporations' practical politics courses were advised to seek out their precinct leaders and volunteer their services. By virtue of hard work and expenditure of time they would achieve a place in the local party hierarchy.[11] As they labored longer in the vineyard, so would they eventually rise to positions where nominations for public office were decided. The theory, in short, was one of infiltration. If businessmen applied themselves to party work they would ultimately gain party power. If tens of thousands of loyal corporation people did this throughout the country, then both major parties would be induced to nominate men sympathetic

---

[9] This is the general tenor of J. J. Wuerthner's *The Businessman's Guide to Practical Politics* (1959). Wuerthner, a General Electric executive, suggests that all too many Congressmen have become "COPE-tivated." *Ibid.*, p. 21.

[10] The nonpolitical character of white-collar employees is analyzed in my *Politics and the Corporation* (1958). Over 40,000 copies of this pamphlet were ordered by companies and trade associations, presumably in the hope that they might obtain some clues on how to politicize their people.

[11] This was the emphasis in the most widely used textbook, a series of eight pamphlets entitled "Action Course in Practical Politics," which was prepared by the U.S. Chamber of Commerce. In a report dated November 1959, the Chamber indicated that the textbook had been used by 107 corporations.

to business. Not only was this corps of potential infiltrators available, but it was equipped with middle-class talent and middle-management skills. With the expectation that such an injection of party workers into the political system would pay off, hundreds of corporations gave their white-collar employees released time to take the courses. Among the enthusiastic firms were General Electric, Ford, Alcoa, A. T. & T., American Can, Gulf, Johnson and Johnson, Republic Steel, Chrysler, Dow Chemical, Equitable Life, General Dynamics, Inland Steel, International Harvester, General Foods, Shell Oil, U.S. Rubber, Jones & Loughlin, Richfield Oil, New York Central, Eli Lilly, Kimberly Clark, Standard Oil of California, Carrier, and Olin Mathieson.[12]

Legislative activities: lobbying

On the whole, however, most corporations are willing and able to work with whichever officeholders the electorate puts into power. A lobbyist for one large company stated the typical viewpoint: "Our job is to work with the elected officials after they are elected, whether they are communists or Democrats or Republicans or Progressives. If they represent districts in which we have operations, it is our duty to work with them." [13] In this sense corporations are nonpartisan: they have discovered that both Democrats and Republicans, liberals and conservatives, are willing to give them a respectful hearing. For example, the American Can Corporation has branches in 153 Congressional districts in 26 states. The various managers of these plants and offices were circularized by the company reminding them of their political responsibilities: "We asked 153 of these men— managers in plants and offices throughout the country—to act as official spokesmen for our company and establish direct relationships with the 153 Congressmen and 52 Senators representing the areas in which our facilities are located." [14] Under this kind of policy a corporation can establish a network of grass-roots lobbyists working to promote the company's interests at the local level. But it must also be granted that the political policies of American Can or any other large corporation are drawn up at the company headquarters in New York or some other distant city. A

---

[12] In a report dated August 1959, the Effective Citizens Organization listed 87 corporations which had set up political training programs for white-collar employees. The E. C. O., which is supported mainly by large companies, runs periodic workshops at which corporation representatives are taught how to teach practical politics. For a general evaluation of the program in one area, see Joel Aberbach, "Businessmen in Politics: A Syracuse Study." Senior Honors Thesis in the Department of Government, Cornell University, 1961. This study is based on questionnaires received from 578 Syracuse businessmen who took a practical politics course.

[13] Quoted in Paul W. Cherington and Ralph L. Gillen, "The Company Representative in Washington," 39 *Harvard Business Review*, 112 (1961).

[14] William Stolk, "The Responsibility of Business in Public Affairs." Speech delivered before the Chemical Specialities Manufacturers Association, May 20, 1959.

local branch manager approaching a Congressman expresses not so much local sentiment as the ideas of top management.

In the past corporations were rather diffident about their lobbying activities in Washington. In recent years, however, more and more companies have decided to register openly as lobbies and to have their spokesmen declare themselves officially as lobbyists. During 1959–60 some of the companies registering under the Federal Regulation of Lobbying Act were: The Alleghany Corporation, American Airlines, American Broadcasting Company, American Can, American Smelting and Refining, American Telephone and Telegraph, Anaconda, Atlantic Refining, Bendix Aviation, Cities Service, DuPont, Ford, General Electric, General Motors, Gulf, Hilton Hotels, Monsanto Chemical, Pacific Gas and Electric, Phillips Petroleum, RCA, Smith-Corona Marchant, Southern Pacific Railroad, Standard Oil of California, Standard Oil of New Jersey, and Westinghouse.[15]

Legislative activities: public relations

"Our conception of practical politics is that if you have a sound enough case to convince the folks back home, you don't have to button-hole the Senator. He will hear from home, and he will respect very highly the opinions he gets from that quarter." In this way did Leone Baxter, public relations counselor to West Coast corporations, define the basic operating principle of grass-roots lobbying.[16] But it is not enough to have a "sound case." That case must be communicated in a persuasive way to the "folks back home" all up and down the country. Long convinced of the efficacy of advertising, an increasing number of corporations are now attempting to sell the public on political issues. If, through public relations campaigns, the grass-roots are set tingling then it is believed that lawmakers will take the cue.

Forays into the public relations field by corporations are easy enough to detect: after all, if a message is intended to reach the general public then it should not be hard for a student of the political process to place himself on the receiving end as well. In 1950 the House Select Committee on Lobbying Activities polled 173 corporations to determine the extent of their efforts to influence legislation.[17] Sixty-five of these companies indicated that they sought to create public sentiment favorable to their own

---

[15] "Lobby Round-Up," *Congressional Quarterly Almanac*, pp. 690–703 (1959); pp. 667–677 (1960). It should be noted that corporations that engage in lobbying are not required to register as lobbies. For their "principal purpose," whatever else it may be, is not influencing legislation.

[16] Leone Baxter, "How the Story was Presented to the People." Speech delivered before the Southern Public Relations Conference, May 8, 1951.

[17] U.S. House of Representatives, Select Committee on Lobbying Activities, 81st Congress, 2nd Session. *House Report No. 3137* (1950).

legislative objectives. General Motors, for example, distributed 630,000 copies of President Charles E. Wilson's testimony on the proposed Taft-Hartley bill. New York Central included 2,000,000 slips in its ticket envelopes seeking to enlist their riders' opposition to the federal transportation tax. Schenley Distilleries, aided by the Carl Byoir public relations firm, gave away over 11 million leaflets asking their customers to write their Congressmen for a reduction in liquor taxes. Pacific Gas and Electric, a client of Whitaker and Baxter, sent out 28 mailings to its million-odd customers attacking the tax-free status of public power projects. These flyers included reprints of articles and editorials ranging from the *Wall Street Journal* to the Woodford (California) *Record*, from the *Reader's Digest* to the Hamilton (Illinois) *Press*. The theory was that if millions of train riders, liquor drinkers, and power users were led to an understanding of the issues at hand, they would contribute to a public ferment which would eventually attract Congressional attention. On this assumption the corporations spent generous sums to reach and persuade the man-in-the-street—or, more precisely, the man-on-the-commuter-train, the man-in-the-bar, and the man-in-front-of-the-television-set.

A more explicit instance of the public relations approach to legislation can be found by turning to the 1955 activities of the large oil companies at the time the Fulbright-Harris bill was being considered.[18] This act would have exempted "independent" natural gas producers from rate regulation by the Federal Power Commission, and its passage was as earnestly desired by the major corporations in the oil and gas industry as it was by their smaller brothers. For reasons of their own these companies decided that it would be imprudent for them to approach the public in their own names. The campaign was carried out by the innocuous sounding (if rather pretentious) "Natural Gas and Oil Resources Committee," and the statement was issued that this body was supported by over 1200 individual and corporate contributors. What was not publicized was that of the almost $2,000,000 raised by the NGORC, 80 per cent of the money came from 26 large corporations. Humble Oil and Refining (88 per cent of which is owned by Standard Oil of New Jersey) gave $175,000; the Texas Company gave $153,000; Shell Oil gave $138,000; Standard Oil of California gave $119,000; Socony-Mobil Oil gave $114,000; and Stanolind Oil and Gas (a subsidiary of Standard Oil of Indiana) gave $100,000. The campaign was not partisan in that it offered no contributions to the candidates of either party; nor did it engage in the direct legislative contacts commonly defined as lobbying. The sole purpose of the NGORC pro-

[18] The information on the Fulbright-Harris campaign has been taken from several sources: Robert Engler, *The Politics of Oil* (1961); Irwin Ross, *The Image Merchants* (1959); and U. S. Senate Special Committee to Investigate Political Activities, Lobbying, and Campaign Contributions, 84th Congress, 2nd Session. *Hearings* (1956).

gram was to influence public opinion. "Not one cent of our funds has been spent for campaign contributions or legislative contact work," its chairman, President of Continental Oil, was able to point out. Instead, the NGORC retained a professional public relations firm to take the oil companies' story direct to the American people.

Hill and Knowlton, Inc., the public relations firm, spent $800,000 on advertising alone. By the end of a year they could report that an educational film produced by them called "You, the People" had been shown 230 times on television and the companies' case was aired on 475 radio broadcasts as well. On these shows a housewifely-looking actress would be told the facts of life under government regulation and by the end of the recital she had become an enthusiastic convert to the NGORC side. "You know something," she would declaim. "I find this so interesting I'm going to quiz my husband about it this evening. I'll bet *he* doesn't know anything—even less than I—because he doesn't do the housekeeping!" Contacts were made, in addition, with 3400 daily and 4300 weekly newspapers, resulting in over 1700 editorials favorable to the companies' cause. Over 120 business and civic groups in 34 states were induced to pass favorable resolutions on the Fulbright-Harris bill. All of these efforts were aided by recruiting 2100 field-workers from the oil and gas companies, who were given released time from their jobs to cultivate editors and local organizations. Assuming that these employees, mainly salesmen and middle-management people, earned salaries averaging $8000 a year, this meant that the corporations were giving the campaign $67,200 each working day that the program was in operation. Hill and Knowlton planned and organized the entire operation, but they insisted that a different image be presented to the public. "The program should reflect that it is being conducted on behalf of thousands of producers, large and small, and not just a few 'big companies' . . . ," one of their bulletins said. "There should be a conscious effort to subordinate the New York headquarters and to reflect the grass-roots support for the program."

It is, of course, impossible to estimate how many people were reached by the NGORC campaign. Nor of those who were reached in one way or another, can it be ascertained how deep was the penetration of the message or how far the public's mind was persuaded to a new way of thinking. Even the Hill and Knowlton executives who directed the campaign had to admit that, in purely scientific terms, "we wouldn't tell you that we had changed opinions two points or ten points or thirty points." Yet in terms of legislative results, the formation of the NGORC and the retention of Hill and Knowlton seem to have been worth the investment of time and money. A bill liberating "independent" natural gas producers from federal rate regulation was passed by the House of Representatives in 1955 and by the Senate the following year. The vote in the Senate was

53–38, a margin sufficiently ample to suggest that it would probably have passed even without the help of the public relations campaign. But the House presented an altogether different story: there the vote was 209–203. Had but four Congressmen voted the other way the bill would not have been passed. While a wide variety of pressures were at work on the Congress in connection with this legislation, it is not too much to credit the NGORC-Hill and Knowlton campaign with being the factor that persuaded any four of the 209 Representatives who supplied the crucial votes.[19] At all events, Senator John McClellen voiced the feelings of many of his colleagues when he concluded that the legislative activities of the oil industry "might well be calculated to wield more influence on Congress than direct lobbying."

THE CORPORATION AS A REPRESENTATIVE INSTITUTION

Prior to embarking on legislative campaigns corporations must decide on their political positions. To favor or to oppose a particular bill, to demand that certain legislative policies be initiated, to support the candidacy of one or another individual—these are decisions that men must make. When a corporation takes a stand it should not be necessary to point out that that stand is decided upon by a handful of individuals in its top management. A corporation is hierarchical and oligarchical, and policy is made by the policy-makers. However if corporations are to claim the political freedoms of speech and petition, they must also establish that they are representative institutions.[20] The political legitimacy of the American Medical Association and the National Association of Real Estate Boards is gained by demonstrating that they voice the sentiments of the individual citizens who compromise their memberships. It is with the active or tacit consent of several hundred thousand doctors or realtors that these organizations petition legislators and address the public. The internal structure of associations such as these are democratic in theory and federative in constitution. If this is true more in principle than in practice, the fact

[19] President Eisenhower, who was planning to sign the bill, felt obliged to veto it because of the overzealous lobbying tactics of the Superior Oil Company. Superior's offer of a campaign contribution to a Senator, however, was not a part of the NGORC campaign.

[20] To be sure, the Courts construe a corporation as a "person" under the Fourteenth Amendment. However this means that it is an economic and legal person, able to make contracts and to sue and be sued. But a corporation cannot, by virtue of its economic and legal personality, thereby claim the political and constitutional rights of a citizen. Senator Albert Gore has put it this way: "A corporation, as such, is a legal entity, carrying with it many benefits and privileges under the law, and in economic and business transactions. I doubt, however, if the law should ever permit corporations to exercise any of the rights and functions of citizenship. It is a legal fiction. A corporation is not a citizen." U. S. Senate Subcommittee on Privileges and Elections, 84th Congress, 2nd Session. *Hearings* (1956), p. 382.

remains that the vast majority of the memberships concur in what is said in their names. Furthermore, an interested and energetic realtor or physician can rise in the organization structure to a place where he can participate in the councils where association policy is made. Opportunities for democracy are generally present, and in internal government the vote of any one member counts as much as any other. In these ways, then, voluntary and even quasi-voluntary associations of citizens serve as extensions of the personalities of their members. Such associations have political rights because they speak and act on behalf of discrete individuals. They are, in short, representative institutions even if the decision-making powers on political matters are delegated to full-time bureaucrats or part-time officers.

A corporation has no such basis for political legitimacy, and the reasons for this need be only briefly outlined at this juncture.

Does a corporation represent its employees?

Corporation political activities cannot claim, with any degree of consistency, to represent the views or sentiments of a majority of employees. In no case is the labor force polled before a company takes it position on legislation. Support for "right-to-work" laws may be General Electric's official stand; however, it is reasonable to conclude that most GE workers have rather a different opinion on this subject. There are of course instances when the survival of a company or an industry seems to be at stake, and in these cases management and employees may well agree on a course of political action. And on certain social issues there may be a consensus among all levels of the company. But the fact remains that policy positions are taken by exclusive management decision with no thought of taking, even less of abiding by, a sounding of employee opinion. The instances where company stands do happen to reflect the majority viewpoint among workers cannot be used to justify those instances where they do not.

Furthermore, there is every reason to believe that a corporation would dispense with employees if it possibly could. Workers are, after all, no more than an additional cost of production, and corporations have taken every advantage of opportunities to replace obstreperous men with obedient machines. It is true that a corporation can claim that it provides jobs and that its well-being must be promoted if employment is to be continued. But it is also the case that it would welcome the chance to operate with no employees at all. At all events, until internal mechanisms for consultation and consent are established for the labor force, a corporation cannot claim that its political activities represent the views of those who work for it. As matters now stand it is best to assume that most workers do not think of themselves as working for the company: they are working for a living.

Does a corporation represent its stockholders?

Nor can it be claimed that a corporation represents its stockholders. This proposition should need little explanation at this late date.[21] Legal ownership and effective management have little or nothing to do with one another in the current stage of corporate development. Managers recruit and promote themselves with no interference from stockholders, and company policy is made by the men who will carry it out. A large corporation will have over a hundred million shares of stock outstanding and will have upwards to a million owners. Such a dispersion of ownership, it is now acknowledged, means that power gravitates to the full-time executives who not only run the company but also make up the agendas for the board of directors' and stockholders' meetings. Furthermore the individual stockholder attending the annual meeting—few do—has power not as a person but in proportion to the number of shares he holds. When votes are cast, each stockholder throws an unequal weight into the balance, depending on the breadth of his portfolio. In addition, almost half of the stockholdings in American corporations are held not by people at all but by other corporate entities. According to a 1959 survey taken by the New York Stock Exchange, 47.4 per cent of the outstanding shares were held by fiduciaries, stockbrokers, security dealers, nominees, and institutions.[22] This means that when a vote is taken at an annual meeting the ballots of the myriad Smiths and Jones and Browns are joined by those of Merrill Lynch and Metropolitan Life and Ford Foundation. The reality is that while individual stockholders support the existing management as an act of habit or inertia, institutional stockholders do so as a matter of considered policy. "We believe in investing in management," a vice president of a large insurance company said. "If the management is sound, we believe in supporting management. If the management should not prove to be capable, we try to be out of the situation before it becomes evident publicly." [23] The upshot is that the acquiescence of individual stockholders coupled with the interest of institutional stockholders gives management a free hand.

One illustration may make the functioning of this process clear. The 1959 annual meeting of the Standard Oil Company of New Jersey was a model affair. The event was well-publicized and almost 4000 people made the trip to Lawrenceville, New Jersey, where they foregathered in

[21] See Joseph Livingston, *The American Stockholder* (1958).
[22] New York Stock Exchange, *Shareownership in America: 1959*, p. 33.
[23] Quoted in Livingston, *op. cit.*, p. 156.

the prep school's field house. The proceedings were amicable enough until someone rose to attack Jersey Standard's decision to contribute $175,000 to Radio Free Europe the previous year. This individual disagreed with the political tone of Radio Free Europe, and he felt that the corporation's donation represented neither his sentiments nor the best interests of the United States. After a reply from the rostrum and a desultory discussion the question was put to a vote. The result: 168 million for continuing contributions to Radio Free Europe, 5 million against.[24] The balloting was, of course, by shares rather than by counting the heads of the shareholders. (Were it by stockholders as individuals, management would still have won but the strength of the opposition would have doubled.) A point to remember is that standing quietly at the back of the Lawrenceville field house, were several men from the larger brokerage houses, insurance companies, and banks. And these men, while not stockholders in Jersey Standard themselves, put an end to the nonsense by voting the institutional shares on management's side. But it is of little value to suggest that the frankly political decision to support Radio Free Europe is "representative" in the sense that it echoes the sentiments of the institutions which hold Jersey Standard shares. For Lehman Brothers, the Chase Manhattan Bank, and even the Sears Roebuck Pension Fund are constituted along much the same lines as Jersey Standard itself.

If a corporation wishes to claim that its political activities are legitimate, that they represent the views of the citizens who hold stock in the company, then it may achieve such a status for itself by taking the following steps: (1) Individual stockholders must be polled to discover whether they consent to the company's taking a particular political position, and the company may embark on its activities if it secures the consent of a majority. (2) In such a balloting, votes must be counted on the arithmetical basis of each stockholder having one vote rather than on the geometric basis of shareholding. (3) Each stockholder who agrees with the political position and activities the company intends to take must expressly agree that his prorated share of the campaign costs for that year be subtracted from his dividend check. (4) Institutions must be excluded from voting. It is quite clear that no corporation will adopt a program even remotely like this. But in refusing to do so they forfeit their claim to be speaking on behalf of the citizens who are their stockholders.[25] They can no longer regard themselves as extensions of the political personalities

---

[24] Standard Oil Company (New Jersey), *Report of the 77th Annual Meeting,* May 27, 1959, pp. 18–21.

[25] Michael Reagen states the matter well: "We think of the corporation as an association of capital rather than of people. This is formally true of the only elections held in a corporation, those of the board of directors, where the balloting is on a basis of one share of stock, one vote—not one man, one vote." "The Seven Fallacies of Business in Politics," 38 *Harvard Business Review* 60 (1960).

of their owners, and this means that they have no right to the constitutional freedoms of speech and petition.

Does a corporation represent social values?

A corporation might agree that its political activities are engaged in without the consent of its employees or stockholders, but that it is nevertheless a "representative" institution because it embodies and upholds the values of the society of which it is a part. "The modern large industrial corporation is in some respects a public institution," intones William T. Gossett, Vice President and General Counsel of Ford. "It is a key economic unit in our society: it holds power in trust for the whole community." [26] The theory here is that corporate power is conjoined with social responsibility, that economic function is guided by a moral conscience. This notion of representation is aristocratic rather than democratic; it suggests that an institution need not speak only for a living constituency but for the interests of those dead, those now living, and those yet to be born. The test of rhetoric such as this is not whether A. T. & T. collects Christmas presents for poor children or whether General Motors gives scholarship funds to M.I.T. If a corporation is going to enter the political arena, then it must—if it seeks to gain legitimacy as a representative institution—demonstrate that its obligations do not cease once its own interests have been effectively promoted. To be representative of social values a corporation must use its power to give meaning to ideas transcending production and profits.

One cannot, unhappily, move back and forth between the "democratic" and the "aristocratic" mood in an effort to make the best of both worlds. If corporations were democratic in their internal structures then they could at least claim that they were adhering to employee sentiment when they pursued particular policies. But General Motors does not poll its workers to determine whether company money should go to M.I.T. This being the case it cannot plead that it is reflecting the opinions of its employees when it refuses to support values that happen to be unpopular with the majority. In many instances such values should be supported despite popular opposition to them, for in these situations the majority is wrong. If corporations elect to take the aristocratic stance, as all the talk of stewardship and management professionalization implies, then they must remember that aristocrats are not bound by the whims and prejudices of the average man. To represent enduring and worthwhile social values requires a willingness to act with courage and to run the risk of criticism and unpopularity.

In this sphere, however, large firms have been remarkably silent. Two

[26] William T. Gossett, "The Role of the Corporation in Public Affairs," *The Business Lawyer*, November 1959, p. 97.

instances will have to suffice: the first is civil liberties and the second is civil rights.

A free society should not impair an individual's pursuit of his livelihood simply because his political views deviate from the dominant ideas in the community. Whatever the causes of the attacks on civil liberties in recent years, corporations have done nothing to oppose them and have almost invariably acquiesced in the face of this pressure. General Electric, for example, made it an official company policy to dismiss any employee who pleaded the Fifth Amendment at a hearing of a legislative investigating committee. U.S. Steel, Westinghouse, Radio Corporation of America, and Bethlehem Steel were other companies that fired employees because they remained silent when Congressional committees put questions to them. A private organization that offered to run loyalty checks on company personnel was able to sell its services, so it claimed, to General Motors, du Pont, F. W. Woolworth, Metropolitan Life Insurance, Reynolds Tobacco, and Bendix Aviation. A notorious instance of corporate acquiescence occurred when General Foods cancelled the contract of a television actress whose name had been "listed" as belonging to some purportedly subversive organizations. The fact that this actress was and is a loyal citizen, that the insinuations about her past were groundless, carried no weight with General Foods. She had, through no fault of her own, become a controversial figure. She had to be fired:

> The use of controversial personalities or the discussion of controversial subjects in our advertising may provide unfavorable criticism and even antagonism among sizable groups of customers. Such reaction injures both acceptance of our product and our public relations. General Foods advertising, therefore, avoids the use of material and personalities which in its judgment are controversial.[27]

All in all, the corporate record on civil liberties has been less than an aristocratic one. The obsession with avoiding controversy clearly has led to the elimination of individuals and the suppression of ideas that might in any way upset entrenched sensibilities. It was a small businessman, not a large corporation, who gave Alger Hiss a job on his release from prison. It has been independent producers, not the major companies, who have hired blacklisted screenwriters. No corporation has come to the defense of its employees who have run afoul of legislative committees and certainly none has offered financial support to an employee when he needed it. The United Automobile Workers Union, by way of contrast, not only kept on the payroll one of its organizers who had been cited for contempt by a Congressional inquiry, but it also paid all of his legal expenses up to the Supreme Court—where he was acquitted in the now-famous *Watkins*

---

[27] Statement of Charles Francis, Chairman of the Board of General Foods. Quoted in Merle Miller, *The Judges and the Judged* (1950), p. 45.

case. It is of some interest that the U.A.W., an organization far more susceptible to both membership opinion and public opinion than a corporation like General Foods, should have expressed such a concern for the civil liberties of one of its employees.

The freedom of Americans belonging to minority groups to live on an equal footing with their fellow citizens is hampered by entrenched forces which are satisfied with things as they are. While the problem of civil rights is national in scope, attention is usually focussed on the Southern states where the condition of inequality is rampant. Since the end of World War II Northern-based corporations have been opening many branch plants in the South. In return for tax concessions and a docile labor force, these companies have agreed to accept the racial patterns of the region. In some areas the branch plants of corporations do not hire Negroes at all, in others they are kept in custodial positions.[28] More than this, the metropolitan corporations strike up an alliance with the provincial legislatures, the one accepting white supremacy and the other keeping public expenditures to a minimum. This is particularly true in a state like Alabama:

> . . . the Black Belt counties would not be able to maintain their stranglehold and their retrograde influence on state policy were it not for a powerful ally, the big industry of Birmingham. The biggest of Birmingham's "big mules" is United States Steel, whose subsidiary Tennessee Coal and Iron, dominates the city economically and, to a considerable extent, politically. The "big mules" and the Black Belt cooperate and, together, usually run the state. . . .[29]

Corporations have the power to enforce the principle of equality in hiring and upgrading, but with one or two exceptions they have decided to play along with the practice of white supremacy. To be sure, as in the case of civil liberties, company policies guaranteeing civil rights would encounter local opposition. But if, as Mr. Gossett of Ford claimed, a large corporation "holds power in trust for the whole community" then it is reasonable to expect that such power will be used to promote the values inherent in the nation's Constitution. However the rhetoric is vapid: a corporation is, by construction and temperament, unfitted to represent the fundamental values of a free society.

Were the corporation to assume the role of public trustee, its political activities might then be cloaked with legitimacy. It might even without benefit of a democratic constituency, assert its claims to freedom

---

[28] See Herbert Hill, "The Negro in Industry," *The New Leader*, May 6, 1957, pp. 3–5. There is no evidence that matters have changed appreciably since Hill's article appeared. There is not much reason to believe that recent administration directives to certain defense contractors will have a widespread impact among corporations with Southern plants.

[29] Harrison Salisbury in *The New York Times*, April 13, 1960, p. 33.

of speech and petition. For in that case its entry into politics would, at least in part, involve promoting the basic values of society. Not only is there hardly any sign that this has occurred in the past or will in the future: there are indications that when corporations do speak politically they are apt to hide their identity. Thus companies like Shell and Standard Oil of California did not address the public openly and boldly in their own names but rather sheltered themselves behind a "Natural Gas and Oil Resources Committee." Montgomery Ward and Sears Roebuck, in their campaign to secure greater subsidies for the Parcel Post system, financed a "National Council on Business Mail" and let it do their talking for them. The Pennsylvania Railroad, in its effort to impose weight-restrictions on the long-haul trucking industry, joined with other railroads in hiring a public relations agency to persuade citizens and apply pressure to state legislatures. This firm not only made sure that attacks against the trucking industry were not attributed to the railroads but it established letterhead groups like the Empire State Transport League and New Jersey Automobile Owners, Incorporated to carry out the anti-truck campaign. Indeed, the Pennsylvania Railroad went so far as to conceal from its stockholders the fact that $300,000 of the corporation's money was spent on political public relations of this kind.[30] In sum, it is difficult to see how corporations can demand the right to free speech if they lack the courage to speak out in their own names.

The American corporation is in politics: its resources and its power are used to influence the course of legislation and public policy, to give shape to the public mind. But the corporation cannot be conceived of as a representative instituton: it speaks for no identifiable constituency and it cannot claim to promote the values of society as a whole. The corporation is not a citizen, and yet it takes full advantage of the Constitutional protections for free speech and the right of petition. It is the burden of this argument that the corporation is not entitled to these political rights: it is not an individual with mind or tongue, it is not a citizen with liberty to gain or lose. Corporation power is real and its political expressions have had a demonstrable impact on public policy. This power, as currently exercised, is illegitimate. It may only be made rightful if certain stringent conditions, all of which have been outlined here, are met. As of this date there is no sign that corporations are willing or able to meet those requirements.

[30] See my "Pressure Politics in Pennsylvania," in Alan Westin, ed., *The Uses of Power* (1961).

4

The Influence of Legal Realism
on William O. Douglas [1]

John W. Hopkirk

For a number of years Associate Justice William O. Douglas has stood out on the Supreme Court of the United States as a man given to open and vigorous statements regarding desirable public policy. It is no secret that in some circles he is regarded as championing his positions on the Court to an "activist" extreme which transcends the limits of desirable judicial behavior. Careful examination of Douglas' legal training and development is particularly interesting for what it reveals concerning Douglas' approach to the law and his view of appropriate judicial behavior. While examination of such material will not resolve argument regarding a Justice's proper behavior on the Supreme Court, it should help in an understanding of how an individual such as Douglas sees his role as a Justice.

Douglas' view of his role was fostered by virtually all of his legal training and reinforced continually by his work as a legal scholar. Available evidence reveals a continuing emphasis upon getting at the realities behind particular legal disputes and judging those realities in the light of desirable public policy. This approach to the law will here be traced in three facets of Douglas' life prior to joining the Court: first, as a disciple

[1] Material in this essay is adapted from a dissertation presented to the Faculty of Princeton University in partial fulfillment of the requirements for the degree of Doctor of Philosophy. While many individuals assisted me in its preparation, I owe a special debt to Alpheus Mason, under whose direction the dissertation was prepared.

of Underhill Moore; second, as a young legal scholar at Columbia and Yale Law Schools; third, as an investigator of bankruptcy laws.

DOUGLAS AS A DISCIPLE OF UNDERHILL MOORE

During Douglas' last two years at Columbia Law School he served as research assistant to Underhill Moore, who was a restless pioneer in new fields of legal research. If any single person can be said to have shaped Douglas' approach to the law that person was Underhill Moore. Douglas himself testifies to this great influence in a preliminary footnote to an essay applying their approach to problems of business law. There he states that "if there is any merit in the ideas expressed here, credit should largely go to Prof. Underhill Moore, . . . whose pioneer work in this field accomplished much more than merely to prophesy a new alignment." [2]

Moore was one of the leaders among the group of scholars, often called "legal realists," who were becoming increasingly dissatisfied with traditional methods of legal analysis and with the legal education which perpetuated those methods. As "realists" they sought to relate legal studies more closely to sociological and economic facets of the problems with which they dealt. They had an unquenchable desire to know more of the facts about the actual workings of the legal system.

Some of the "realists," including Moore and Douglas, have sometimes been called "functionalists" because they viewed the goal of their fact-finding as better understanding of the functions which legal institutions (such as that of bankruptcy) were actually fulfilling in our society.

In his own writing Douglas' mentor emphasized the need to eliminate any element of the mysterious, the metaphysical, or the ideal, which might enshroud principles employed in legal thinking. Moore wrote:

> To say that a legal institution—private property, the federal government of the United States, Columbia University—exists is to say that a group of persons is doing something, is acting in some way. . . . A legal institution is human behavior. [3]

Directing his attention to one of the concepts most often thrown up as a barrier to government regulatory activity Moore observed:

[2] "A Functional Approach to the Law of Business Associations," 23 *Illinois Law Review* 673, note (1929). Compare Douglas, "Vicarious Liability and Administration of Risk—I," 38 *Yale Law Journal* 584, note (1929). Moore's influence on Douglas is attested to by both Carrol Shanks, who was Moore's second research assistant at the same time and who subsequently collaborated with Douglas in organizing courses and writing case books (Interview, Newark, New Jersey, May 18, 1953), and by Judge Charles E. Clark, who was Dean of the Yale Law School during Douglas' period as law professor there (Interview, New Haven, Connecticut, June 10, 1953).

[3] Underhill Moore, "The Rational Basis of Legal Institutions," 23 *Columbia Law Review* 609 (1923).

Private property may be a useful concept for some purposes, but it is an intellectual device which must not be allowed to obscure the duty not to commit a nuisance on one's land, the liability to the police power and to the power to tax, the disability to alienate in certain modes. . . .[4]

Moore considered that a lawyer's main job, the giving of advice to clients, was in essence the making of judgments as to probable judicial behavior. Probabilities such as this could best be studied through use of statistics. To attain accurate results in such endeavors Moore believed that legal scholars would have to take into account events which are studied by many disciplines, "anthropology, anthropogeography, sociology, and psychology, psychiatry and perhaps other biological sciences."[5] His belief that lawyers would find great difficulty in learning modern methods of scientific research reportedly even led Moore to remark that "I don't believe any man with law training should be elected to a law faculty."[6]

DOUGLAS AS A YOUNG LEGAL SCHOLAR AT COLUMBIA AND YALE

Douglas helps reshape legal instruction at Columbia

After a short period as an associate in one of Wall Street's largest law firms, Cravath, de Gersdoff, Swaine, and Wood, Douglas soon returned to Columbia Law School as a full-time faculty member. There he soon indicated his own concern over the state of legal research. Showing the influence of Underhill Moore, he made clear a conviction that legal problems could be studied significantly only against a background of social and economic events. One major theme which seems to run through Douglas' work at this stage of his development is the need to end the study of abstract legal problems *in vacuo*. Only by placing a subject such as bankruptcy in its broader setting, by studying factual situations rather than abstract definitions, will the student grasp the significance of what he learns. This viewpoint is brought out as Douglas criticizes a new textbook which he feels is inadequate preparation for the intelligent handling of an ordinary bankruptcy case.

> It is one thing to start a machine and see it run. It is another thing to be able to operate a machine once started. It is one thing to learn how to allege in a petition an act of bankruptcy; it is another to be able to recognize a fraudulent conveyance or preference. It is one thing to learn the definition of insolvency; it is another to be able to analyze the "value" concepts involved. . . . It is one thing to learn the definitions of void-

---

[4] *Ibid.*, p. 613. See also Felix Cohen, *op. cit.*, and note the favorable use of the quotation in Douglas, "Stare Decisis," 49 *Columbia Law Review* 735, 736 (1949).
[5] Underhill Moore and Gilbert Sussman, "The Lawyer's Law," 41 *Yale Law Journal* 566, 576 (1932).
[6] Charles E. Clark, "Underhill Moore," 59 *Yale Law Journal* 189, 190 (1950).

able preferences; it is another to be able to make logic or at least under-standable policy out of decisions based on complex facts.[7]

Douglas was not left to attempt a wholesale revision in approach by himself. On December 20, 1926, the Columbia Law Faculty held the first in a two-year series of conferences on their educational program.[8] In these conferences we again see indication of Douglas' emphasis on legal study which will relate the legal materials as closely as possible to the relevant social forces in the world beyond the law.

While the conferences were not a sign of unanimity of faculty opinion on the approach to legal problems, Karl Llewellyn soon thought he saw the chance for agreement on these two principles: first, "work throughout the school [was] to be directed, in teaching and in research, at setting law against the background of the society in which law is found"; second, "legal materials [were] to be regrouped to make feasible their study in conjunction with the relevant nonlegal materials, with special reference to the effects of law, and to possible means of better legal adjustment." [9]

Douglas participated in special committees planning curriculum revision within the field of his own special interest, business law. After some initial work with his associate Carrol Shanks under the chairmanship of Underhill Moore, Douglas was appointed chairman of a new committee on the field of Business Organization.[10] We find Douglas' committee clearly endorsing the functional approach in their conclusions to a study of marketing procedures observed from three alternative standpoints: the functions involved, the agencies performing the task, and the characteristics of the units being marketed.

If we examine these three bases from the point of view of the permanence of the data concerned, we conclude that *functions* or *basic processes* (such as demand creation, transportation, storage, etc.) are the most permanent or enduring. The functions being performed in 1927 are the same functions that were performed in the earliest days of an ex-

---

[7] Douglas, "L. E. Joslyn, *Student's Manual of Bankruptcy Law and Practice*," 22 *Illinois Law Review* 347 (1927). See also reviews of "Holbrook, Evans, and Aigler, *Cases on the Law of Bankruptcy*," 37 *Yale Law Journal* 685 (1928), and of William E. Britton's *Cases on the Law of Bankruptcy* in 24 *Illinois Law Review* 121 (1929).

[8] A set of duplicated or typescript copies of many documents dealing with these con-ferences is available in the Law School Library at Columbia. They are bound in two groups:
    a. Columbia University, School of Law, Faculty Conferences on Legal Education, 1926–27. *Documents*.
    b. Columbia University, School of Law, Faculty Conferences on Legal Education. *Memoranda and Special Faculty Reports*.
For the beginning of the conferences see *Documents*, "Memorandum to the Law Faculty."

[9] *Memoranda*, Doc. 28-1, "Preliminary Report of the Committee on Program."

[10] *Documents*, 4 and *Memoranda*, Doc. 28-3.

change society. Quite enduring, but nothing like as enduring as functions, are the unit characters (such as perishability, bulk, etc.) of goods. . . . Least enduring of all are the agencies used. The chain store, the department store, and many others of these devices did not exist yesterday and may not endure until tomorrow.[11]

In this atmosphere, Douglas was completing assembly of the elements that were to be important in his legal philosophy. However, this enthusiasm for linking the law to sociology and economics, shared with some of his older colleagues such as Underhill Moore and Karl Llewellyn, was not common to all members of the faculty. Disagreement boiled up among them regarding a successor to Dean Huger W. Jervey, who was retiring because of ill health. If a candidate's views satisfied one group, the same opinions seemed to provoke virtually unassuageable doubts in the minds of the other faction. Nicholas Murray Butler, impatient with the lack of agreement, apparently decided that he would have to act himself.[12]

The news that Butler had appointed Young B. Smith as Dean [13] seemed a special rebuff to the sociologically oriented members of the faculty. The new Dean had made no secret of the feeling that while individuals such as Moore provided a useful new approach, it should be only one viewpoint among others presented at the law school. Smith apparently felt that Moore and Walter Wheeler Cook wanted to make their approach the only method by which legal material was presented.[14] Douglas, one of the younger members of the offended group, quickly resigned from the faculty.

Douglas matures his legal philosophy at Yale

News of the discontent at Columbia spread fast. Robert M. Hutchins, just at the outset of his career, had been made Acting Dean of the Yale law faculty. With a number of other members of the Yale staff he had kept a sympathetic eye on the work of Columbia's sociologically oriented legal scholars. In their visions of the future, the group saw the Yale Law School as a center for research and teaching directed along similar lines

[11] *Documents,* 35. See also *Documents,* 26, "Business Associations: Devices for Organizing for Management, for Limiting Risk, and for Assembling Capital."
[12] Useful background regarding this controversy can be found in A. T. Mason, *Harlan Fiske Stone* (1956), pp. 128–130, and in the footnote on p. 139. Many of the maneuvers reported in connection with the dispute can be learned only from those close to the actual protagonists. I am indebted for additional insight into the material on which this account is based to Judge Charles E. Clark of the United States Court of Appeals, Second Circuit. Judge Clark was Dean of the Yale School of Law from 1929 to 1939. Naturally I do not wish anyone to hold him accountable for the final form which I have given to these facts. Interview, New Haven, June 10, 1953.
[13] *The New York Times,* May 8, 1928, p. 24, col. 8.
[14] Mason, *op. cit.,* p. 129.

of interest. They now concluded that the time was ripe for the realization of their project.[15]

Hutchins hoped to lure as many of the Columbia dissidents as possible to Yale, and at the same time sought to establish a center where research scholars could join with men from many other disciplines in a co-ordinated study of man's problems. While hard at work on these projects he accidentally met Douglas and fell into conversation, an encounter which persuaded Hutchins that Douglas was just the man to help revamp Yale's courses in corporation law.[16]

Shortly after Douglas' switch to Yale the plan for a social-science research center was rounded out also, providing facilities which would help Douglas to further his interests in linking law with other social sciences. The Laura Spellman Rockefeller Fund granted $7,500,000 to Yale in 1929 "for the establishment of an Institute of Human Relations in which the University's resources for the investigation of man's behavior from the individual and social viewpoints will be concentrated." [17]

The nature of law—Douglas' version

We have already seen a glimpse of Douglas' approach to the law reflected in the reviews he had been publishing in legal periodicals. For him law is to be defined according to the functions it performs in society; it is to be studied by investigating precisely how those functions are carried out; it is to be judged by its effectiveness in fulfilling those functions.

In reviewing *The Lawful Pursuit of Gain* by Max Radin, Douglas speaks of "law in the broader sense" as "the control exercised by all groups in society (including but not restricted to courts, legislatures, and other governmental agencies) on other groups and on individuals." [18] In a 1933 article he quotes with approval Arnold's view that, to the prosecutor, the criminal law is not to be viewed as "something to be enforced because it governs society, but as an arsenal of weapons with which to incarcerate certain individuals who are bothering society." [19]

As Douglas resumed the task of transforming his views on legal education into specific courses he again joined with Carrol Shanks, his asso-

[15] For this I have relied primarily on information supplied by Judge Clark.

[16] Jack Alexander, "Washington's Angry Scotsman," 215 *Saturday Evening Post* 9, 106 (October 17, 1942); interview with Judge Clark.

[17] Yale University, "Catalogue of the School of Law, 1929–30," *Bulletin of Yale University*, 25th Series, No. 25 (July 15, 1929), p. 30. See also *The New York Times*, February 24, 1929, Sec. 10, p. 1, col. 2.

[18] Douglas, Review of *The Lawful Pursuit of Gain* by Max Radin, 44 *Harvard Law Review* 1164, 1165 (1931).

[19] Thurman Arnold, "Law Enforcement—An Attempt at Social Dissection," 42 *Yale Law Journal* 1, 9 (1932). Quoted by Douglas and G. E. Bates, "The Federal Securities Act of 1933," 43 *Yale Law Journal* 171, 211 (1933).

ciate from the days of research and teaching at Columbia. Shanks, working in the New York law office of Root, Clark, Buckner, and Ballantine, rejoined Douglas in New Haven during the years 1929 and 1930. Shanks taught some of the classes in corporation law. Together they finished evolving the rationale for a series of casebooks which would be suitable for their new courses, finding that none on the market was adequate for their purposes.

While crystallizing their ideas, Shanks and Douglas exposed them from time to time to the criticism of their colleagues in the legal profession.[20] One such exposition was printed in the *Illinois Law Review* for March 1929. Under the heading, "A Functional Approach to the Law of Business Associations," Douglas set forth, *first*, the inadequacies of existing schemes for organizing the subject matter of this field and, *second*, the advantages of the approach which he and Shanks envisioned as remedying these ills. The article is interesting as Douglas' first broad statement of his approach to the law.

As Douglas reviewed the past study of business law, he found that it had crystallized into four major fields. Two of these, *corporation* and *partnership*, were concerned with possible *forms* of business organization. Two others, *agency* and *master and servant*, dealt with "tools for expediting business" operations. The significant thing to be noted, in Douglas' opinion, was the effect of this crystallization on the manner in which problems of business law were visualized in the classroom, the law office, and the judicial chamber. With emphasis on form:

> The kind of organization, its nature, its quality, its limitations, were analyzed. The analysis took the form of rules; the rules became the theology. The analysis, the rules, the theology emphasized the business unit. It was this. It was not that. It could do this. It could do not do that. It was different from this but similar to that. It—and its qualities and its characteristics—were the keystone of the law of business associations. The habit of thought crystallized.[21]

Such developments were anathema to Douglas. In his opinion their fatal weakness was the resulting loss of contact with reality, the inability of the law to adapt to a constantly changing world:

> The theology obscured thinking. It instituted an endless process of refinement. It continued by its own momentum. The theology complete in itself left no room for growth. Postulates became firmly fixed. The flexibility required for adaptation to an ever-changing economic order was lacking. Creation of new postulates in the light of new facts became increasingly difficult.[22]

[20] Interview with Carrol Shanks.
[21] 23 *Illinois Law Review* 673, 674 (1929).
[22] *Ibid.*, pp. 674–675.

To Douglas' way of thinking a complete reorganization of thought was required if legal minds were to be freed from these stultifying habitual ways of thought. He further hoped to achieve a formula which would aid in keeping the new materials from again losing touch with the problems of any given day, a formula which would bring something of the ever-changing nature of the economic world to the law itself. This, he felt, might be attained by developing a set of categories and classifications which would focus attention on the economic and social forces involved in the cases of business litigation:

> That would lead rather to a consideration of the phenomena observed in the organization and operation of a business than of the mere form itself of business. That would result in observations of the things men attempt to do and are found doing when engaging in business. That would lead to the emphasis being placed on the end sought. . . . That would shift the emphasis from forms of business units to the uses to which the units are put. That would discard at one sweep the theological refinements of the concepts. Instead of having his mind cluttered up with many analytical distinctions (ofttimes metaphysical) the student would start with considerations more fundamental. The process would be concerned almost solely with the incidents of economic, social, and business problems; with a consideration of the social controls over such economic, social, and business forces; with the results of such controls. Around such incidents would the legal and nonlegal material be grouped.[23]

With such a technique of study, Douglas felt, the attention of all would be directed to answering two general questions of major importance:

> (1) what are the socially sanctioned ways in which this activity can be conducted? and (2) what social regulations of such activity are necessary in order to protect the investor, to safeguard those with whom the business will come into contact and to make the undertaking of business not too burdensome? [24]

As the young Yale professor saw it, the material, both legal and nonlegal, concerning business organization fell into three categories. These categories, one might say, subsumed within them the various phases of a business's activities from birth to death.

The first was "the assembly of resources," either at the inauguration of an enterprise or when, for any purpose, it sought additional capital at some later time. This, like the other two processes, was one "common to all" and "unknown to none." The logical Douglas mind broke it down further into two main operations, long-term financing and short-term financing.[25]

The second phase of business life Douglas singled out for study was

23 *Ibid.*, pp. 675–676.
24 *Ibid.*, p. 677.
25 *Ibid.*, p. 676

"the 'control' or 'direction'" of the enterprise as a going concern. Such control need not be looked at in a narrowly legal fashion either. When regarded in a broader way the problem to be studied would resolve itself into the investigation of "allocation of 'control' among labor, creditors, employees, investors, and the state," groups which all could be found sharing to varying degrees in the "direction" of virtually any business of the time.[26]

Last of the three functions involved in the life cycle of a business firm was that of allocating losses should the enterprise fail. Douglas suggests that a company might be considered "as a group composed of all employees, all creditors, all investors and the state," each with an economic stake in the business.[27] Worker, creditor, stockholder, and bondholder all have aided in conducting the business. If losses occur how much shall each group sacrifice of the value it has contributed to the enterprise?

> To hide [this question] under the guise of what is a partnership or what is a corporation is to fail to focus on the social regulatory function which the judicial process is performing through these various legal devices.[28]

Look at the matter in the fashion Douglas suggests and the "rules of law will be studied not as ends in themselves but as part of the allocation process."[29]

Douglas felt that with such a grouping of problems it would be difficult to avoid considering the nonlegal materials, study of which was essential to understanding. With such an approach it would be harder to remain oblivious to alterations in economic and social conditions, alterations which might render prior studies of a problem obsolete.[30]

Soon Douglas and Shanks had a stream of casebooks organized along the above lines flowing from the presses of legal printing houses. Perhaps the volumes were compiled a trifle more hastily than would have satisfied some, including the authors in their more leisurely moments. But with

---

[26] *Ibid.*, pp. 679–680.

[27] *Ibid.*, p. 679.

[28] *Ibid.*, p. 680.

[29] *Loc. cit.*

[30] *Ibid.*, p. 681. For similar functional treatment of other problems see Douglas, "Vicarious Liability and Administration of Risk," 38 *Yale Law Journal* 584–604, 720–745 (1929). Other examples of his views on business law at this time can be found in the following reviews:

Shareholders' Money, by Horace E. Samuel, reviewed in 34 *Columbia Law Review* 788 (1934).

Cases on the Law of Bankruptcy, by William E. Britton, reviewed in 24 *Illinois Law Review* 121 (1929).

Cases and Materials in the Law of Corporate Financing, by Adolph A. Berle, Jr., reviewed in 17 *Virginia Law Review* 625 (1931).

no materials available which completely met the needs of their students, the authors felt that something had to be prepared quickly.[31]

The casebook series met with widespread approval. Comment, both good and bad, suggested that the authors were reaching their goal. Elihu Root, Jr., reviewing *Cases and Materials on the Law of Financing Business Units,* paid the editors a high compliment.

> This volume is one of a series which approaches in a novel manner the teaching of corporate law. The manner of approach is novel, but it is so sensible and obvious that it is a wonder that it has not been tried before. In my early practice . . . there were no good practical works on corporate law in general circulation. . . . A few years ago there were delivered at the City Bar Association a series of very able lectures on the practical aspects of corporate law. They have been a boon to all of us. It seems to me that the new series of texts and materials by Douglas and Shanks does for teaching very much what those extraordinary Bar Association lectures did for practice.[32]

A reviewer of *Cases and Materials on the Law of Management of Business Units* felt that it represented "a high degree of success" in placing the legal problems "on a practical business plane" and was "the first effective introduction" into law school teaching of materials of many phases of recent corporation law.[33]

In evaluating *Cases and Materials on the Law of Corporate Reorganization,* Robert T. Swaine noted the inadequacies of the typical law curriculum as a means of preparing the law graduate to deal adequately with the problems he would encounter in practice. Douglas and Shanks, he felt, had assembled the materials necessary to do an adequate job.[34] Arthur Stone Dewing of the Harvard Business School felt that the latter portions of the material in this book "dealing specifically with reorganization procedure, have never had such a complete or balanced treatment." [35]

The books did not receive unalloyed praise. One of the more critical comments by E. Merrick Dodd, Jr., is interesting because of its similarity in tone to more recent criticism of the Douglas approach. Speaking of the organization of the chapter on sales in the book on corporate reorganization, Dodd observes:

> The effect is to center the student's attention at the outset on the sub-

---

[31] Douglas and Shanks, *Cases and Materials on the Law of Financing Business Units* (1931); *Cases and Materials on the Law of Management of Business Units* (1931); *Cases and Materials on the Law of Corporate Reorganization* (1931); *Cases and Materials on Losses, Liabilities, and Assets* (1932); by Douglas, with Charles E. Clark as co-author, *Cases on the Law of Partnership* (1932).

[32] 41 *Yale Law Journal* 481 (1932).

[33] N. Isaacs, 41 *Yale Law Journal* 150 (1931).

[34] 32 *Columbia Law Review* 402 (1932).

[35] 45 *Harvard Law Review* 1138, 1139 (1932).

stantive issue of the fairness of the plan and to leave for later treatment the procedural devices of judicial sale and intervention by dissenters by means of which the issue of fairness is normally brought before the court. This method has undoubted advantages, especially from the standpoint of those who regard business law as primarily applied economics. On the other hand, it has the serious disadvantage for one who is teaching students to be lawyers rather than financial experts of making it difficult to bring out clearly the extent to which the existing procedural devices affect both the theory and the practice of the courts with respect to what constitutes unfairness.[36]

DOUGLAS AS INVESTIGATOR OF BANKRUPTCY LAWS

Douglas' interest in business law led him into the major research project in which he was involved while at Yale, an investigation of the causes of business failures, their social and economic effects, the legal and nonlegal methods of preventing them.[37] Once again, the study illustrates Douglas' concern with the social impact of the law. The study was announced as part of a new legal curriculum at the Law School. The project was to embrace within it "the functioning of the whole credit system of the country." It was to take the administration of the bankruptcy act as a point of origin since that was "the point where the credit system breaks down and credit losses are suffered and felt." [38] The study was noteworthy both for its approach to problems of public policy involved in the administration of the bankruptcy laws and for the social-science research techniques it employed, techniques which represented real pioneering in their day.

Bankruptcy study—the approach employed

It was a real stroke of fortune that Douglas began a comprehensive study of the bankruptcy laws in the late 1920's. The oncoming depression soon made this problem one of the popular subjects of the day.

Douglas' views and the co-operation of his research staff were sought in many quarters. His investigations assumed major proportions.

The Yale Institute of Human Relations saw in them the opportunity to engage in social-science research of broad scope and implications. A popular magazine became interested. Under the title, "Have You the Right to Be in Business?" it published an article presenting the gist of Douglas' discoveries on the question of why people go bankrupt.[39]

The Bar Associations of New York and Bronx Counties, with William

[36] 17 *Cornell Law Quarterly* 317, 318 (1932).
[37] *The New York Times*, February 7, 1928, p. 46, col. 3.
[38] 3 *Journal of the National Association of Referees in Bankruptcy* 48 (1929).
[39] M. K. Wieshart, "Have You the Right to Be in Business?" 110 *American Magazine* 26 (August, 1930).

J. Donovan as counsel, were studying bankruptcy administration in the Southern District of New York. They called on Douglas and his assistants for information concerning bankruptcy proceedings in the courts of other jurisdictions.[40]

In mid-1930 President Hoover authorized his Solicitor-General, Thomas D. Thacher, to investigate exhaustively "the whole question of bankruptcy law and practice." Thacher, who had had some contact with Douglas while presiding at the New York hearings in 1929, soon had Douglas and his staff working for him.[41]

As Douglas' field studies expanded they were combined with research being carried on by the Department of Commerce regarding causes of business failure in retail grocery stores and restaurants. Soon a request came from retail credit associations and other business organizations around Newark, New Jersey, for a study in their area. Judge William Clark, sitting on the bench of the federal district court in Newark, also proved to be interested in a more detailed analysis of the cases of bankruptcy brought before him. These groups decided to co-operate in a study of all bankrupts who came before Judge Clark's court.[42] The Institute of Human Relations saw that there was an opportunity here to engage in intensive study of factors leading to a particular pathological social condition and assumed control of the study for Yale.

The manner in which these investigations were planned and carried forward is a particularly interesting illustration of the degree to which Douglas felt the law must be brought alive by an admixture of materials from the other social sciences. At first a "bankruptcy clinic" was established in Judge Clark's court.[43] Approximately every two weeks it was intended to summon to the court all who had filed bankruptcy petitions since the last meeting of the clinic. This appearance was to constitute the occasion for their regular hearing before the court. In contradistinction to the usual cursory examination, a staff of eight investigators from

[40] *The New York Times*, September 11, 1929, p. 30.

See U.S. Congress, House of Representatives, Committee on the Judiciary, 38 *Public Hearings* before the United States District Court for the Southern District of New York *In the Matter of an Inquiry into the Administration of Bankrupts' Estates,* 71st Congress, 3rd Sess., House Committee Print (1931), p. v., "I wish to express my appreciation also to the Yale Law School for the studies made by certain of its staff, and particularly by Professor William O. Douglas, without whose aid much of our research work could not have been done."

[41] U.S. President, *Message Recommending the Strengthening of Procedures in the Judicial System, together with the Report of the Attorney-General on Bankruptcy Law and Practice,* Senate Document No. 65, 72nd Congress, 1st Session (Washington: U.S. Government Printing Office, 1932), p. 45.

[42] *The New York Times*, November 11, 1929, p. 43.

[43] For the account of the clinic, as it was conceived by its creators, see William Clark, W. O. Douglas, and Dorothy S. Thomas, "The Business Failures Project—A Problem in Methodology," 39 *Yale Law Journal* 1013 (1930).

Yale would ply the bankrupts with a lengthy series of questions. The schedule of questions, drawn up as a result of "conferences with judges, lawyers, economists, psychologists, sociologists, and physicians," was designed to explore areas where each of these professional groups thought some of the explanations for bankruptcy might lie. As the questions were put, the investigator engaged in such cross-examination as he felt was required to bring out all aspects of the debtor's problems.

Following the examination of the bankrupt himself the investigators were to turn their attention to such books and records as the bankrupt might have possessed, to information on their trade practices obtained from creditors, the Better Business Bureau, and trade associations. Social welfare and medical services were to be consulted for possible information on illness and/or need for social service. The location of the insolvent business was to be surveyed so that the appropriateness of its locale for service to its intended clientele might be examined. The investigators felt that only two things still were lacking to round out their sources of information. They regretted that "the facilities for giving intelligence tests are not adequate, nor has a practical method of securing necessary observation by a mental hygienist yet been devised." [44]

At least some of the collaborators regarded the study as more than an opportunity to obtain a limited amount of quantitative data on bankrupts. They also saw it as an opportunity for pioneering in unearthing hypotheses about the antecedents of bankruptcy—little known at the time—and for testing the reliability and effectiveness of various types of questions and data-collecting devices. This interest was a fortunate one for the equanimity of the investigators; after two or three sessions, comprehending study of only fifty-eight bankrupts, the clinic was abandoned "for political reasons." [45]

Following the closing of the clinic three other information-gathering techniques were employed: a personal interview with the bankrupt, the mailing of a questionnaire to the bankrupt with a letter from the project staff explaining the purpose of the study and requesting completion and return of the form, and, in substitution for the staff letter, a letter from the bankruptcy court directing the bankrupt to fill out and return the questionnaire. From the results of this experience it was possible to enlist the co-operation of Solicitor-General Thacher, as a consequence of which 910 more cases were studied within the jurisdiction of the Federal District Court in Boston.[46]

[44] *Ibid.*, p. 1018.
[45] Dorothy S. Thomas, "Some Aspects of Socio-Legal Research at Yale," 37 *American Journal of Sociology* 213, 217 (1931).
[46] See Douglas and D. S. Thomas, "Business Failures Project—an Analysis of Methods of Investigation," 40 *Yale Law Journal* 1034 (1931).

The bankruptcy studies gave Douglas a great deal of additional sophistication concerning research techniques. One valuable source was his acquaintance and collaboration with a young sociologist associated with the Institute for Human Relations, Dorothy Swaine Thomas. Dr. Thomas was interested in the effects of economic hardship on individuals and society,[47] and was naturally interested in Douglas' research on bankrupts. To Douglas and other members of the law school staff with whom she worked, Dorothy Thomas brought understanding of the problems and techniques of social-science research, particularly research of a statistical nature.[48] This real interdisciplinary co-operation helped to keep the work of Douglas and others on a methodologically sound basis.[49]

Direct work through the Institute offered less to Douglas and other faculty members, they soon concluded. Efforts to develop organized interdisciplinary collaboration, a goal virtually revolutionary for the academic world of the time, were groping and frequently not too successful. A meeting would be held at which a particular individual would discuss the project he was trying to investigate. Douglas, for example, might bring up some of his recent work in the bankruptcy investigation. A public-health specialist would suggest, "You'd better see what condition the homes of the bankrupts are in." [50] A psychiatrist, pursuing some theory of his own, might suggest that the investigators find out whether or not the bankrupts were constipated.[51] Much of this sort of "cross-fertilization" was not too helpful.

Open disenchantment with the Institute's possible contributions to legal research increased when it became clear that little of the Institute's resources would be available for the financing of legal research. Aside from some assistance for the Business Failures Project, there was only a moderate grant to Underhill Moore for his study of commercial bank credits, and a small sum which enabled Borchard to complete his study of the errors of criminal justice, whence came *Convicting the Innocent.*[52]

---

[47] A few years before she published *Social Aspects of the Business Cycle* (1925).

[48] See her book, *Some New Techniques for Studying Social Behavior* (1929).

[49] Observation of Donald Slesinger, interview, New York, New York, June 29, 1953. Mr. Slesinger was for some time executive secretary of the Institute of Human Relations.

Slesinger apparently should receive more credit than he would give himself. See the acknowledgment in Charles E. Clark and W. O. Douglas, "Law and Legal Institutions," 2 *Recent Social Trends in the United States* (1933), p. 1430, note 1.

[50] Interview with Dorothy S. Thomas, Philadelphia, Pa., May 29, 1953.

[51] Interview with Donald Slesinger. When lawyers complained to Judge William Clark, in whose court the bankruptcy study was made, he, less interested in such problems, put an end to inquiries as to whether or not the bankrupts were constipated. Telephone conversation, Princeton, N. J., June 26, 1954.

[52] Edwin M. Borchard, *Convicting the Innocent* (1932).

Bankruptcy study—implications for public policy

Very early in Douglas' study of bankruptcy and reorganization problems his alertness for special questions of public policy in the law became apparent. In an early examination of equity receiverships in Connecticut, Douglas found that, even though such receiverships could only be instituted if the assets of a business exceeded its liabilities, the general creditors of the concerns involved received only 16.8 per cent of their claims.[53] Did this mean that the costs of administering the receivership or the generally unsatisfactory profit-and-loss position of the business would have made it more desirable from the standpoint of the creditors to have proceeded directly to bankruptcy, accompanied by immediate liquidation of the assets of the enterprise? [54]

Douglas was quite aware of the broader issues. Naturally, in a given case, a receivership, which made it possible to dispose of the business as a going concern, might bring more of a return to the creditors and stockholders. Most interestingly, while recognizing that the workers "do not have an investment in the business in the legal or popular sense," Douglas felt they possessed a "prospective income" from it which gave them a status in the enterprise with a "measurable degree of permanency."

> A liquidation which would cause an immediate displacement of labor with little chance of an early absorption of the displaced labor might argue for such an attempt [to rehabilitate the business or to sell it as a going concern] even though it would not be deemed good judgment if the interests of creditors and stockholders alone were considered.[55]

As the bankruptcy study progressed, Douglas found that many businessmen were menacing their actual or putative creditors by failing to keep books of account and, oblivious to their financial condition, were plunging headlong down the road to insolvency. He found them relying excessively on credit, at times speculating on the stock exchange or at the race track with funds owed these creditors. Careful supervision of discharges in bankruptcy was needed to make sure that the careless or criminal bankrupt did not escape to continue his game of fleecing creditors.

[53] W. O. Douglas and J. H. Weir, "Equity Receiverships in the U.S. District Court for Connecticut, 1920–1929," 4 *Connecticut Bar Journal* 1, 6, Table I (1930).

[54] *Ibid.*, p. 8.

[55] *Ibid.*, pp. 8–9. Douglas' friends, for the most part, do not recall his having at this time any particular concern with the broader problems of society beyond the sphere of corporation law. Because of that it is particularly interesting to note the regard he displays here for the interests of the workers. Interviews: Charles E. Clark, Carrol Shanks, Abe Fortas (Washington, D.C., June 16, 1953), Wesley A. Sturges (New Haven, Conn., June 11, 1953), Donald Slesinger.

Nevertheless, Douglas felt that the law should be generous in many cases. Frequently it appeared that creditors were encouraging reckless ventures.

> If conditions generally are anything like the New Jersey situation and creditors are making it easy for marginal entrepreneurs to enter business, it would seem unwise to penalize too severely the debtor. So long as the barriers against entering business are down, ill-advised and poorly executed undertakings will continue. So long as the prevalent notion of freedom of opportunity prevails (in practice as well as theory) it seems harsh to impose on the foolish (and sometimes unfortunate) severe penalties for their improvidence. If creditors are creating or contributing to the situation, they should not be allowed their pound of flesh.[56]

Another result of Douglas' functional research into bankruptcy operations was the discovery that the institution was being employed by wage earners and other persons not engaged in business as a means of escaping liability for judgments in automobile accident litigation, a problem which has received much attention in more recent years. As Douglas pointed out, here was a problem unforeseen at the time the Bankruptcy Act was passed in 1898. The increasing financial burden of automobile accidents demanded legislative consideration on its merits. For that reason there should be reconsideration of whether or not the bankruptcy laws should be used to escape from such judgments.[57]

Problems related to bankrupt lessees provided another interesting illustration of the way in which functional analysis might suggest a new approach to legal problems. By 1933 the economic crisis was creating serious difficulties for business landlords, who found bankruptcy increasingly being used as a means of avoiding corporate leases. Considering the problem from the standpoint of the economic operations involved, Douglas, collaborating with Jerome Frank, agreed that while leases must be open to revision if businesses were to avoid being smashed on the rocks of the depression, firms must not be permitted to use the technicalities of bankruptcy as a means of escaping entirely from such obligations. The co-authors produced strong arguments for their view that landlords were entitled to the same treatment at law or in equity as all other creditors of corporations, neither being denied a hearing nor allowed to retain a subsequent right to harass those who had received the assets of the defunct bankrupt. Their insistence on the necessity of preventing legal technicalities from obscuring the economic realities of the situation can be seen in some of their concluding words:

---

[56] Douglas, "Some Functional Aspects of Bankruptcy," 41 *Yale Law Journal* 329, 351 (1932).

[57] *Ibid.*, pp. 342–343. When the Court considered New York's financial responsibility law Douglas re-emphasized his view that Congress should give consideration to this problem before the courts permitted a reduction in the scope of the relief afforded by a discharge in bankruptcy. *Reitz v. Mealey*, 314 U.S. 33 (1941).

Landlords are as much in business with their tenants as any other creditors. In reorganizations they should be accorded the same treatment as any other creditor. The feudal aspects of their legal rights and duties should not obscure the dominant business and economic characteristics of their position. As frequently as not they are in as precarious financial position as their tenants, having equally unbearable burdens of overhead. In fact, in innumerable instances the so-called landlord is none other than a group of bondholders who have financed the building. It is the interest of those bondholders that is ultimately at stake; and pitted against that interest is the interest of the lessee which in turn represents the investments of other creditors, bondholders, and stockholders. The problem becomes, then, one of wholesale reorganization with discrimination against no type of creditor.[58]

OTHER INFLUENCES ON DOUGLAS AT YALE

Many other influences at Yale helped to create a general atmosphere conducive to weeding out the last vestiges of legal scholasticism. The emphasis on realistic study of legal institutions was all-pervasive.

In tackling the questions of the social impact of law-making there was constant collaboration within the faculty. The emphasis of their work being upon these social aspects of the law, attention tended to be drawn to public rather than private law. Several courses were added not ordinarily found in the law curricula of the era—labor regulation, taxation, administrative law, trade regulation (i.e., public control of business).[59]

A number of unusual additions to the teaching staff occurred around 1930. Walton Hamilton was one. Thurman Arnold was another. Arnold, hearing some lectures given by a young lawyer down in New York City, brought him up to Yale as a research fellow.[60] That lawyer, the late Jerome Frank, it is highly significant to note, was collaborating with Douglas at Yale in the period immediately following publication of *Law and the Modern Mind,* one of the most radical views of the nature of the judicial process ever to have been offered to the public.[61]

Douglas himself helped to establish collaboration with the Harvard Graduate School of Business Administration, first on an informal basis,

[58] Douglas and Frank, "Landlords' Claims in Reorganizations," 42 *Yale Law Journal* 1003, 1049–1050 (1933).
[59] Interview with Walton Hamilton, Washington, D.C., June 17, 1953.
[60] Interview with Jerome Frank, New Haven, Conn., June 11, 1953.
[61] See Douglas and Frank, *op. cit.,* for evidence of their work together. Frank's association with both Douglas and Yale continued to be a close one. Frank reluctantly agreed to join Douglas as a Securities and Exchange Commissioner in 1937 only when Douglas, convinced that Frank was the man he needed, got F.D.R. to draft him. This ended Frank's hope of being able to devote himself again to private practice. Appointed to the Second Circuit Court of Appeals in 1941, he lectured at Yale fairly regularly from 1946 until his death, having an office in the Law School building. Interview with Jerome Frank.

and then through an abortive combined degree program.[62] Together with Roger Foster, Thurman Arnold, and Walton Hamilton, Douglas journeyed up to Cambridge in a dilapidated Ford to make their initial contacts. For Douglas this led to collaboration over a period of years with George Bates of the Harvard Business School.[63]

With Judge Charles E. Clark, sometime Dean of the Law School, Douglas supervised a study of the actual work of the federal courts for the National (Wickersham) Commission on Law Enforcement, an investigation which led to establishment of regular statistical reporting on the nature and disposition of proceedings in the federal judicial system.[64] The pair also had a chance to broadly review current legal developments in our society in a survey of "Law and Legal Institutions" for President Hoover's Research Committee on Recent Social Trends.[65]

CONCLUSION

By 1933 Douglas was finishing ten years of intensive legal study and research in the school of functional realism and its implications for public policy. As he prepared to shift from the academic arena to full-scale application of his techniques and policy to our nation's affairs there was little reason to doubt the nature or regularity of his views, for one school of the law had impressed itself on him from all sides. His first teacher and legal employer, Underhill Moore, had started him off. Early teaching days at Columbia had centered on a reassessment of legal curricula. His associates at Yale, collaborators in legal research, and the nature of his projects had all combined to the same end. Thus it was that Karl Llewellyn felt he could speak with full confidence a few years later concerning the newly appointed member of the Supreme Court.

> His unique character consists in being the first high judge trained from the beginning in the modern realistic approach to legal techniques.
>
> Keeping one's self always alive to the realities under words and never getting tangled in the words as such, has hitherto been in law a product of self-teaching, a mark of individual power, and an occasion for effort.
>
> Mr. Douglas grew up in law with no touch of tradition to the contrary to be unlearned.[66]

[62] *The New York Times*, February 20, 1933, p. 17, col. 5.

[63] Interview with Walton Hamilton. Similar co-operation had been started at Columbia, with a co-operative seminar on business organization, before Douglas left. See Columbia University, President and Treasurer, *Annual Report to the Trustees for the Year Ending June 30, 1925* (1926), p. 90.

[64] Interview with Judge Clark. Consult: National Commission on Law Observance and Enforcement, *Reports*, Vol. 2, No. 7, "Progress Report on the Study of the Federal Courts" (Washington: U.S. Government Printing Office, 1931), and the final report: American Law Institute, *A Study of the Business of the Federal Courts* (1934).

[65] See Clark and Douglas, "Law and Legal Institutions," *loc. cit.*

[66] Letter to the Editor, *The New York Times*, April 2, 1939, Sec. 4, p. 8, col. 5.

5

The Amicus Curiae Brief:
From Friendship to Advocacy*

Samuel Krislov

I

When a history of political science is written, public law will remain an area of primary focus. It is noteworthy that an iconoclastic spokesman for the "new political science," Charles Hyneman, has already singled out the field of public law with his observations that:

> Our literature on this subject is voluminous. It is frequently said that this part of our literature is in quality of analysis the best that American political scientists have produced. . . . The cumulative effect of this literature has been to illuminate brilliantly what judges have done to the national Constitution and what they have done to legislation tested against that Constitution.[1]

It is not unworthy of notice that public law remains one of those rare fields where political scientists have moved into a discipline and made a creative contribution that superseded what relatively established scholars had already contributed. All too often political science has been on the other end of the stick, with psychology, anthropology, sociology and eco-

* The author wishes to acknowledge the assistance of the Michigan State All-University Research Fund, and the granting of released time for the undertaking of the project of which this is a part. Also, the permission to reprint from volume 72 of the Yale Law Journal is appreciated.

[1] This appears as part of Hyneman's considered evaluation of the field, *The Study of Politics* (1959), p. 41.

nomics pre-empting, through superior intellectual creativity, an area of scholarly endeavor.[2]

The public law pre-eminence has been due to the contributions of a succession of creative minds. Beard, Powell, Goodnow, and Freund, among others, loom as writers and political scientists who brought insight and power to bear in the articulation of a *political* analysis of the legal and constitutional sphere.[3] To this process the Corwin-Mason tradition has made a rich contribution.

While in most of his writings Edward Corwin remains a legal analyst of mordant style and logical keenness, he scattered brilliant, intuitional perceptions of political controversy throughout his work. Nor were those unintegrated into his general approach. Since his analysis pierced the skin of logic and asked the further question of the source of illogical excrescences, he inevitably was driven to political interpretations as a consistent extension of his system of analysis. Thus Corwin's work burst the bounds of the prevailing legalism of his day. What Beard's ideology functionally did for *An Economic Interpretation of the Constitution,*[4] Corwin's relentless iconoclasm forced to develop and form between the lines in such work as his "The Constitution as Instrument and Symbol." [5] Benjamin R. Twiss' *Lawyers and the Constitution,*[6] the first approach to an interest group activity analysis of the Supreme Court, is, after all, basically an elaboration of a sentence by Corwin.

The biographical absorption of Mason has disguised for most people his essential preoccupation with the political process. *Brandeis: A Free Man's Life,*[7] gives some glimpse of the complex patterns of affiliation and competition that constitute the political life of a great society; but the essential discreetness so pre-eminent in Brandeis made full-scale revela-

[2] See the dire warning by Arthur Vanderbilt to his fellow legalists in his *Men and Measures in the Law* (1949), p. 54. "Constitutional law along with other branches of public law is in danger of becoming the exclusive property of the political scientist, to whom we owe much in this field." Actually, Vanderbilt was principally writing of the past. By 1949 the lawyers were beginning—as Vanderbilt expressly urged them—to assimilate the findings of the social scientists (*Ibid.*, p. 61), while in political science public law was beginning to lag behind.

[3] Compare Howard Jay Graham, "Procedure to Substance—Extra-Judicial Rise of Due Process, 1830–1860," 40 *California Law Review* 483, 486 (1952). ". . . law review constitutional history seldom has been institutional history; the political juices, and even the chronology, generally are lost in extracting the rules. . . . Constitutional Law, in more senses than one, emerges as digested politics!" And contrast the implied evaluation of political science in the pre-eminent inclusion of essays by Corwin, Cushman, J. A. C. Grant, *et al.*, in the *Selected Essays on Constitutional Law* assembled in 1938 by the Association of American Law Schools.

[4] Charles A. Beard, *An Economic Interpretation of the Constitution* (1913).

[5] Edward S. Corwin, "The Constitution as Instrument and as Symbol," 30 *American Political Science Review* 1071 (1936).

[6] Benjamin R. Twiss, *Lawyers and the Constitution* (1942).

[7] Alpheus T. Mason, *Brandeis, A Free Man's Life* (1946).

tions difficult. The blend of Stone's garrulousness and Mason's perspicacity, in turn, contributed to what is beyond doubt the wealthiest mine of information about the political nature of the Supreme Court ever assembled. In some ways even more revealing are such derivative works as *The Supreme Court: Vehicle of Revealed Truth or Power Group, 1930–1939*,[8] which shows an intense fascination for personal maneuver and interplay on the part of both the indirect subject of the lectures, Harlan Fiske Stone, and the author as well; it is C. P. Snow with some of the narrator's moralizings left out.

All of this provided the background for an interest group approach to law and social problems. As early as 1935, Karl Llewellyn had "rediscovered" the work of Arthur Bentley. Llewellyn accepted it as a basis for his analysis of law and the interest group hypothesis. "The Constitution as an Institution," he suggested, could be entitled "On Rediscovering Bentley." [9] The absorption of interest groups into a Veblenian institutional analysis of society, and the patterns involved in law, "law-stuff," and law jobs, became the typical Llewellyn mode of analysis, and remained a foundation of his work until his recent demise.[10] Legal theorists, in short, provided a reasonably consistent analysis of American law in interest group terms for almost a quarter of a century before political science began to accept the same frame of reference.

In 1953 Jack Peltason, himself a student of both Corwin and Mason, called for the application of a Bentleyite analysis of constitutional phenomena.[11] Paralleling this in 1954, Clement Vose began to publish the fruits of his study of NAACP activities in the Restrictive Covenant Cases.[12] Together they provided a theoretical and an empirical model for new types of research in the judicial process. In the ensuing years a more realistic appraisal of participation by the broader spectrum of interests in society has been undertaken. Oddly, this has placed the political scientist more closely in touch with thinking in law schools. There the Pound-Cardozo-Stone notion of "balancing of interests" has long been an ac-

[8] Alpheus T. Mason, *The Supreme Court: Vehicle of Revealed Truth or Power Group, 1930–1939* (1953).

[9] K. N. Llewellyn, "The Constitution as an Institution," 34 *Columbia Law Review* 1 (1934). "Bentley saw and said in 1908 all that should have been necessary to force constitutional law theory into total reconstruction." "Why so profound and incisive a book has found so little echo, I cannot make out. Morris Cohen led me to it. I feel like entitling this paper 'A Rediscovery of Bentley.' "

[10] See the use made in his culminating statement, *The Common Law Tradition: Deciding Appeals* (1960).

[11] Jack Peltason, "A Political Science of Public Law," 34 *Southwestern Social Science Quarterly* 51 (1953); *Federal Courts in the Political Process* (1955).

[12] Clement Vose, "The Impact of Pressure Groups upon Constitutional Interpretation," (unpublished paper, 1954); "NAACP Strategy in the Covenant Cases," 6 *Western Reserve University Law Review* 118 (1955); *Caucasians Only* (1959). See also "Litigation as a Form of Pressure Group Activity," 319 *Annals* 20 (1958).

cepted and acceptable mode of approaching law and society.[13] The products of the school of jurisprudence of interests, and the effects of Von Ihering on legal thought have long been apparent; the reciprocal influence through Bentley on political science has thus placed them in closer touch with each other. It is not an accident that such works as Gross and Truman are popular and highly utilized in law schools. Nor is it completely a coincidence that Stone's "balancing of interests," which loomed so large in Mason's work, should be a tool for political analysis by political scientists.

The present study is conceived of within the framework of the interest group approach to the judiciary, an approach I believe immanent in the works of A. T. Mason. It is also a fragment of a broader work, currently under way, dealing not with the single aspect of use of the amicus curiae brief, but the range of interest group activity, and the styles and extent of participation before the courts—including the lower federal and state judiciaries.

II

Scholars have long been familiar with a phenomenon called "lawyer's history"—a stark, crabbed, oversimplified picture of the past, developed largely to plead a case. In compensation there also exists a less noticed tendency toward "lawyer's contemporaneity," or what might be called "the fallacy of misplaced homogeneity." The pretense by the lawyer that all precedents are, in Holmes' phrase, "born free and equal" all too often produces a curious portrait of a static legal universe where instruments and decisions alike avoid both decay and development. Yet, wise legal scholars have demonstrated many times over the unique insights that imaginative utilization of the genetic method can produce.[14]

One device that has been treated in this antihistorical vein is the amicus curiae brief. Its delusive innocuousness has prevented its being made focus of intensive study. The standard terminology, which has not changed for centuries, as well as the offhand manner of its usual use in court, have not alerted scholars to its importance. Inasmuch as the device was apparently known in Roman law and was an early instrument of the com-

---

[13] See, e.g., Stone's opinion in *Southern Pacific Co.* v. *Arizona*, 325 U.S. 761 (1945); compare Pound's "A Survey of Social Interests," 57 *Harvard Law Review* 1 (1943) and Julius Stone's *The Province and Function of Law* (2d ed., 1950).

[14] For a discussion of lawyers' history, see the entertaining pages 104–147 in Benjamin R. Twiss' *Lawyers and the Constitution* (1942). For a brilliant use of the genetic method, see McIlwain's "Some Illustrations of the Influence of Unchanged Names for Changing Institutions," in Paul Sayre, ed., *Interpretations of Modern Legal Philosophies* (1947).

mon law, the assumption has been facilely made that it has remained functionally unchanged as long as the term has remained constant.

Yet, the mere fact that the Supreme Court of the United States first promulgated a written rule on the subject of such briefs in 1939 and made two modifications of this newly codified provision within a span of twenty years belies the assumption of permanence.[15] Quietly, but unmistakably, such change demonstrates the transition that has occurred and continues to occur in the use of the brief.

The early use of the device is still preserved in the standard definitions, and to be found to this day carefully preserved in such sources as the *Corpus Juris Secundum*. As *Abbott's Dictionary of Terms and Phrases* describes it, the amicus curiae is:

> A friend of the court. A term applied to a bystander, who without having an interest in the cause, of his own knowledge makes suggestion on a point of law or of fact for the information of the presiding judge.

Holthouse's Law Dictionary of older vintage puts it in even more stately fashion:

> When a judge is doubtful or mistaken in matter of law, a bystander may inform the court thereof as *amicus curiae*. Counsel in court frequently act in this capacity when they happen to be in possession of a case which the judge has not seen or does not at the moment remember.

The function was principally one of oral "shepardizing," the bringing up of cases not known to the judge, or providing other aids to precision for a less professional era. The *Yearbooks* cite many instances of such comments by bystanders, including calling attention to manifest error, to the death of a party to the proceeding, and to existing appropriate statutes, as well as acting on behalf of infants.[16] Occasionally, however, other information was adduced. In one instance, Sir George Treby, a member of Parliament, informed the court that he had been present at the passage of the statute whose meaning was contested, and as amicus curiae, wished

---

[15] See Fowler V. Harper and Edwin D. Etherington, "Lobbyists Before the Court," 101 *University of Pennsylvania Law Review* 1172 (1953), probably the pathfinding article on this topic, and Fredrick Bernays Weiner, "The Supreme Court's New Rules," 68 *Harvard Law Review* 20 (1954).

[16] *The Protector* v. *Geering*, 145 *Eng. Rep.* 394 (1656), re manifest error; *Dove* v. *Martin and another*, 1 *Shower* 56 (1689); *Falmouth* v. *Strode*, 11 *Mod.* 137 (Q.B. 1707); 88 *Eng. Rep.* 949, for information as to death of a party in a suit; *Beard* v. *Travers*, 1 *Vesey* 313, 27 *Eng. Rep.* 1052 (Ch. 1749), for participation on behalf of infants, and *The Prince's Case*, 8 *Coke* 1, 29a (1606), 77 *Eng. Rep.* 481,516, on the calling of attention to a statute. The latter case is distinguished for its denouement, with the Court assailing John and Warwick Hele, the amici curiae: "But in truth the Serjeant and his son have not performed the office of a good friend or of a good informer, for they have omitted one clause in the same act . . . and have thereby endeavored to deceive the Court."

to inform the court of the intent of Parliament in passing the legislation.[17] The amicus did not even have to be an attorney to intervene, and the general attitude of the courts was to welcome such aid, since "it is for the honor of a court of justice to avoid error." [18]

Inasmuch as permission to participate as a friend of the court has been and remains a matter of grace rather than right, the courts have from the beginning avoided precise definition of the perimeters and attendant circumstances involving possible utilization of the device. This, of course, increases judicial discretion, while it concomitantly maximizes the flexibility of the device. A recent court opinion suggested this rather sharply:

> If such appearance was as amicus curiae and as a matter of grace, then that grace alone concerns us. Grace doth not abound through the consent of one's adversary. It droppeth withal, like mercy—as the gentle and refreshing dews of Heaven.[19]

A nineteenth century decision illustrates *in extremis* the overwhelming flexibility of such participation. In *Ex Parte Lloyd,* the reporter of the case, a practicing attorney, had further demonstrated his versatility by accepting retainers from both sides, and thus felt himself in a quandary. The Lord Chancellor, sitting in bankruptcy, felt he had no authority to advise an attorney as to which client to represent, but was not to be outdone in this game of shifting roles. He promptly appointed himself amicus curiae and in this second capacity did advise the attorney.[20] In short, through lack of precise rules the courts have developed a highly adaptable instrument for dealing with many of the problems that arise in adversary proceedings.

Perhaps the most significant enlargement of the amicus curiae function came early and was itself a partial resolution of one of the most serious and enduring difficulties with the adversary system. The problem of representation of third parties in a common law suit (and, for that matter, in equity proceedings in class suits where large numbers are involved) is one that does not permit either a quick or easy solution. On the contrary, the difficulties have persisted through the centuries, and devices to mitigate rather than cure have been the rule.

Common law procedures remain peculiarly resistant to the expanding

---

[17] *Horton and Ruesby,* Comb. 3, 90 *Eng. Rep.* 326 (1686).

[18] *The Protector* v. *Geering,* 145 *Eng. Rep.* 394 (Ex. 1656). However, the often-repeated statement of early editions of *Bouvier's Law Dictionary* to the effect that a statute of Henry IV recognizes such a right is held by most competent authorities to be an error. See "Amici Curiae," 34 *Harvard Law Review* 733, 775 n. (1921).

[19] *Ex Parte Brockman,* 233 *Mo.* 135, 154, 134 *S.W.* 977, 982 (1911).

[20] *Ex Parte Lloyd* (1822) note 8, *Mont.* 70 n. Montagu, the Reporter, so records his own perplexity and its resolution, in *Ex Parte Elsee Mont.* 69, note (a) 70 (Ch. 1830).

of the scope of participation and trials. The theory of trial by duel, the basic notion of *Jones* v. *Smith,* precludes the generous view of the right to intervene. "The fundamental principle underlying legal procedure," a court has observed, "is that parties to a controversy shall have their right to litigate the same, free from the interference of strangers." [21] The proposition that the common law knew no intervenors—a proposition regularly advanced by the courts since 1315—may be too sweeping; but if there were exceptions, they were in fringe areas paralleling equity cases, as in dealing with heirs.[22]

As a result of this fight theory of justice, major constitutional decisions on federal tax matters have seen the United States government participate, at least nominally, only as a subsidiary or remote party to the dispute. The most expeditious route to a decision of a tax court has generally been for a stockholder or other interested party to seek to prevent the payment of the contested tax by a corporation or partnership.[23] Such ventures are, at least in some sense, evasions of the spirit of the "real interest" rule; but they have the further fillip of labeling the taxing authority, essentially a stranger, to a proceeding testing the validity of its own revenue measures.

This resistance to the participation of other parties is also reflected in the old federal practice with regard to damage suits against the government. Where the government could not be sued because of legal problems invoked by the incantation of sovereignty, it was often possible to sue a nominal defendant who, if he lost, was then reimbursed by the government. A common nominal defendant was the Postmaster General in cases affecting the operations of his department. Where the Postmaster General had been sued, and died in the course of ensuing legal proceedings, substitution of parties was statutory and tenuous. Several times no appearance was possible on his behalf by the government, and thus in a number of instances—Frankfurter and Landis list seven cases—the United States Treasury suffered because of the untimely death of one who was essentially a fictional participant.[24]

[21] *Consolidated Liquor Co.* v. *Scotello & Nizzi,* 155 *Pacific* 1089, 1093 (1916), 21 N.M. 485, 494–495.

[22] See "Parties," 67 *Corpus Juris Secundum* 975; Raoul Berger, "Intervention by Public Agencies in Private Litigation in the Federal Courts," 50 *Yale Law Journal* 65 (1940). But compare this with Ralph V. Rogers, "Intervention at Common Law," 57 *Law Quarterly Review* 400 (1941). See comments indicating reluctance to permit government participation as late as 1906, in *Brooks* v. *Southern Pacific Co.,* 148 *F. Rep.* 986 (1906).

[23] See, e.g., *Carter* v. *Carter Coal Co.,* 298 U.S. 238 (1936), and the comments thereon in Robert Jackson, *The Struggle for Judicial Supremacy* (1941), pp. 21, 153.

[24] Felix Frankfurter and James Landis, *The Business of the Supreme Court* (1927), p. 271, n. 53.

Examples of this type of complexity and injustice resulting from over-rigid application of the principles of adversary proceedings could, of course, be cited for cases involving private parties as well. Indeed, attention to these problems has been called by defenders of the system, including the judges—to say nothing, of course, of the critics.

In common law the amicus curiae was apparently early utilized to resolve one such complication—namely to call attention to collusive suits. The friend of the court could thus point out either that the proceeding was fraudulent—involving no dispute at all—or that it had threatened to foreclose the rights of third parties through collusion. For example, in *Coxe* v. *Phillips*, a 1736 case, the nominal issue was a suit for debt. Actually the suit was collusive, allowing Mrs. Phillips to embarrass one Muilman, whose marriage to her had been declared null on discovering that she had a living husband. Muilman had then proceeded to marry another woman, to the apparent irritation of Mrs. Phillips. Though on the record not involved as a party, Muilman was able to plead as amicus curiae. He proved successful, not only with regard to vacating the action, but also in having both Coxe and Phillips found in contempt of court.[25]

The incorporation of this new function fundamentally transformed the role of the amicus curiae, and with it the device assumed radically new dimensions which only time made apparent. For in spite of the pretense of service to the court—with the functional relations solely to justice and law—the amicus clearly here had to depart from all-obliging-general-service and was willing now to function in the interest of some party, but not necessarily as his representative. One may cite precedent without participating basically for one interest or another; one may not call "fraud" without basically taking sides. While the courts cling to the proposition that the amicus remains a detached servant of the court—"he acts for no one, but simply seeks to give information to the court" [26]—his services no longer precluded commitment to a cause. Indeed, the very notion of his acting for no one was belied by his rising to do just the opposite—in many instances to act directly and officially as counsel for some party not involved in the case in the official sense. Such a participant might be deemed to extend (and reciprocally to enjoy) "friendship" toward the court, but it would seem that every entrant in the legal arena might expect the same relationship in the very same sense.

Thus, even in its native habitat, the amicus curiae brief went through changes that were profound and were to have profound repercussions.

---

[25] *Coxe* v. *Phillips*, 95 *Eng. Rep.* 152 (K.B. 1736). Earlier a court held that "if an indictment be apparently vitious (be the crime what it will) it ought to be quashed . . . and therefore as amicus curiae anyone may move to quash it," *Rex* v. *Vaux*, 90 *Eng. Rep.* 314 (1686).

[26] *Campbell* v. *Swasey*, 12 *Ind.* 70, 72 (1859).

III

These problems of representation of several interests under a common law system of legal laissez-faire were, if anything, exacerbated by the American system. On the one hand a complex system of entities was created by a federal constitution, with state and national interests all potentially in conflict, and, hence, potentially unrepresented in the course of private suit. Legal doctrines espoused by the Court also multiplied the problem. The assertion of judicial review and a Court role as "umpire to the federal system" meant that disputes of private litigation were to result ultimately in the basic constitutional law of the realm. (This assertion can easily be verified by reading the names of the litigants in the table of contents of any constitutional law text.)

Further, Marshall early and effectively established strict criteria for standing to sue in the federal courts. In *Strawbridge* v. *Curtis*, in 1806, Marshall insisted "each distinct interest should be represented by persons, all of whom are entitled to sue or may be sued in the federal courts." [27] This ruling has not escaped criticism.[28]

While he thus minimized the task of the Court in one sense by excluding certain types of parties, Marshall magnified it in others. He thus clearly and early inaugurated the trend of Court abnegation; Frankfurter and Landis have trenchantly observed that "perhaps the decisive fact in the history of the Supreme Court is its progressive contraction of jurisdiction." [29] By this auto-limitation of Court availability as a forum to "real parties" and "real disputes," Marshall sought to escape from some of the necessities of decision in crucial cases, and in this was, on the whole, successful. The price paid for this, however, is that interests not so tightly self-evident and formally litigious may be quite significant and far-reaching in their practical political effects, dwarfing the purely legal considerations.

Consequently, the corollary of the Frankfurter-Landis dictum is that there has been through history an opposite and almost equal effect. The Court, in contracting jurisdiction in one direction, will often establish criteria by which it may flexibly reclaim authority when it so chooses in opposition to the fundamental tendency of renunciation.

With regard to Marshall's *Strawbridge* decision, the Court's solution has been to establish a number of loose categories by which governmental

[27] *Strawbridge* v. *Curtis*, 7 U.S. (3 *Cranch.*) 267 (1806).
[28] See the account in Nicholas J. Campbell, Jr., "Jurisdiction and Venue Aspects of Intervention Under Federal Rule 24," 7 *University of Pittsburgh Law Review* 1, 4 ff. (1940).
[29] Frankfurter and Landis, *op. cit.*, p. 187.

authority may be vindicated. Thus denied standing under certain rubrics, governmental interests may often be permitted standing through others. The Court has also found a number of devices for relaxing the criteria for standing to sue where deemed desirable for other types of parties as well. These devices have varied over time, and have been implemented with differing vigor in different eras. But the secular trend has clearly been toward the practical evasion of some of the more restraining consequences of a strict interpretation of the decision in the *Strawbridge* case. Oddly, the amicus curiae was not one of the early devices used to resolve the problem in the Supreme Court. Neither has it been always the most frequently utilized. It did not, in fact, make its appearance in the Supreme Court until after 1820.

The scope of participation in cases, however, was expanded as early as the decision in *The Schooner Exchange* v. *McFadden*. In that case the United States' Attorney General was allowed to intervene by way of "a suggestion" in an admiralty suit.[30] Such participation in admiralty actions and in proceedings *in rem* became quite common, and as early as 1834 Story observed of such intervention, "This is very familiar. . . ." [31]

It originally was felt that such exceptions were compelled by the peculiar nature of *in rem* proceedings, but as time went on it began to be realized that it was rather the general exercise of the legal process involved. The recognition that it was the general nature of the judicial process, that it might jeopardize innocent bystanders, compelling this sort of representation, came very slowly. The earlier belief had been based on the assumption that *in rem* proceedings establishing rights of ownership "as against the whole world" peculiarly required the acknowledgment of the right of many others to participate. Since this was a "total" process, there might be more grounds for intervention. Slowly, as cases multiplied in which difficulties were experienced in other areas as well, a recognition of the utility of third party participation became prevalent.[32]

The courts, where obvious injustice will be caused by lack of representation, allowed outsiders to intervene generally by exercise of what was called "the inherent power of a court of law to control its processes." [33] No great ceremony was attendant on this; often the court merely extended the privilege of filing a brief "by leave of the Court." Gradually this development was controlled by a set of increasingly formal rules that were com-

---

[30] *Schooner Exchange* v. *McFadden and others*, 11 U.S. (7 *Cranch.*) 116 (1812).
[31] *Stratton* v. *Jarvis and Brown*, 33 U.S. 4, 9 (1834).
[32] See Benjamin Wham, "Intervention in Federal Equity Cases," 17 *American Bar Association Journal* 160 (1931): "It has grown up almost without legitimate parentage or sponsorship. . . ." See also Edward Elliott, "Interventions in the Federal Courts," 31 *American Law Review* 377 (1897).
[33] *Krippendorf* v. *Hyde*, 110 U.S. 276, 283 (1884).

municated more or less informally to the regular practitioners before the court, or those who habitually handled similar cases on other levels.[34] It was only at a much later date that these tended to be codified.

To meet the problems caused by the straitened processes of court action in an era in which semi-political decisions were increasingly reached, a number of devices were at hand in the law or were created. "The ways of the third party" developed by the courts in this field range widely in degrees of formality. A list suggested a quarter of a century ago included among others: (a) leave to intervene as a party or as a quasi-party (growing out of early equity proceedings, as well as admiralty and perhaps common law proceedings, the right to intervene has become more general, particularly in the twentieth century, but also is based upon legislation); (b) participation as an ancillary party; (c) petition or motion or presentation of claim on a fund; (d) amicus curiae; (e) suggestion or memo; (f) special appearance; (g) class suits.[35]

In addition, one might consider taxpayer suits as some sort of elevation of third parties to participant status. Further, in more carefree and less rigorously legalistic days, when the Attorney General was permitted by law and indeed forced by circumstance to maintain a private practice, it was often possible for him to serve two masters in a case. Sometimes he could advance the cause of the United States by merely acting in the name of a party; this seems to have been the case, for example, in *Gibbons v. Ogden*.[36] In other instances he might represent both the interest of the United States and obtain a fee for private activity as well. The early usages of the third party devices tended to be of these more informal sorts.

So, in *Hayburn's Case* in 1792, Randolph was allowed to move "ex officio" for the government, but the court "entertained great doubt upon his right . . . to proceed" in this manner.[37] The proper mode which seemingly emerged through the years was by route of the suggestion, as in the case of *The Schooner Exchange*, or general courtesy, that third parties were generally permitted to participate. More broadly, in 1821, Pinckney was heard "upon application of the executive" in the case of *The Amiable Isabella*. As the headnote suggests, accommodation of broader interest was commencing in formal fashion, for the reporter states the meaning of

---

[34] Elliott, *loc. cit.*, p. 392. Of course, today codification is virtually required. See James Beck's lament on the absence of a distinctive Supreme Court bar in 1930, estimating the size at that time as at least 30,000. *May It Please the Court* (1930), p. 20.

[35] Anne Bates Hersman, "Intervention in Federal Courts," 61 *American Law Review* 1, 4–6, 161 (1927).

[36] 22 U.S. (9 *Wheat.*) 1 (1824). See James Klonoski, "The Influence of Government Counsel on Supreme Court Decisions Involving the Commerce Power," (Ann Arbor: University Microfilms, 1958), pp. 1, 10, 10 n. 3, and 12; and compare James S. Easly-Smith, *The Department of Justice* (1904), p. 5.

[37] *Hayburn's Case*, 2 U.S. (2 *Dallas*) 408 (1792).

the case to be that "where a case involved the construction of a treaty, the court heard a third argument on the application of the executive government of the United States." [38]

In any event, all of these modes of representation merge into one another, and in various epochs have often been functional equivalents of each other. Even in recent years the precise standing of a party may often be somewhat vague and differently interpreted by the parties and the reporters; the line between an intervenor and an amicus curiae is still often blurred. In former years the lines were even vaguer, and contradictions and anomalies were quite common.

The early Marshall Court was not overly addicted to Latinisms; so it is perhaps not remarkable that it was not until *Green v. Biddle* in 1821 that the amicus curiae formally made its appearance.[39] In that celebrated case a decision relating to land holdings in Kentucky was made without any representation on the part of that State. Repercussions were quickly evident. Coming on the heels of the controversy aroused by the decisions in the southern land cases, the case presented explosive possibilities. It was apparently thought best to provide some forum for opposition. Under instructions from the State of Kentucky, Henry Clay made an appearance as an amicus curiae and sought a rehearing.

On March 12, 1821, "*Clay* (as *amicus curiae*) moved for a rehearing in the cause, upon the ground that it involved the rights and claims of numerous occupants of the land. . . . He stated that the rights and interests of those claimants would be irrevocably determined by this decision of the Court, the tenant in the present cause having permitted it to be brought to a hearing without appearing by his counsel and without any argument on that side of the question." [40]

Faced with this peculiar behavior on the part of one of the nominal participants, strongly suggesting collusion, the Court allowed the extraordinary procedure which would generally not be permitted today. The Supreme Court granted the plea for a rehearing on petition of an amicus curiae.[41] Inasmuch as the amicus curiae is not deemed to be a party, most jurisdictions would not allow him to initiate such an important procedural motion.

Clay, again acting as an amicus curiae, was then later permitted to argue the case. Again in view of the usual attitude that "he acts for no one," "an amicus curiae cannot perform any act on behalf of a party," and that "the court on the suggestion of an amicus curiae can do that only which he

---

[38] *The Amiable Isabella*, 19 U.S. (6 *Wheat.*) 1, 50 (1821). Similarly, in *U.S. v. Mormon Church*, 150 U.S. 145 (1893), "Mr. Solicitor General watched the case on behalf of the United States."

[39] *Green v. Biddle*, 21 U.S. (8 *Wheat.*) 1 (1823), records the events of 1821.

[40] *Ibid.*, p. 17–18.

[41] *Ibid.*

could do without such suggestion," this debut of the amicus curiae in the Supreme Court must indeed be recognized as a dramatic and unusual one.[42]

More conventionally, the Taney Court utilized the device in *Lord* v. *Veazie* in 1850.[43] In that case the Court allowed the suggestion by amicus curiae, and agreed that the suit was collusive. More significantly, the judges were forced to deal with and develop more concisely some of the factors involved in such participation, as a result of the interesting case of *Florida* v. *Georgia*.[44]

The request of the Attorney General of the United States to be heard being opposed by counsel for the two States, the Court was forced to grant or deny permission on its own initiative. Defining the problem, Chief Justice Taney noted that if the United States were merely requesting to be heard, there would presumably be no problem, "for it is the familiar practice of the Court to hear the Attorney General in suits between individuals when he suggests that the public interests are involved . . . not as counsel for one of the parties . . . but on behalf of the United States." [45]

Why then the difficulty in this case? The nub of the problem was the simple fact that the United States as a party had a very real interest in the case and was, by all criteria, at the very least a quasi-party in the guise of an amicus curiae. As Justice Curtis noted in a learned dissent, this presented at least a severely constitutional problem with regard to court jurisdiction as had the case of *Marbury* v. *Madison*.[46] While suits between states fall within the original jurisdiction of the Court, all jurisdictional grants involving the United States mentioned in the Constitution are included within the appellate jurisdiction of the Court. By allowing the United States to participate as amicus curiae, the Court was, in effect, evading the jurisdictional grants of Article III.

In spite of Curtis' high standing as a jurist and the skill and logic of his position, the rest of the Court accepted the amicus curiae as an easy road to solution of this thorny jurisdictional problem. This pattern became an accepted one, and it is today a commonplace for the United

[42] 35 *American and English Annotated Cases*, Vol. 35, 1915A, pp. 193–198; compare *Green* v. *Biddle* (note 39) with *Campbell* v. *Swasey* (note 26).

[43] 8 *Howard* 250 (1850). Somewhat earlier, in *Ex Parte Randolph*, 20 F. Case No. 11558, 2 *Brock* 447 (1834), Nicholas appeared for the United States, stating specifically that "he appeared in the case at the request of the court as amicus curiae and did not feel himself at liberty to make any admissions," p. 453. He did, however, venture the opinion in passing that "it was the fashion of the times to raise constitutional questions and to nullify acts of Congress," p. 470. See also, *In Re Ah Yup,* 1 F Case 223 No. 104 (C. C. Cal. 1878) 5 *Sawyer* 155 (1878), where the entire Bar was invited to make "such suggestions as amicus curiae as occurred to them."

[44] 58 U.S. (17 *Howard*) 478 (1854).

[45] *Ibid.*, p. 490.

[46] *Ibid.*, p. 498.

States to participate in cases arising under the original jurisdiction of the Court.

During the following decade, the amicus curiae device continued to be used to protect governmental interests, notably in connection with grants of land.[47] The flow of litigation engendered by such programs saw the government appearing in third party guises to defend passed allocations or claimed present holdings.

In another far-reaching development, the Taney Court in the case of *The Grey Jacket* faced both ways in dealing with the problem of multiple representation caused by the appearance of more than one United States agency.[48] In this 1867 case, the Attorney General had already been heard on behalf of the United States when the Treasury Department sought leave to be heard on the other side. While the Justices ventured the absolutistic position that "in causes where the United States is a party . . . no other counsel can be heard" in opposition on behalf of any other of the departments of the government, they nonetheless, in fact, allowed the Treasury to be heard for two hours, since "the Court is desirous of all the light that can be derived from the fullest discussion." [49] This phenomenon of adverse representation by different departments of the government taking opposite stands before the Courts, rather than resolution within the executive branch, was then unusual, and remains "comparatively infrequent."

Paralleling the courtesies extended to the United States, the problem of accommodation of state interests became more acute. Some of these advantages accrued to the state government through the familiar pattern of active participation of state counsel as attorneys for private litigants or by admission of state attorneys into proceedings without formal categorization of the extent of participation. In 1864, for example, with constitutionality of a state statute at issue, the Attorney General of California filed a brief.[50] During the 1880's the Court began to grant leave directly to state counsel to vindicate state rights before the Court as a regular pattern.

At the same time, and continuing until legislation clarified the situation—legislation which occurred principally in this century—the Court began to extend the right of participation of private litigants. At times as intervenors, at times as amici curiae, depending on the situation and requests of the litigants or agreements of the counsel, litigants of similar

---

[47] See, e.g., *Dubuque and Pacific Railroad Co. v. Litchfield*, 64 U.S. 68 (1859); *Platt v. Union Pacific R. R. Co.*, 99 U.S. 48 (1879); *Mining Co. v. Consolidated Mining Co.*, 102 U.S. 167 (1880).
[48] 72 U.S. 342 (1866).
[49] *Ibid.*, p. 371.
[50] *Steamship Co. v. Jolliffe*, 69 U.S. 450, 454 (1864).

cases pending before the lower courts and parties to lower court proceedings in the same case who were not overtly impleaded in the instant Supreme Court case were all allowed to state their views by brief and/or oral presentation. Others claiming to be "real parties" in the case, or who could be directly injured by a decision, were sometimes extended similar privileges.[51]

Such third party activity was not uniformly evident in all types of cases, and certain types of litigation typically had more considerable numbers of such complexities. Patent matters often involve ultimate parties, such as holders of the patent; land cases raised similar issues to those raised in admiralty situations. Some types of cases are, strictly speaking, *in rem* proceedings; others approached this category in consequences. Tax cases had extremely wide ramifications, and causes involving Indians and their rights were preternaturally involuted, presenting all types of problems in representation.[52]

IV

Beginning in the last quarter of the nineteenth century, and increasing in effect through the twentieth, two significant developments combined to emphasize third party participation. The formation of the Department of Justice in 1871 meant that broader vindication of governmental rights was feasible. With the increase of staff came the development of a broader "public interest" approach to government litigation, which supplanted an emergency attitude of vindication only where absolutely necessary.[53]

Charles J. Bonaparte's administration as Attorney General was a particularly aggressive one with far-reaching developments in cases involving Negro rights and vindication of federal legislation before the courts. He, if anyone, seems to have been the innovator of a positive use of governmental amici briefs, not merely to vindicate specific statutes, but with a broader aim of effectuating major social changes and implementing broad public interest policies. Following the advice of Moody, who as Attorney General decided to concentrate on Supreme Court action, and who concluded at the time of his elevation to the Court that even more intense

---

[51] See Austin W. Scott, "Actions at Law in the Federal Courts," 38 *Harvard Law Review* 1 (1924), for a good statement of the transition from Court rules to legislative action, and the reciprocal influence of the two processes, as well as the leading articles by James W. Moore and Edward H. Levi, "Federal Intervention," 45 *Yale Law Journal* 565 (1936), and 47 *Yale Law Journal* 898 (1938), for legislation dealing with private and public intervenors.

[52] See, e.g., *Bate Refrigerating Co. v. Hammond*, 129 U.S. 151 (1889); the *White-Smith Music Co. v. Apollo Co.*, 209 U.S. 1 (1908) (where Victor Herbert was amicus curiae); and the discussion in the *Northern Security Co. v. U.S.*, 191 U.S. 555 (1903).

[53] See Easly-Smith, *op. cit.*, and Klonoski, *op. cit.* (note 36).

focus would have been rewarding, Bonaparte in twenty-seven months conducted fifty-six cases before the highest tribunal, and personally argued forty-nine of them.[54]

Specifically, the United States as a third party actually was the principal litigant in such cases as the *Employer Liability Cases* [55] and *Bailey* v. *Alabama*.[56] And Bonaparte personally figured as an important ally in *Buchanan* v. *Warley*,[57] which tested the constitutionality of segregated residence laws attempting to establish Negro ghettoes through local legislation. The practice of governmental pleading in significant public causes, where only very broad social problems and a generalized public interest is involved, has become standard procedure—as illustrated by such cases as the school segregation, racial covenant, and redistricting litigation. While it is possible to argue that the Justice Department files in such cases only where the weight of logic or political strength is obvious, the fact remains that the United States as amicus curiae has been associated on the whole with a remarkable string of successful litigation.

Another major development has been the emergence of the administrative state. Regulatory agencies enforcing and establishing administrative policies have necessarily been involved with a broad complex of interests. Their policies, in turn, effect a broader skein of interests, in both direct and indirect fashion, than those of the older executive agencies. In short, the activities of these agencies have involved potential interests and actual

[54] See Charles Bonaparte, "Experience of a Cabinet Officer Under Roosevelt," 79 *Century Magazine* 752 (1910).

[55] 207 U.S. 463 (1908). The conclusion that the United States was, in fact, the principal litigator is derived from a number of factors. Bonaparte's 114-page brief amicus completely dwarfs the skimpy argument of the nominal litigants. Further, an indication of such partnership appears both here and in *Johnson* v. *South Pacific Co.*, 196 U.S. 1 (1904). In both instances the printing order numbers indicate that the litigant's briefs and those of the United States as amicus (in the latter case as "a suggestion") were printed together. The numbers on the *Employer Liability Cases* were 22410–07 for plaintiffs, 22411–07 on the government brief. The briefs in both instances were filed on the same day. A letter from E. E. Morsberger of the U.S. Government Printing Office (Jan. 7, 1960) indicates no records are available to show whether government briefs were continuously printed at the Government Printing Office during the period involved.

[56] 211 U.S. 452 (1908); 219 U.S. 219 (1911). Wickersham for the Taft Administration continued aggressively with the case, and the U.S. brief sustains the major part of the legal argument.

[57] 245 U.S. 60 (1917). Attorney General Charles Bonaparte wrote a series of articles in the *Baltimore Sun* that was strongly relied on and quoted extensively in the amicus brief of the Baltimore NAACP. Brief of Baltimore NAACP as Amicus Curiae, pp. 24–30, *Buchanan* v. *Warley, supra*. The case seems to have been a perfect forerunner of subsequent civil rights litigation, down to participation of various neighborhood "welfare associations," a group of legal scholars advocating Negro rights, and the accusation by the City of Baltimore as amicus curiae that "outside agitation," notably Senator Clapp of Minnesota, had really fostered the litigation.

participants beyond the normal course of individual social and political interaction with governmental agencies.[58]

The fact that this has been explicitly recognized has also reinforced the trend. Many administrative agencies, by legislative provision or on their own initiative, have broadened the base of official participation in litigation before them. They, thus, have actually mobilized and alerted groups to issues and stakes involved in a stage prior to judicial litigation. So alerted, groups and individuals have sought access to judicial decisions and means of strengthening favorable policies, both at the administrative level and, by extrapolation, at the judicial level.[59]

Over and above these developments, in a manner difficult, if not impossible, to disentangle, was the change in tactics and structure of interest articulation in American politics as a whole that occurred during the latter quarter of the nineteenth century. As Harold Lasswell has noted, that period saw a transformation of dominant modes of interest activity. The emphasis shifted from personal face-to-face contacts (not excluding corruption) to impersonal, organized, and systematic bureaucratically-undertaken and bureaucratically-oriented activity.[60] This transformation is usually recognized only implicitly by commentators when accounted for in terms of reaction, either to industrialization or bureaucratization—that is, as the product of either the industrial or the organizational revolution.

The advantages that accrue to bureaucratically sophisticated groups in other political arenas became evident in the judicial sphere as well. Involved are such factors as: sensitivity to the possibility of raising new issues (whether for offensive or defensive purposes); the ability to mobilize resources (including human resources), and to bring to bear expertise, memory, or files; and the organizational flexibility to respond quickly and

---

[58] For some of the interest group complexities caused by administrative programs, see e.g., J. P. Comer, *Legislative Functions of National Administrative Authorities* (1927), pp. 198–270. Compare Samuel Huntington, "The Marasmus of the I.C.C.," 61 *Yale Law Journal* 467 (1952). The Huntington indictment and the notion of interest groups as capturing such agencies, found throughout political science literature, has some connotations of an a priori analysis; note that, as early as the twenties, Progressives opposed creation of a Commerce Court on the ground that it would be controlled by special interests. See Frankfurter and Landis, *op. cit.*, pp. 157 ff.

[59] In some instances governmental agencies may only participate as third parties, with the U.S. Department of Justice entrusted with the real responsibility of litigation. See Robert L. Stern, " 'Inconsistency' in Government Litigation," 64 *Harvard Law Review* 758 (1954). The I.C.C. recognizes, for example, the right of complaint of any person, company, mercantile organization, manufacturing society, body politic, municipal organization, carrier, or state commission. See I. L. Sharfman, *The Interstate Commerce Commission* (1931), pp. 152 ff. Even the process of adjudication and the opinions of the commissioners encourage litigants. See Lowell Mason, *The Language of Dissent* (1959), p. 28.

[60] Lasswell, Review of Blaisdell, *American Democracy Under Pressure*, 107 *University of Pennsylvania Law Review* 295 (1958).

sensitively before policy is set, or where timing is vital, in order to achieve maximum results. These are vital in all political matters, and in this the legislature, judiciary, and administration remain similarly responsive. Though spun off from each other through time, these three processes still retain many of the marks of their Procrustean origins.

A transitional link between governmental agents acting as interest articulators and normal interest group activity in the judicial sphere was the participation of governmental officials in the guise of organized groups. So, in 1913 the railroad commissions of eight states were conjoined in a single amicus curiae brief.[61] The 1916 term of the Court saw the National Association of Attorneys General participate in cases, as well as groups of Attorneys General.[62]

Among the private interest groups which were the first to utilize the opportunities of broader access were included, nonexhaustively, racial minority groups, securities and insurance interests (often involved in litigation), railroad interests, and miscellaneous groups under severe attack, notably the liquor interests in the first quarter of this century. Sheer familiarity with the intricacies of the existing system, strong dissatisfaction with it, and relative desperation, seemingly can all function as sufficient motives for the seeking out and the finding of new channels of influence for self-protection or aggrandizement.

The first example of minority group activity appears to have been the participation of the Chinese Charitable and Benevolent Association of New York in immigration cases. Beginning in the 1904 case of *Ah How (alias Louis Ah How)* v. *U.S.*, Mr. Max J. Kohler was to intervene in such cases, explaining that:

> The peculiar character of these Chinese Exclusion cases, involving arrests or exclusions of Chinese persons, frequently indigent travellers far from their home, and beyond the convenient reach of relatives and friends, as well as of witnesses in their own behalf, has made it desirable for the Chinese persons of the City of New York and its immediate vicinity, by concerted action and mutual aid, to assist each other . . . and accordingly at or about August 1, 1903, your petitioning corporation did retain Mr. Max Kohler . . . to defend Chinese persons arrested within or prevented from entering the United States. . . .[63]

The identification of the NAACP with such briefs is, however, not merely a contemporary one, for that organization has, almost from its in-

[61] The *Minnesota Rate Cases*, 230 U.S. 352 (1913); *Missouri Rate Cases*, 230 U.S. 474 (1913).

[62] *Caldwell* v. *Sioux Falls Stock Yards Co.*, 242 U.S. 559 (1917); and *Hall* v. *Geiger-Jones Co.*, 242 U.S. 539 (1917), where both the National Association of Attorneys General and the Investment Bankers Association of America filed briefs; and *Utah Power and Light* v. *U.S.*, 243 U.S. 389 (1917).

[63] *Ah How* v. *U.S.*, 193 U.S. 65 (1904); Brief of Mr. Max J. Kohler for the Chinese Charitable and Benevolent Association of New York, *Records and Briefs*, p. 2.

ception, participated as amicus curiae in litigation. An early case in point is *Guinn* v. *U.S.*, the famous Grandfather Clause case, where the NAACP justified its participation on the grounds that "the vital importance of these questions to every citizen of the United States, whether white or colored, seems amply to warrant the submission of this brief." [64]

Highly regulated groups also were early participants. Since before the turn of the century [65] litigation involving the ICC regulatory powers has involved extensive nonparty participation of interest groups (though not necessarily as amicus curiae).[66] Following the principle enunciated by Merle Fainsod that interest structure often arises in response to governmental patterns, the transportation industry has continued to be the most highly and intricately organized area of the interest group spectrum.[67] Not only has there been continued representation paralleling the political struggles of the railroad versus the trucking interests, and railroad executives versus laborers, or even individual members versus leaders; but also the report of *Noble* v. *United States* records the appearance on opposite sides of the fence of both the Regular Common Carriers Conference of the American Trucking Association and the Contract Carriers Conference of the ATA.[68]

While stockholders and committees and rival companies began to participate as third parties in the last quarter of the nineteenth century, organized financial groups and associations became active later, noticeably appearing in the Court after about 1917.[69] *Hamilton* v. *Kentucky Distilling Co.*, involving the constitutionality of liquor prohibition, saw participation of interested organizations in 1919, as did the *Pacific States Telephone and Telegraph Co.* v. *Oregon* in 1912, with public service and ideologically oriented groups being the principal actors.[70]

That the transitional dates tend to cluster closely indeed about the time of Brandeis' effective use of the amicus curiae brief on behalf of the National Consumers League in *Muller* v. *Oregon* in 1908 will not escape the careful reader. But it is difficult to assess how strong a causal relationship there is, for Brandeis insisted on appearing for the State of Oregon, and

[64] 238 U.S. 347 (1915); Brief for NAACP as amicus curiae, *Records and Briefs*, p. 2. Incidentally, an individual amicus curiae in that case asked the Court to declare the Fourteenth Amendment not legally adopted. See brief of H. Adriaans, *Records and Briefs*.

[65] *I.C.C.* v. *Cincinnati, N. O. & T. Pac. Ry.*, 167 U.S. 479 (1897).

[66] *I.C.C.* v. *Chicago, R.I. & Pacific Ry.*, 218 U.S. 88 (1910).

[67] Fainsod, "Some Reflections on the Nature of the Regulatory Process," 1 *Public Policy* 296, 299 (1940).

[68] *Noble* v. *U.S.*, 319 U.S. 88, 89 (1943).

[69] See note 62. At least so far as I have been able to determine, these cases mark the first instances of such appearances.

[70] 223 U.S. 118 (1912). Among others briefs were filed for "the American Bureau of Political Research" and the People's Rule League of America."

as far as the Court is concerned, there were no indications of his being in reality an amicus curiae. Such an arrangement was, for Brandeis, a condition of his participation in that "the status of appearing as an official participant on behalf of the state seemed to him an important element of strength for the defense." [71] However, as early as 1916 Frankfurter called attention in print to the fact that Brandeis' essential role was that of amicus curiae.[72]

Yet another type of interest was to be heard from. In 1925 the *Myers Case*, which tested the limits of legislative control over the power of executive appointment and removal, presented peculiar dilemmas of representation. Legislative interests were presumably to be defended by the plaintiff, and the executive position directly by the Department of Justice. Quite naturally Congress was restive under the arrangement, and the President Pro Tem of the Senate and the Chairman of the House Judiciary Committee were conferring with regard to possible action, when the Court, apparently on its own initiative, appointed George Wharton Pepper as amicus curiae to present the legislative point of view.[73] Such representation has been periodic since that time, including an extended oral presentation on one occasion by the Chairman of the House Judiciary Committee.[74]

Thus, by the mid–nineteen-twenties, the major types of political interests had all witnessed at least one major instance of representation before the U. S. Supreme Court. Throughout the subsequent years the number of cases in which such briefs were filed grew in number, as did the

---

[71] A. T. Mason, *Brandeis: A Free Man's Life*, p. 248; Vose, "The National Consumers League and the Brandeis Brief," 1 *Midwest Journal of Political Science* 267 (1957); Josephine Goldmark, *Impatient Crusader* (1953), p. 163.

[72] Felix Frankfurter, "Hours of Labor and Realism in Constitutional Law," 29 *Harvard Law Review* 353, 372 n. (1916).

[73] See *The New York Times*, Feb. 3, 1925, p. 2, col. 2; and Frankfurter and Landis, *op. cit.*, p. 311, 312, for an account of the Myers case. Further political interest representation was secured in *Secretary of Agriculture* v. *Central Roig Refining Co.*, 338 U.S. 604 (1950). Puerto Rico was here allowed formally to intervene to protect its interests after an effective plea that pointed out that: "Puerto Rico has no access to the political process. . . . In the Congress the territory has only a Resident Commissioner, who by courtesy of that body—there is no law on the subject—is indulged in a seat in the House of Representatives but has no vote. As a 'discrete and insular minority' . . . the people of Puerto Rico must depend upon the courts." Memo by the Government of Puerto Rico, *Records and Briefs*, p. 21.

[74] See *Jurney* v. *MacCracken*, 294 U.S. 125, 128 (1935), for presentation by Representative Hatton W. Sumners. In *Murdock* v. *City of Memphis*, 87 U.S. (20 *Wall.*) 590 (1875), Mr. Philip Phillips orally, and Mr. B. R. Curtis through a posthumous brief, participated as friends of the court. The statement of Wiener (note 15), p. 81 n., that Pepper was the only instance of oral presentation by an amicus curiae other than the Attorney General is in error. Wiener, *The Supreme Court's New Rules*, 68 *Harvard Law Rev.* 20, 81 n. 303 (1954). Cf. Reynolds Robertson, *Appellate Practice and Procedure in the Supreme Court of the United States* (Rev. ed., 1929), p. 202.

number of such briefs filed in cases. By the 1930's such briefs were commonplace, and by the late 1940's they were beginning to be regarded by the Court as potential sources of irritation, at the same time that they were increasingly of significance to the outcome and directly even cited as justification for the granting of certiorari.[75]

Paralleling the development of the brief was a revealing change in nomenclature. The amicus curiae essentially stood in a professional relation to the Court and organizations were not regarded as amici, but rather the lawyer himself. Throughout the last half of the nineteenth century the Court, the Reporter, and the brief cling to this approach. As late as 1919 the attorneys in the *Prohibition Case* styled themselves as "both of Washington, D.C., amici curiae, *and* general counsel to the National Association of Distillers and Wholesale Dealers." [76] Apparently without self-consciousness, such identifications have been totally forgotten. By the 1930's, the open identification of an amicus brief with an organizational sponsor was quite commonplace.

The attribution of a brief to an organization belies the essentially lawyer-like role of the amicus, but realistically embraces and ratifies the transformation of the actual pattern of behavior and its new function. The amicus is no longer a neutral, amorphous embodiment of justice, but an active participant in the interest group struggle.

Where the stakes are highest for the groups, and where the needs on the part of the judges for information and for the sharing of responsibility through consultation are all at a peak, access has appropriately, and almost inevitably, been at its greatest. Occasionally a lower court will refuse an amicus brief for being "excessively partisan." [77] Again, a state court will, like the Michigan court, strike their permission to participate in view of the fact that a party "is acting (though under disguise) not as a friend of the court but as a friend of one of the contestant litigants before said court." [78]

The Supreme Court of the United States makes no pretense of such disinterestedness on the part of "its friends." The amicus is treated as a

---

[75] See Wiener, Harper, and Etherington (note 15); also, Peter Sonnenfeld, "Participation of Amici Curiae . . . 1949–1957," *Working Papers in Research Methodology*, No. 3 (1958), for instances of abuse by amici curiae. See *Pennsylvania* v. *Nelson*, 350 U.S. 497 (1956), and *Georgia* v. *Evans*, 316 U.S. 159 (1942), for instances where amici curiae were cited as evidence in justification for granting review.

[76] *Hamilton* v. *Kentucky Distilleries Co.*, 251 U.S. 146 (1919). This identification is reprinted only in 40 S. Ct. 107 (1919) and not in the official reports.

[77] See *First Citizens Bank & Trust Co.* v. *Saranac*, 246 App. Div. 672 (3d Dept., 1935).

[78] Brief for respondent, *City of Grand Rapids* v. *Consumers Power Co.*, 216 Mich. 409 (1921), 185 N.W. 852 (1921) *Records and Briefs*, p. 59. The court rejected the contention made by the petitioner that he was an intervenor on the basis of insufficient interest and rejected the contention that he was an amicus curiae on grounds that his interest was too partisan for him to be anything but an intervenor.

potential litigant in future cases, as an ally of one of the parties, or as the representative of an interest not otherwise represented. At this level the transition is complete; at the other court levels it is in process. So the institution of the amicus curiae brief has, indeed, moved from neutrality to partisanship, from friendship to advocacy.

III

Federalism

6

The Lawyers Need Help
with "the Lawyer's Clause"

Harold W. Chase

INTRODUCTION

It is appropriate for a former student of Alpheus T. Mason to sound a call to political scientists to give attention to the "lawyer's clause" of the Constitution. Professor Mason passes on to his students his own enormous and abiding interest in the nature and problems of federalism. Also, by word and example, he has refused to be intimidated by lawyers' assertions that issues in large part legal should be left to the lawyers alone. In that connection, I can still vividly recall a seminar in which an outraged Professor Mason took lawyer Charles P. Curtis to task. With a mixture of disdain and disbelief he read for us in a voice dripping sarcasm the last sentence of Curtis' bibliography in *Lions Under the Throne*. That sentence read: "Corwin has written sundry short books." [1]

For years, political scientists have been content to leave research and writing on the full faith and credit clause to the lawyers. Perhaps, Justice Jackson's famous sobriquet for the clause has tended to intimidate political scientists.[2] But whatever the reasons for the reticence in the past, political scientists should break the shackles of their own diffidence and give attention to (1) the problems which the clause has been hopefully employed to meet and (2) the problems inherent in the clause itself. These

[1] Charles P. Curtis, *Lions Under the Throne* (1947), p. 361.
[2] Robert H. Jackson, "Full Faith and Credit—The Lawyer's Clause of the Constitution," 45 *Columbia Law Review* 1 (1945).

are not legal problems pure and simple; they are, as will be demonstrated in this essay, primarily problems in intergovernmental relations. To achieve solutions to them which will be more effective than present ones, the knowledge and research skills of the political scientists will be as important as the special knowledge and skills of the lawyers. In this connection, I am reminded of the remark of a distinguished law professor. After listening to the statement of my thesis, he suggested that I entitle the piece, "The Lawyer's Clause Is Too Important To Leave To The Lawyers." I suspect his suggestion was made tongue-in-cheek. But the old saw about truth and jest immediately pops into mind.

THE FUNDAMENTAL PROBLEMS

Two fundamental problems arise in any federal system composed of states, whatever the number, which have their own comprehensive body of law and their own judiciary. Briefly, they are: (1) what effect must state agencies (including courts) give to judgments of Other-State courts?; (2) what effect must state courts give to Other-State law in deciding a case where it is appropriate to consider the law of the other state?

How did the Framers of our Constitution meet these problems? Despite valiant attempts to divine what the Framers meant to do when they incorporated the full faith and credit clause in the Constitution, no one has come up with a definitive answer which has received general acceptance as such.[3] Perhaps, the reason is that writers have tried to prove too much, that the Framers really had no clear-cut idea of what they were trying to accomplish. As Justice Jackson succinctly put it: "I find no satisfactory evidence that the members of the Constitutional Convention or the early Congress had more than a hazy knowledge of the problems they sought to settle or those which they created by the faith and credit clause."[4]

Whatever their intent or lack of it, the Framers did provide a constitutional provision requiring that "Full faith and credit shall be given in each state to the public acts, records, and judicial proceedings of every other state" and empowering Congress to "prescribe the manner in which such acts, records and proceedings shall be proved, and the effect thereof."[5]

---

[3] For assessments of the Framer's intent see Edward S. Corwin, " 'The Full Faith and Credit' Clause," 81 *University of Pennsylvania Law Review* 371 (1933); Max Radin, "The Authenticated Full Faith and Credit Clause; Its History," 39 *Illinois Law Review* 1 (1944); Kurt H. Nadelmann, "Full Faith and Credit to Judgments and Public Acts: A Historical-Analytical Reappraisal," 56 *Michigan Law Review* 33 (1957); James D. Sumner, Jr., "The Full Faith and Credit Clause—Its History and Purpose," 34 *Oregon Law Review* 224 (1955).

[4] Jackson, *op. cit.,* p. 6.

[5] Constitution, Article IV, Section 1.

Acting under its constitutional mandate, the First Congress enacted the following law in 1790:

> . . . the acts of the legislatures of the several states shall be authenticated by having the seal of their respective states affixed thereto: That the records and judicial proceedings of the courts of any state, shall be proved or admitted in any other court within the United States, by the attestation of the clerk, and the seal of the court annexed, if there be a seal, together with a certificate of the judge, chief justice, or presiding magistrate, as the case may be, that the said attestation is in due form. And the said records and judicial proceedings authenticated as aforesaid, shall have such faith and credit given to them in every court within the United States, as they have by law or usage in the courts of the State from whence the said records are or shall be taken.[6]

Here, too the intention of those who framed the proposal was not crystal clear. What exactly did they mean by the words "the said records and judicial proceedings . . . shall have such faith and credit given to them *in every court* within the United States, *as they have by law or usage in the courts of the State from whence the said records are or shall be taken?*" (emphasis supplied). It would appear they meant their words to be taken literally.[7] But any hope that the law would be interpreted literally and rigidly—if, indeed, there was such a hope—was dashed the first time the Supreme Court expounded at length on its meaning. The Supreme Court in 1839, described by Corwin as being "in the grip of States' Rights prepossessions," [8] decided in *M'Elmoyle* v. *Cohen* that "the statute of limitation of Georgia can be pleaded to an action in that state founded upon a judgment rendered in the State of South Carolina." [9] Traveling to that conclusion, the Court explained "By the law of the 26th of May, 1790, the judgment is made a debt of record, not examinable upon its merits, but it does not carry with it into another state the efficacy of a judgment upon property or persons to be enforced by execution. To give it the force of a judgment in another state, it must be made a judgment there, and *can only be executed in the latter as its laws permit*" (emphasis supplied).[10]

A more intriguing mystery of the Act of 1790 is whether or not the word "acts" was deliberately or inadvertently omitted from the sentence requiring that court records and judicial proceedings be given full faith and credit.[11] Did they feel that, since the constitutional clause already required it, there was no reason to require it again? But could not the same be said for judicial records and proceedings?

[6] 1 *STAT.* 122 (1790).
[7] Jackson, *op. cit.,* p. 7.
[8] Edward S. Corwin, *The Constitution and What It Means Today* (1954), p. 158.
[9] 13 Peters 312, 328 (1839).
[10] *Ibid.,* p. 325.
[11] Nadelmann, *op. cit.,* pp. 60–62, 81–85.

Patently, the vagueness about the meaning of the constitutional pro-vision and the statute of 1790 gave wide scope to the judiciary to develop their "real" meaning. Congress has been reluctant to provide direction for the courts even when the Supreme Court partially nullified the Act of 1790.[12] From 1790 until 1948, Congress did virtually nothing regarding full faith and credit.[13] In 1948, Congress amended the 1790 law to require that acts of state legislatures receive full faith and credit in Other-State courts.[14] It has been suggested that even here Congress was merely codi-fying the law and making no substantive changes.[15] In any case, it is clear that the courts have played the leading role in attempting to resolve the two fundamental problems described earlier. How well have they done the job?

THE SPECIFIC PROBLEMS

A. *Full faith and credit as to judgments*

On the whole, the meaning of the full faith and credit clause as to judgments has been well settled and settled well by case law.[16] Credit for it must go not only to the judges but to the lawyers who contributed much by their efforts (1) to restate the law of Conflict of Laws and (2) to achieve uniform state law on enforcement of foreign judgments.

In the early 1920's a group of prominent American judges, lawyers, and law teachers (I do mean prominent, note these names: Root, Wickersham, Stone, Cardozo, John W. Davis, Leffingwell, Williston, Beale, Pound, and Wigmore), organized the American Law Institute "to promote the clari-fication and simplification of the law and its better adaptation to social needs, to secure the better administration of justice and to encourage and carry on scholarly and scientific legal work." [17] Toward that end it was decided that the organization undertake "to produce a restatement of certain phases of the law that would tell judges and lawyers what the law was." [18] This the organization did and continues to do. As to Conflict of Laws, a Restatement was completed in 1934, and supplements in 1948. Currently a new Restatement is in the mill. Some measure of the impact of the original Restatement on Conflict of Laws may be indicated by the

---

[12] Corwin, *op. cit.*, p. 388 and Jackson, *op. cit.*, p. 7.

[13] Sumner, *op. cit.*, p. 236 and Nadelmann, *op. cit.*, p. 81.

[14] 62 *STAT.* 947 (1948).

[15] Nadelmann, *op. cit.*, pp. 81–85.

[16] Herbert F. Goodrich, *Handbook of the Conflict of Laws* (1949), Chapter 15. George Stumberg, *Principles of Conflict of Laws* (3rd ed. 1963), Chapter 5. James D. Sumner, Jr., "Full Faith and Credit for Judicial Proceedings," 2 *U.C.L.A. Law Review* 441 (1955).

[17] Herbert F. Goodrich and Paul A. Wolkin, *The Story of The American Law In-stitute, 1923–1961* (1961), p. 7.

[18] *Ibid.*, p. 8.

fact that it has been cited in over 3000 court decisions.[19] But, perhaps, as one critic has suggested, frequency of citation is no real measure of how many times "the Restatement 'rule' has affected decision." [20] Nonetheless, it stands to reason that the proceedings leading up to the Restatements as well as the Restatements themselves were bound to be read, thrashed out in private conversations, and discussed at professional meetings, and, consequently, to influence profoundly the sitting judges.

The Uniform Law movement had an even earlier beginning. Before the turn of the century, the American Bar Association took the lead in seeking to have states set up Commissions on Uniform State Laws for the purpose of promoting "Uniformity in State Laws on all subjects where uniformity is deemed desirable and practicable." [21]

Once Commissions were established by a few states, the practice of holding an annual Conference of Commissioners was begun. The Conference undertook as early as the 1890's to prepare drafts of uniform laws and continues to do so to this day. Since 1936, the Conference has additionally taken on the assignment of drafting Model Acts and promoting uniformity of judicial decisions. As one would expect, "Commissioners are chosen . . . from among leading lawyers, judges and teachers of law." [22]

To the extent that states have uniform laws and state courts interpret them uniformly, many of the problems inherent in the execution of judgments in a federal system will be mitigated. With that theorem in mind, how you evaluate the contribution of the Uniform Law movement depends upon whether you see the glass with some water in it as being part-full or part-empty. There is a whole host of uniform acts which have been recommended for adoption by all states and which have been enacted by varying numbers of states. Very few, however, have been enacted by all or nearly all the states.[23] Unfortunately, there have been only desultory efforts to promote uniformity of judicial decisions.[24] Whatever the shortcomings by way of actual accomplishment, the Uniform Law movement has helped to create an awareness of the difficulties where states in a federal system go their own merry way. And, surely, this aware-

---

[19] *Ibid.,* p. 39.

[20] Alan Milner, "Restatement: The Failure of a Legal Experiment," 20 *University of Pittsburgh Law Review* 795, 799 (1959).

[21] "Uniformity in the Law—The National Conference of Commissioners on Uniform State Laws," 19 *Montana Law Review* 149, 152 (1958). For a good short history of the movement see, "Address of the President" in National Conference of Commissioners on Uniform State Laws, *Handbook,* 1940, pp. 35–39.

[22] "Uniformity in the Law," p. 153.

[23] National Conference of Commissioners on Uniform State Laws, *Handbook 1962,* pp. 341–388 and chart.

[24] See reports or evidence of no reports by the Committee on Uniformity of Judicial Decisions in National Conference of Commissioners on Uniform State Laws, *Handbook* for each year 1937–1962.

ness has helped to shape the case law on the enforcement of foreign judgments.

Despite the earlier acknowledgment that the law as to the execution of Other-State judgments is on the whole well-settled and settled well, perhaps it is possible to streamline procedures and reduce uncertainties which stem from the present law. True, clumsy procedures and uncertainty may be grist for the lawyer's mills, but if they are unnecessary, they should be intolerable to intelligent people in a free society. In this connection, why shouldn't a judgment rendered in a *bona fide* court of one state be directly enforced in another state? Goodrich summed up the law on the question concisely:

> When a court in a state renders a judgment in a suit before it, and the cause of action arose in the state, and both parties to the suit live there and are present in court and the judgment is not paid, and it is sought to be enforced in another state, or some question as to its effect arises in another state, there arises one of the most common situations dealt with in Conflict of Laws. What effect is to be given in one state to the judgment or decree rendered in another? In no common law jurisdiction may a successful plaintiff have execution proceedings in one state upon a judgment rendered in another. This is true even between states of the United States. The judgment creditor cannot have the judgment debtor's property seized by an Ohio Sheriff to satisfy a Michigan judgment; still less could a Michigan officer make the service in another state.[25]

What this means as a practical matter is that to effectuate a judgment in a second state, it is necessary to institute a fresh action in a court of the second state. This, of course, raises the additional and important question of how much full faith and credit the court of the second state must accord to the judgment rendered in the court of the first state. Fortunately, the courts have spelled out the case law on the question so well that Professor Stumberg has been able to sum it up in just three sentences, admittedly, the sentences are long and heavily-laden with footnotes which are not incorporated in this quotation:

> A valid judgment may be relied upon for domestic purposes as a defense or bar to proceedings on the original cause of action, and where it is in favor of the plaintiff, it may form the basis of a new cause of action or execution may be levied upon it. A judgment to pay money rendered in a sister state is not subject to execution abroad, but a valid judgment, entitled to recognition, operates as a bar to further proceedings upon the original claim, both at home and abroad, and when such is its effect where entered, a judgment in favor of the plaintiff is said to merge the original cause of action so that, while suit may not be brought on the original claim, an action lies in another state on the judgment. As between the states, permissible refusal to give effect to a final unconditional judgment rendered in another state is limited to situations where the foreign court

---

[25] Goodrich, *op. cit.*, p. 601.

lacked jurisdiction; where, under certain circumstances, there was fraud; where the judgment is penal; and to a limited degree, where the local judicial machinery is such that the judgment cannot be enforced.[26]

On its face, it would appear that the need for a second action to make a *bona fide* judgment effective does not square with the requirements of the jet age. There is no point in belaboring the obvious—the interaction between persons, companies, and corporations of different states grows by geometric proportions. In like measure, modern conveyances allow people to move about with an ease and speed which is still a cause of wonderment to this writer, who sits and writes in Minneapolis some few hours after leaving New York.

Bench and Bar, with some notable exceptions, have seemed to take it for granted that the direct enforcement of state judgments in other states is undesirable.[27] In any case, there is precious little evidence that they have pressed for such a goal.[28] From the outset the courts have accepted the idea that Other-State judgments will not be enforced by direct execution of them.[29] The lawyers accepted this view without question in the Restatement.[30] Even in the Uniform Enforcement of Foreign Judgments Act, adopted by the National Conference of Commissioners on Uniform State Laws in 1948, an effort was made to expedite the enforcement of judgments, but by offering "a type of relief *almost as efficient as would be the case if execution could be issued directly on the foreign judgment.*" (emphasis supplied).[31]

Why not go all the way and provide for the direct execution of Other-State judgments? Interestingly enough, it is difficult to find a persuasive argument in the literature against doing so. Consequently, it is instructive to canvass lawyers on the question. When pressed, some lawyers will concede that there is probably no good reason for preserving the status quo. Others feel compelled to defend it; the reasons proffered are far from convincing. It is suggested, as if it ended the matter, that direct execution would curtail state sovereignty. So it does. But in 1964, are we going to accept the notion that a state is sovereign in the old classic sense? Is Congressional action in respect to the Civil Rights Acts any less an invasion of state sovereignty than an act of Congress requiring the direct execution of Other-State judgments? It may be asserted that we must preserve and respect state differences in law and customs as they sometimes bear on

[26] George W. Stumberg, *op. cit.*, pp. 108–111.
[27] Sumner, *op. cit.*, pp. 494–499.
[28] *Ibid.*
[29] Nadelmann, *op. cit.*, pp. 62–71.
[30] American Law Institute, *Restatement of the Law of Conflict of Laws* (1934), p. 517.
[31] National Conference of Commissioners on Uniform State Laws, *Handbook 1948* (1948), p. 159.

judgments rendered. The assertion may be festooned with an array of hypotheticals drawn from the world of hyperbole rather than the real world. Does it really make sense to encourage diversity in the law and customs of the states at a time when we are increasingly drawn together as a people by the economic and social realities of life? If so, what is the logic for promoting or tolerating the Uniform Law movement? It may be argued, on the other hand, that there really is no problem, since the second proceeding in most cases is in actuality *pro forma.* If such be the case, why go through the motions?

Another line of argument is that a second proceeding enables one to challenge on due process grounds the first proceeding and that this is a necessary safeguard. James D. Sumner, Jr., professor of law, gives a good answer to this argument:

> The present method for enforcing sister state judgments in the United States serves no useful purpose. It is a hangover from the days when sovereign countries cast suspicion on the judicial proceedings of other nations. Each country presumably had the egotistical notion that there was no assurance that justice would be rendered elsewhere. . . . Within the United States the administration of justice is safeguarded by many provision [*sic*] of the Federal Constitution, and the process is supervised by the Supreme Court. . . .[32]

The most telling argument for the present system is that the direct enforcement of Other-State judgments may cause hardship for a defendant who, in order to protect his interests might be forced by the system to appear in far-away courts even to challenge the court's jurisdiction. The problem of jurisdiction will be dealt with shortly. For the present, suffice it to say that hand-in-hand with a provision requiring the direct execution of Other-State judgments would have to go some provisions for better determining on what basis courts could take jurisdiction. Also, there would have to be provisions to insure adequate service. Admittedly, whatever is done about these matters, direct enforcement would undoubtedly in some cases make for inconveniences for a defendant. But these inconveniences must be measured against the enormous inconveniences of the present system, as well as the fact that being forced to appear in court in any jurisdiction is inconvenient. In the real world, is it necessarily more difficult for a Minneapolitan to appear in Chicago than in Duluth? In the jet age, it is unlikely. How about the inconvenience of a second proceeding, or the inconvenience for the plaintiff who goes to a *bona fide* court, obtains a *bona fide* judgment, only to discover he must don his boxing gloves for another round? The lack of certainty about the conclusiveness of a first judgment, even if it is not immediately challenged, can be a real hardship. And how convenient is it to have the kind of zany jockeying for

[32] Sumner, *op. cit.*, pp. 496–497.

first judgment that now takes place? This jockeying described in detail in an interesting law journal note is worth pondering:

> The general law today is that full faith and credit need not be given until a judgment is rendered. When the same cause of action between the same parties is litigated in two or more states, the first judgment rendered must be given faith and credit in other suits, regardless of when the case was commenced. In this "first judgment" rule, rights of the litigants may depend on mere chance or accident beyond the control of the courts or parties, since a court with an overcrowded docket is delayed in trying a case and thus rendering a judgment.
>
> Under the first judgment rule the defendant, in the first action, is encouraged to bring a second suit for the same cause of action, like divorce, in another state with the hope of obtaining judgment first, thus defeating the prior suit. Not infrequently this second suit results in a default judgment since the original plaintiff may rely on the first action. Or the defendant in each action will use such delaying tactics as are available in order to obstruct the rendering of a judgment, while his own suit is being tried.
>
> Another disadvantage of the prevailing first judgment rule is that it enables the plaintiff to bring an action in one court, and if by chance he should be able to catch the defendant in another jurisdiction more favorable to his interests, he may bring a second suit while the first is still pending; and a third and fourth. This not only results in a multiplicity of suits for the same cause of action between the same parties, dissipating the time and energies of a number of courts, but it encourages the plaintiff to use surreptitious means of "catching" the defendant in the more desirable judisdiction. It is quite clear that "courts of justice were instituted to afford speedy and effectual remedy for the redress of wrongs, and not to afford a litigious person the means of oppression."
>
> Another inherent difficulty of the first judgment rule is that two courts might render judgments on the same day, or so near in time that the successful suitor in one court is unable to set up his judgment as a bar to the other, thus giving rise to conflicting judgments. Or one court may issue an injunction against the prosecution of a foreign suit to which a counter injunction may be issued by the foreign court, thereby creating a struggle for power.[33]

Surely, one of the predictable results of the direct execution of Other-State judgments would be that it would cut down on the amount of litigation we now have. Lawyers would no longer advise clients to remain at home and start an action locally when served by a competent state court elsewhere. Nor would it be possible to wait for a second judicial proceeding to challenge a court's jurisdiction. It would have to be done at once or not at all.

It is significant that the Commissioners on Uniform State Laws in constructing "a type of relief almost as efficient" as direct execution of Other-

---

[33] "Full Faith and Credit Clause Reanalyzed: The Finality Doctrine Denounced—Judicial Proceedings Redefined," 54 *Northwestern Law Review* 211, 237–239 (1959).

State judgments felt compelled to point out in a prefatory note that: "The mobility, today, of both persons and property is such that existing procedure for the enforcement of judgments in those cases where the judgment debtor has removed himself and his property from the state in which the judgment was rendered is inadequate." [34] Significant, too, is the fact that in 1948, Congress provided for the direct execution of the judgments of a federal court in any district of the United States.

> A judgment in an action for recovery of money or property entered in any district court which has become final by appeal or expiration of time for appeal may be registered in any other district by filing therein a certified copy of such judgment. A judgment so registered shall have the same effect as a judgment of the district court of the district where registered and may be enforced in like manner. A certified copy of the satisfaction of any judgment in whole or in part may be registered in like manner in any district in which the judgment is a lien.[35]

Equally instructive is the fact that two other federal systems, The Federal Republic of Germany, and Australia with its vast geographic area, have effectively required the direct execution of Other-State judgments.[36]

Although the question is sometimes raised about Congress' constitutional power to provide the requirement suggested, it would appear that the full faith and credit clause does specifically grant Congress the power "to prescribe the manner in which such . . . proceedings shall be proved, *and the effect thereof."* (emphasis supplied).[37]

B. The jurisdiction problem

As indicated by Goodrich, "the full faith and credit clause of the Constitution and the legislation thereunder do not preclude an inquiry into the question of jurisdiction of the first court to render the judgment sought to be enforced in the second state. If there was no jurisdiction, the judgment is not entitled to faith and credit." [38] The fact that a court may later find that an Other-State court did not really have jurisdiction has led, in the past at any rate, to some puzzling and harsh results, particularly in divorce cases. What follows here is not meant to imply that the jurisdiction problem only applies to judgments in divorce cases.[39] But since di-

[34] National Conference of Commissioners of Uniform State Laws, *Handbook 1948* (1948), p. 156.

[35] 62 *STAT.* 958 (1948).

[36] Robert R. Bowie and Carl J. Friedrich, eds., *Studies in Federalism*, (1954), pp. 131, 146.

[37] Walter W. Cook, "The Powers of Congress Under the Full Faith and Credit Clause," 28 *Yale Law Journal* 421, 430 (1919).

[38] Goodrich, *op. cit.*, p. 611.

[39] For discussion of another fascinating example of the problem of jurisdiction as it applies to judgments, see Don Hopson, Jr., "Cognovit & Judgments: An Ignored Problem of Due Process and Full Faith and Credit," 29 *University of Chicago Law Review* 111 (1961).

vorce cases are dramatically illustrative of the problem and substantively important because of the high incidence of divorce, the jurisdiction problem will be discussed almost exclusively in terms of judgments rendered in divorce cases.

The ludicrous decision in the second *Williams* case, which upheld a conviction for bigamous cohabitation in North Carolina of a couple who had obtained divorces from their respective spouses in Nevada, is too well known to be recounted.[40] Since it is downright foolishness to tolerate a system in which it is possible for individuals to obtain a divorce in a *bona fide* court, have every reason to believe that they have been legally divorced and then later be imprisoned for bigamous cohabitation upon remarriage, it is not surprising that the courts endeavored to clean up the mess that was the law regarding jurisdiction in divorce cases at the time of *Williams II.* As Stumberg pointed out: "in subsequent cases the Supreme Court held that if respondent appears in the earlier proceedings to contest jurisdiction upon a contention of lack of domicile by the plaintiff an adverse ruling is *res judicata* and the decree may not be questioned elsewhere." [41] But this still leaves some questions open. One, although it is apparently settled that a decree obtained under the circumstances described by Stumberg cannot be questioned by another person, is it clear that a state cannot question it? There are those who think a state can.[42] Two, what about the *ex parte* proceeding? Law Professor Henry H. Foster, Jr. reports on the basis of a "hurried check by a student assistant" that:

> A spot check of the decisions since the *Williams* cases indicates that as a practical matter *ex parte* judgments are rarely disturbed and that almost no criminal prosecutions have occurred. In the relatively few cases where the validity of a sister state's *ex parte* divorce has been challenged, however, the majority have held the *ex parte* decree was without jurisdiction. Over 90 per cent of such cases have been actions where the stay-at-home spouse was seeking to impose or enforce the duty to support, and a few cases have involved workmen's compensation claims or wrongful death actions.[43]

Is the situation now "well enough" so that the old maxim about leaving "well enough" alone applies? Hardly! The reason that jurisdiction of the first court is so rarely challenged is because of a wondrous contrivance of the Supreme Court, the divisible divorce. Human nature being what it is, it is rare for spouses to want to stay married to someone who no longer wants them. Consequently, the real contest in divorce cases is not over

---

[40] *Williams* v. *North Carolina,* 325 U.S. 226 (1945).

[41] Stumberg, *op. cit.,* p. 300.

[42] George W. Stumberg, "The Migratory Divorce," 33 *Washington Law Review* 331, 340 (1958).

[43] Henry H. Foster, "For Better or Worse? Decisions since *Haddock* v. *Haddock*," 47 *American Bar Association Journal* 963, 965 (1961).

the marital status, but rather over such issues as division of property, alimony, and child custody. In essence, the divisible divorce concept boils down to this. A Second-State court can consider the divorce itself, i.e., the rending of the marital status, as one matter and support, property settlement, and child custody as a separate matter, if their disposition by the First-State court is challenged where the Second-State court has a legal basis for taking jurisdiction. Consequently, a Second-State court will only rarely countenance a challenge to the First-State court's jurisdiction as to the divorce itself. As to the whole host of issues which inhere in divorce cases, like alimony and child custody, a Second-State court which has reason to take jurisdiction does not have to grant *full* faith and credit to the Other-State court's disposition of these matters.[44] This, of course, in effect is a denial that the Other-State court had exclusive jurisdiction as to these matters. The rationale of the Supreme Court for the divisible divorce was first provided in a case involving support. The Court said that since the abandoned spouse was a resident of the second state, that state "was rightly concerned lest the abandoned spouse be left impoverished and perhaps become a public charge. The problem of her livelihood and support is plainly a matter in which her community had a legitimate interest." [45] The Supreme Court proudly went on to hail its own wisdom in splitting divorce down the middle: "The result in this situation is to make the divorce divisible to give effect to the Nevada decree insofar as it affects marital status and to make it ineffective on the issue of alimony. It accommodates the interests of both Nevada and New York in this broken marriage by restricting each State to the matter of her dominant concern." [46] The fact remains, the husband obviously only went to Nevada to obtain the divorce. Under those circumstances what was Nevada's interest other than maintaining the profitable state divorce mill? Of course, Nevada would have a real interest where the party seeking the divorce really came to Nevada to live.

The divisible divorce concept can hardly be considered a satisfactory solution. What it means as a matter of fact is that two courts frequently become involved in proceedings where one court could properly do the job.[47] Not only that, it leaves the way open to more uncertainty than is essential. A person can obtain an *ex parte* decree in a *bona fide* court and not know for some time, if ever, whether or not important elements of the decree are worth the paper they are written on. Not only that, but until the matter is cleared up once and for all, there is a vast army of indi-

[44] *Ford v. Ford*, 83 S. Ct. 273 (1962).
[45] *Estin v. Estin*, 334 U.S. 541, 547 (1948).
[46] *Ibid.*, p. 549.
[47] See David Seidelson, "Full Faith and Credit: A Modest Proposal . . . Or Two," 31 *George Washington Law Review* 426, 476–496 (1962).

viduals who are in jeopardy of criminal action by their respective states, when and if the states' prosecutors choose to act. As Foster summed it up: "The net result is that today, in the *Williams II* situation, we have the possibility of divisible divorce, and in the case of support and child custody, divisible incidents as well. In the field of divorce law we certainly are not 'one nation indivisible'." [48]

It might be easy for some to write off the difficulties a divisible divorce creates for a run-away spouse on the grounds that the difficulties serve him or her right. But in addition to these difficulties, there is an aggravated evil of enormous dimensions to which the divisible divorce concept contributes. As indicated, one can now be pretty certain that a "quickie" divorce obtained in a divorce-mill state will enable a man or woman to rid himself or herself of an unwanted spouse, even though the questions of alimony, child custody, and the like are not resolved. Consequently, people still flock to the divorce-mill state, making a mockery of the law for all to see, and undermining faith in the fairness and wisdom of the judiciary. What does it contribute to public confidence in the law and judiciary, when the Governor of a great state will allow his attorney to make an appearance in his behalf in an Other-State court, where his wife is seeking a divorce, in order to escape the law of the state of which he is Governor? For, to rephrase the classic words of Mr. Bumble, if the law believes that the reason the first Mrs. Rockefeller instituted proceedings in a Nevada court was because she had come to make her permanent home in Nevada, "the law is a ass, a idiot." The Commissioners on Uniform Laws summed up very well the evils inherent in such shenanigans in a Prefatory Note to the Uniform Divorce Recognition Act:

> Public opinion increasingly recognizes the ills which spring from this situation. Those able to embark on divorce-seeking tours obtain a discriminatory advantage over their fellow-citizens. Respect for local law is destroyed. The effectiveness of state policy is broken down. The autonomy in local affairs which is the object of federalism is subverted. Since the "quickie" divorces are obtained in large measure by persons whose conduct is regarded as "newsworthy" the resultant publicity helps to establish a pattern of disrespect for law and social institutions. The impression of well-to-do and influential elements of the community is that they need not be hampered by inconvenient restrictions of their local laws of reform. . . .[49]

Unfortunately, under present circumstances, even in the rare instances where courts in a divorce-mill state get their backs up because someone has "misled" them as to his or her domiciliary intentions, they only confuse the issue more. Regard the curious result in the recent case, *Hartigan* v.

[48] Foster, *op. cit.*, p. 966.
[49] The National Conference of Commissioners on Uniform State Laws, *Handbook 1947* (1947), p. 174.

Hartigan.[50] Mrs. Hartigan of New York went to Alabama to obtain a "quickie" divorce. She claimed there that she was a *bona fide* resident of Alabama. Her husband "filed an answer and waiver in which he admitted the jurisdictional facts but denied the other allegations . . . and agreed that the case 'may be carried forward to its final determination and decree of divorce issued without other notice. . . .' " [51] In due course, Mrs. Hartigan was granted the divorce and alimony. Later, Mr. Hartigan remarried and fathered a child in the second marriage. When Mr. Hartigan filed a petition in the same Alabama court for a change in the amount of alimony, the court decided that the original decree had been fraudulently obtained because Mrs. Hartigan had not in fact met the residence requirements and vacated the *original* decree. This decision was upheld by the Supreme Court of Alabama. The fact that Mr. Hartigan had remarried and the decision made him a bigamist and his child a bastard gave the Alabama Supreme Court some concern, but not enough, apparently, to overrule the lower court decision. Needless to say, the decision created more problems than it solved and the Alabama Supreme Court has since qualified its decision in the *Hartigan* case.[52]

Another significant aspect of the divisible divorce is the concern it has caused the lawyers about the ethics involved in suggesting to clients that they escape the laws of their own state by seeking "quickie" divorces elsewhere by lying about their domiciliary intentions.[53] It is hard to quarrel with the notion that a lawyer should truthfully acknowledge to a client that under the present state of the law, he or she can obtain a "quickie" divorce in another state and that the divorce will stick, because that is the fact of the matter. But, this is not to say, that the system that puts lawyers in the position of advising their clients to commit perjury is a healthy one.

Probably, there is no easy solution to the problem of jurisdiction. Most lawyers presumably, would be quick to reject what appears to be the most simple solution as also being the most simple-minded. Why not try to establish a basis for jurisdiction, so that in a particular case only the courts of one state could take jurisdiction? It would be particularly desirable to have jurisdiction clearly lie in the courts of one state, if there were to be direct execution of Other-State judgments. Is it possible to find such a basis? Currently, as Stumberg summarizes it: "Presence, domicile, . . . consent, and certain types of acts have been held sufficient to

---

[50] 128 So. 2d 725 (1961).

[51] *Ibid.,* 727.

[52] "Migratory Divorce: The Alabama Experience," 75 *Harvard Law Review* 568, 571 (1962).

[53] Henry S. Drinker, "Problems of Professional Ethics in Matrimonial Litigation," 66 *Harvard Law Review* 443 (1953) and Committee on Professional Ethics, Association of the Bar of the City of New York, *Opinions* (1956), pp. 436, 568–569.

confer jurisdiction." [54] But does it have to be that way? What would be the consequence of a requirement that cases could only be brought in the state in which the defendant was domiciled? Surely, there would be cases where this might be inconvenient to the plaintiff, but on the overall would the inconveniences be as great as those brought about by the present practice? To be sure, there are other practical problems, like deciding which state was home state for a corporation doing business in many states. Consequently, it would probably be necessary to draw up a complex set of criteria upon which jurisdiction would be based, indicating priorities where several claims of jurisdiction could be made. In addition, provision would have to be made for allowing a party to plead that it was inconvenient for him to appear in the designated forum, just as he can under present law.

Congress would appear to be the best agency for drawing up the criteria. And for the task, the Congress could use the Australian Service and Execution of Process Act as an analogue, though not as a model. The Australian law spells out a more rational basis for jurisdiction than our case law does, but it does not establish priorities between conflicting bases of jurisdiction.[55] It would seem that Congress has the power under the full faith and credit clause to prescribe that only the proceedings of a court having jurisdiction as defined by Congress must be accorded full faith and credit. If this position is not accepted, and if it is desirable to set up a more precise basis for jurisdiction, then why not seek a constitutional amendment? Professor Walter W. Cook, many years ago, suggested another interesting possibility—expand the jurisdiction of the federal courts in diversity of citizenship cases.[56] This suggestion has considerable appeal. Why not consider going further and *requiring* that all diversity of citizenship cases be settled in federal courts? This would require a tremendous expansion of the federal judiciary, but who is prepared to argue that such a solution is not preferable to what we have now?

It goes without saying that, along with the provisions determining which state courts would take jurisdiction in a particular kind of case, there would have to go some provisions providing for a high standard of service. In this respect too, the Australian law is instructive. That law provides that:

> When no appearance is entered or made by a defendant to a writ of summons served on him . . . if it is made to appear to the Court from which the writ was issued or a Judge thereof . . .
> (g) that the writ was personally served on the defendant; or in the case of a corporation served on its principal officer or manager or secretary within the State or part in which service is effected; or

[54] Stumberg, *Principles of Conflicts of Laws*, p. 69.
[55] *Australia, Commonwealth Acts*, V, 4026 (1953).
[56] Walter W. Cook, *op. cit.*

(h) *that reasonable efforts were made to effect personal service* thereof on the defendant, *and that it came to his knowledge* or in the case of a corporation that it came to the knowledge of such officer as aforesaid . . .

such Court or Judge may on the application of the plaintiff order from time to time that the plaintiff shall be at liberty to proceed in the suit. . . .[57] [emphasis supplied].

Whatever is done about jurisdiction, it would appear desirable to do something about divorce law specifically. For, even if jurisdiction in divorce cases is settled, the lack of uniformity will continue to have a devastating effect on the people's conception of our judicial system, because of the high incidence of divorce and the incredible mobility of the American people. If the jurisdiction problem is not improved, then it is absolutely essential that something be done about the divorce laws. Here, too, we can learn from the Australians.[58] Under the full faith and credit clause, Congress could pass a law indicating the substantive requirements which must be met for a divorce decree to receive full faith and credit. One such substantive requirement might be a year's waiting period. Apparently, there is good reason for believing that Congress has the constitutional power to enact such legislation.[59] It is commonly argued, however, that Congress would never be able to pass such legislation, since it would make divorce easier in the populous states where there is a large Catholic population. But is it inconceivable that Catholic and non-Catholic opponents of easy divorce laws could be persuaded that a moderate, sensible, and uniform approach is preferable to the present system? This may be hard to believe in view of the lack of success to obtain support for more sensible divorce laws in the past. But is it not relevant to consider, in this connection, the point stressed by the Commissioners on Uniform State Laws, that one of the biggest obstacles to obtaining reform has been that the more substantial and articulate people in the states with rigid divorce laws do not have to be concerned because they can afford to go elsewhere for divorces? Would it not have had some consequence on reform in New York, if the Governor had been unable to obtain a divorce because of New York law?

C. The full faith and credit clause as it applies to choice of laws

The choice of laws problem is well-illustrated in the familiar *Alaska Packers* case.[60] The important facts in that case will be recalled. An

---

[57] *Australia, Commonwealth Acts, loc. cit.*

[58] "Divorce—Australian Statute Establishes Uniform Federal Law for Marital Actions," 74 *Harvard Law Review* 424 (1960); Erwin N. Griswold, "Divorce Jurisdiction and Recognition of Divorce Decrees—A Comparative Study," 65 *Harvard Law Review* 193 (1951).

[59] Edward S. Corwin, *op. cit.*, p. 165.

[60] *Alaska Packers Assn. v. Industrial Accident Commission*, 294 U.S. 532 (1935).

employee had entered into a contract of employment in California and then went off to fulfill that contract by working in Alaska. The contract contained a provision stipulating that the employer and employee would be bound by the provisions of the Alaska Workmen's Compensation Law. Later the employee came back to California, where he applied to the appropriate agency for compensation for injuries received in Alaska. The stipulation in the contract binding employer and employee to Alaska law was meaningless in California because California's Workmen's Compensation act provided that (1) The California Commission "shall have jurisdiction over all controversies arising out of injuries suffered without the territorial limits of this State in those cases where the injured employee is a resident of this State at the time of injury and the contract of hire was made in this State, . . ." and (2) "No contract, rule, or regulation shall exempt the employer from liability for the compensation fixed by this Act." [61] But despite California law, the injury did in fact occur in Alaska and a good argument could be made, and in fact was made by the employer, that law of Alaska should be accorded full faith and credit in the California courts and applied in the case. In short, there were in this case, as in many others, legitimate grounds for the court to apply either one of two jurisdictions' conflicting laws. Under the circumstances of the case, which law were the California courts required to accept as controlling? Eventually the Supreme Court of the United States had to supply the answer. The answer was that ". . . the conflict is to be resolved, not by giving automatic effect to the full faith and credit clause, compelling the courts of each state to subordinate its own statutes to those of the other, but by appraising the governmental interests of each jurisdiction, and turning the scale of decisions according to their weight." [62] But this answer is no solution at all for the general problem of choice of laws. It is an invitation to litigate each of the myriad of choice-of-law cases, which are bound to rise in the present system, through the courts all the way to the Supreme Court of the United States for final resolution.[63] Take for example, the *Pearson* case which attracted so much attention several years ago.[64] A widow, whose husband had been killed in an airplane crash in Massachusetts, was granted a $160,000 award by a jury in a New York court. Although the crash occurred in Massachusetts, the husband had bought the ticket in New York and the plane had taken off from La Guardia Airport in New York. Since a Massachusetts statute limited recovery in such cases to $15,000 at that time and New York's law did not,

---

[61] *Ibid.*, p. 538.
[62] *Ibid.*, p. 547.
[63] Jackson, *op. cit.*, pp. 14–16 and Brainerd Currie, "Notes on Methods and Objectives in the Conflict of Laws," *Duke Law Journal* 171–174 (1959).
[64] *Pearson* v. *Northeast Airlines*, 309 F. 2d 553 (1962).

the airline appealed the decision on the grounds that Massachusetts law should have been controlling in this case. A three-judge panel of the United States Court of Appeals, Second Circuit, reversed the decision and remanded the case. When the case came again to the Court of Appeals, the full court heard the case, explaining that "The issue being one of great significance—the constitutional power of the states to develop conflict of laws doctrine—it was ordered upon application by the plaintiff-appellee and the affirmative vote of a majority of the active judges of this circuit, that the appeal be reheard *en banc.*" This time the court reversed itself. It cited with approval the reasoning of a lower court in a parallel case: "An air traveler from New York may in a flight of a few hours' duration pass through several commonwealths. His plane may meet with disaster in a state he never intended to cross but into which the plane has flown because of bad weather or other unexpected developments, or an airplane's catastrophic descent may begin in one state and end in another. The place of injury becomes entirely fortuitous." [65] Eventually the case was brought to the United States Supreme Court which denied certiorari.[66] The case is recalled here not for the outcome on the merits but rather to make the point that at the late date of 1962, lawyers and judges were still not quite sure which state's law would apply in such a situation and the case was not resolved until it went all the way to the Supreme Court.

Justice Jackson summed up the unhappy state of affairs nineteen years ago; his summary is still applicable:

> That the Supreme Court should impose uniformity in choice-of-law problems is a prospect comforting to none, least of all to a member of that body. I have not paid any exaggerated tribute to its performance thus far in this complex field. But the available courses from which our choice may be made seem to me limited. One is that we will leave choice of law in all cases to the local policy of the state. This seems to me to be at odds with the implication of our federal system that the mutual limits of the states' powers are defined by the Constitution. It also seems productive of confusion, for it means that a choice among conflicting substantive rules depends only upon which state happens to have the last word. And that we are not likely to accept such a principle is certainly indicated by the Court's sporadic interferences with choice of law, whether under the rubric of due process, full faith and credit, or otherwise. A *second course is that we will adopt no rule, permit a good deal of overlapping and confusion, bar any reason by which the one or the other course is to be guided or predicted. This seems to me about where our present decisions leave us.* Third, we may candidly recognize that choice-of-law questions, when properly raised, ought to and do present constitutional questions under the full faith and credit clause which the Court may properly decide and as to which it ought at least mark out reason-

[65] *Ibid.,* p. 561, note 15.
[66] 83 S. Ct. 726 (1963).

ably narrow limits of permissible variation in areas where there is confusion. [emphasis supplied].⁶⁷

In addition to the solution offered by Justice Jackson, a simpler approach
begs for consideration. Why should not Congress attempt to prescribe by
statute which state's law should apply in choice-of-law problems? Perhaps
such a law would have to be very comprehensive and complex. On the
other hand, maybe it could be relatively simple. For example, what would
be wrong with a pat and unassailable requirement that questions regarding
contracts will always be governed by the law of the state in which they are
made, or alternatively, by the law of the state in which they are performed?
Certainly, such an inflexible requirement would lead to some unhappy
results. Perhaps, Professor George W. Stumberg is correct in concluding
that:

> Always to allocate to a single state the power to create rights and duties
> appears, at first blush, a simple expedient. To do so may seem to render
> the decision-making function easier. Once the necessary connecting link
> has been determined, application of the proper law follows mechanically
> as a matter of course. An objective of the *Restatement, Conflict of Laws*,
> as originally promulgated in 1934, was to give lawyers and judges a help-
> ing hand by furnishing a complete guide through the labyrinths that run
> through the crooks and crannies of conflict of laws. However, no satis-
> factory detailed guide can be formulated by resort to a priori hypotheses
> that only the law of this or that state or country can control in a given
> situation. To attempt to do so is unrealistic in the light of the
> cases. . . .⁶⁸

On the other hand, it might provide some alleviation to a situation so
bad as to merit the following accolade from Stumberg in his well-regarded
hornbook:

> One attempting to describe the reactions of American courts in general
> to the question of what law determines the validity of a contract in Con-
> flict of Laws could not well improve upon the cautious statement made
> approximately thirty-five years ago by an eminent authority [Goodrich]
> that it is "the most confused subject in the field of Conflict of Laws. Not
> only do rules vary in different jurisdictions but decisions in the same court
> often enunciate inconsistent theories upon the subject." ⁶⁹

Nor does the approach employed in the new Draft Restatement promise
to solve more problems than it raises. It is suggested there "that all matters
of validity *and* effect are governed by the local law of the *state of most
significant relationship* with the exception of minute details of performance
which are still said to be governed by the local law of the place of per-

---

⁶⁷ Jackson, *op. cit.*, pp. 26–27.
⁶⁸ George W. Stumberg, "Choice of Law and the Constitution," 10 *Journal of Public
Law* 289, 296–297 (1961).
⁶⁹ Stumberg, *Principles of Conflict of Laws*, p. 225.

formance. . . ." [70] (emphasis supplied). Just how well will parties to a contract (and their lawyers) be able to determine in advance which state will bear "the most significant relationship" in the event of controversy over the contract?

Alas, lawyers might be too quick to disregard a suggestion that an attempt be made to seek Congressional action to supplant court-made choice-of-law rules, particularly where it is made by a nonlawyer, as too naïve to merit serious consideration. For that reason, I scurry to latch on to the apron strings of Professor Brainerd Currie, certainly, one of the most knowledgeable lawyers in this subject-matter area. He has suggested good reasons for such an approach:

> But the assessment of the respective values of the competing legitimate interests of two sovereign states, in order to determine which is to prevail, is a political function of a very high order. This is a function which should not be committed to courts in a democracy. It is a function which the courts cannot perform effectively, for they lack the necessary resources. Not even a ponderous Brandeis brief could marshal the relevant considerations in choosing, for example, between the interest of the State of employment and that of the State of injury in matters concerning workmen's compensation. This is a job for a legislative committee, and determining the policy to be formulated on the basis of the information assembled is a job for a competent legislative body in Congress; but it has not seen fit to exercise its powers under the full faith and credit clause in such a way as to contribute to the resolution of true conflicts of interest.[71]

He goes on to conclude that "We would be better off without choice-of-law rules. We would be better off if Congress were to give some attention to problems of private law, and were to legislate concerning the choice between conflicting state interest in some of the areas in which the need for solution is serious." [72]

THE LIMITATIONS OF THE LAWYERS

It goes without saying that solutions to the problems raised in this essay will only be reached with the help of lawyers. At the same time, there is good reason to believe that they will not be solved by the lawyers alone. First of all, among the practitioners, there is a pronounced defensive attitude about the law as it is. The writer canvassed a host of them in

---

[70] American Law Institute, *Tentative Draft, Restatement of the Law, Second Conflict of Laws* (1960), p. 4.

[71] Brainerd Currie, *op. cit.*, pp. 176–177.

[72] *Ibid.*, p. 177. For an exceptionally fine critique of Currie's views on solving conflicts problems, generally, see Michael Traynor, "Conflict of Laws: Professor Currie's Restrained and Enlightened Forum," 49 *California Law Review* 845 (1961). Also, see 63 *Columbia Law Review* 1212 (1963).

a subjective, nonsystematic, nonscientific way about the problems presented earlier. The position generally taken is that (1) the law on the matter is about as good as human beings can devise in a complex federal system; (2) the law is well understood by lawyers and that, practically, the problems suggested are exaggerated; (3) if you cannot "see" that propositions one and two are valid it's because you do not understand "The Law." This attitude is manifested in the Uniform Laws and Restatement undertakings. In neither effort have the lawyers really taken a good hard look at the whole problem of full faith and credit with an eye to suggesting profound and fundamental change, if study indicated such was needed. The Uniform Laws Commissioners nibble at the problem with an approach which on its face appears hopeless. The approach is based on the idea that we can get around the problems arising from federalism by obtaining passage of identical legislation in fifty different states, rather than by one solid effort at the national level. In the language of the dice table, this is doing it "the hard way." Although Commissioners have achieved some positive results, the record is not very impressive.[73] A Restatement by definition can never really be much more than a restatement of current law. Perhaps the restaters can push for change in areas where the courts have left ambiguities, but however much they may wish to do, they have no mandate to rewrite the law wholesale and they have not done so.[74] This is the important point. The approach does not provide an opportunity for a fresh, wide-ranging inquiry. And such an inquiry into the problems presented here seems desirable.

Do the lawyers have good reason to be complacent? Let Justice Jackson answer that question.

> To a foreign observer the United States may well appear to be "a nation concealed under the form of a federation." However true this may be as to political power and economic controls, it is far wide of the truth as to the administration of internal justice among our forty-eight state legal systems. Indeed, today in respect to our legal administrations we have not achieved a much "more perfect union" than that of the colonies under the Articles of the Confederation. We have, so far as I can ascertain, the most *localized* and *conflicting* system of any country which presents the external appearance of nationhood. *But we are so accustomed to the delays, expense, and frustrations of our system that it seldom occurs to us to inquire whether these are wise, or constitutionally necessary.* [emphasis supplied].[75]

[73] National Conference of Commissioners on Uniform State Laws, *Handbook 1962* (1961) pp. 341–388.

[74] Albert A. Ehrenzweig, "American Conflicts Law in Its Historical Perspective—Should the Restatement be 'Continued'?" 103 *University of Pennsylvania Law Review* 133 (1954), and Alan Milner, "Restatement: The Failure of a Legal Experiment," 20 *University of Pittsburgh Law Review* 795 (1959).

[75] Jackson, *op. cit.*, p. 18.

Nor can the lawyers who have become judges be relied upon to resolve these problems with the vaunted case-by-case approach. Where drastic change may be necessary, the case-by-case approach leaves much to be desired. But let the highly-regarded Judge Roger J. Traynor make the case for me. He writes that "Only occasionally does a judge have the luxury of expounding on the law that might be rather than the law that is." [76] Then in speaking hopefully and optimistically about what courts may do in the future, he indicates clearly the reasons why they haven't and probably will not solve the problems described earlier:

> Meanwhile the courts could do much more than they have done toward a rapprochement of states in the optimum development of common law. The more courts strive for the optimum development, the more they will liquidate local anachronisms that breed conflict. *The more they realize that judicial law-making is something more than parroting the once timely wisdom of their predecessors or perpetuating their sometimes unfortunate foolishness, the more they will come to share at least the idiom of their own day and therefore common rules.* If I speak confidently and not hypothetically of such a prospect, it is because of a belief that law schools are training future lawyers and judges who will be ready, willing, and able to analyze universal problems in a universal language that transcends archaic modes of thought and the patois of their own provinces. [Emphasis supplied].[77]

True, Judge Traynor concludes that state courts *probably* should continue to be the agencies for resolving the conflicts problems, but the host of caveats he attaches to the suggestion would indicate something less than full confidence that the courts will do it and do it well.[78]

In sum, to the nonlawyer the efforts of Bench and Bar in resolving the problems of federalism conjure up a picture of methodical and unimaginative men slowly and carefully doctoring a tree here and a tree there while the forest is being ravaged by a pestilence. Maybe it is the best way—but it's hard to believe that it is.

WHAT POLITICAL SCIENTISTS CAN CONTRIBUTE

As indicated at the outset, the problems which the lawyer's clause has been employed to meet, as well as the problems which have grown out of the application of the clause, are problems in intergovernmental relations as well as legal problems. In attempting to solve these problems, it would seem appropriate to call on the expertise, talents, and research know-how

---

[76] Roger J. Traynor, "Is This Conflict Really Necessary?" 37 *Texas Law Review* 657, 664 (1959). For additional explication on the limitations within which judges must work, particularly in the conflicts area, see Brainerd Currie, "Justice Traynor and the Conflict of Laws," 13 *Stanford Law Review* 719, 719–723 (1961).

[77] *Ibid.*, p. 665.

[78] *Ibid.*, p. 675.

of those political scientists who have made the study of intergovernmental relations, public law, and comparative government their major concern. One of the astounding things to this writer is how little attention Bench and Bar have given to what other federal systems have done about the problems highlighted in this essay. Justice Jackson pointed out the obvious very well, when he wrote: "Perhaps the best perspective for judging whether our society is being well served by its present legislative and decisional law under the faith and credit clause is a comparative study of the methods and degree of integration employed by other peoples whose heritage and jurisprudence are comparable to our own." [79] Is it not of some significance that in Australia, with its large area, judgments are directly executed in any state? [80] Is it not worth exploring how well the Australian practice as to jurisdiction and service, described earlier, really works?

As to choice of laws, where Brainerd Currie has suggested that policy is best made by a legislative body, he has in essence pointed out a role for the political scientist who can help marshal the data and devise the ways to evaluate it as scientifically as possible, so that in measuring the competing interests of states we can rely on objective criteria rather than subjective impressions.

Finally, the political scientist can design and execute research which would measure the consequences of the present arrangement, would attempt to predict the practical effect of the direct execution of judgments, as well as the other alternate arrangements worthy of exploration. Patently, a cooperative effort by lawyers and political scientists would be ideal. The political scientists can raise the questions and make proposals which would make the lawyers go back to first things. At the same time, in such a complex area the lawyers' talents and knowledge would serve to make certain that grandiose schemes would run the gauntlet of practical considerations. For the cooperative effort envisioned, there is an analogue. Back in 1952, the Graduate School of Public Administration and the Law School of Harvard University, upon a request from the American Committee on United Europe, and with the assistance of a grant from the Ford Foundation, joined together to do a first-rate study on federalism.[81] Because their objective was to "provide detailed comparative material for the deliberations on the European constitution," [82] they ranged far and wide and dealt only briefly with the problems raised in this essay. Evidently, it is possible under some auspices to get distinguished lawyers and political scientists together, for the group included lawyers like Paul Freund, Edward McWhinney, Louis B. Sohn, Arthur E. Sutherland, and Alexander Bickel;

[79] Jackson, *op. cit.*, p. 18.
[80] Robert R. Bowie and Carl J. Friedrich, eds., *Studies in Federalism* (1954), p. 131.
[81] *Ibid.*, p. xxvii.
[82] *Ibid.*, p. xxvi.

among the political scientists engaged in the project were Carl J. Friedrich, Robert G. McCloskey, Gottfried Dietze, Lawrence Fuchs, Albert Mavrinac, Stanley Rothman, Judith Shklar, and Herbert Spiro.[83]

If such an undertaking can be started, the approach which is most appealing would be one where the group first attempted to determine what arrangements they would recommend if we were not bound by history, law, and precedent. After determining the ideal solution, it would be time enough to consider whether or not it would be possible to achieve the ideal. Nor should constitutional considerations be a bar in any area. The Constitution has and can be amended. Lawyers may receive with ill-grace the suggestion that we need to get back to first things. Again, to seek refuge from their fury, I turn to Brainerd Currie:

> I have been told that I give insufficient recognition to governmental policies other than those which are expressed in specific statutes and rules; the policy of promoting a general legal order, that of fostering amicable relations with other states, that of vindicating reasonable expectations, and so on. If this is so, it is not, I hope because of a provincial lack of appreciation of the worth of those ideals, but because of a felt necessity to emphasize the obstacles which the present system interposes to any intelligent approach to the problem. Let us first clear away the apparatus which creates false problems and obscures the nature of the real ones. Only then can we effectively set about amelioriating the ills which arise from a diversity of laws by bringing to bear all the resources of jurisprudence, politics, and humanism—each in its appropriate way.[84]

Of course, it is entirely possible that nothing would be gained by such an endeavor, that, perhaps, we now have the best of all possible worlds. But it would certainly be reassuring if this turned out to be the case after intensive study.

In lieu of a cooperative undertaking, political scientists are urged to declare open season on the lawyer's clause. Let us not be intimidated. Let us give it the same attention and scrutiny we have given to other important parts of the Constitution. If we can point the way to better solutions to full-faith-and-credit problems convincingly enough, we might get the support of the Bench and Bar. And whether they generally realize it or not, they can use our help. As Currie put it so well—we can "set about ameliorating the ills effectively only by bringing to bear all the resources of jurisprudence, politics, and humanism—each in its appropriate way." [85]

[83] *Ibid.*, p. vii.
[84] Currie, *op. cit.*, p. 181.
[85] *Ibid.*

7

Intergovernmental Cooperation

and American Federalism

Richard H. Leach

Ever since the birth of the Republic, the concept of federalism has been a subject of debate in the United States, a debate made all the more intriguing by what Professor Mason once called the "irreconcilable ambiguity" the framers of the Constitution wrote into that document in 1787.[1] For while they visualized two levels of government exercising power over the nation's affairs, they failed to make clear which of them—the Union or the states—was to be the focal point of the system they created. Neither in Article IV, which is certainly among the least revealing parts of the Constitution, nor in Article VI, section 2, known as the "supremacy clause," did they deal to any great extent in specifics, and nowhere else in the document did they address themselves directly to the question of federalism at all. Even the addition of the Tenth Amendment in 1791 served only to confuse, not to enlighten. The result of this constitutional smog was on the one hand that federalism developed following no very clear or necessary plan and on the other that a continuing quest for definitive answers was set in train. Through the years, federalism remained a topic of absorbing interest and concern to Americans, with the consequence that a considerable body of literature, exploring both the main road and many a by-path of federalism, was gradually built up.

Concern about federalism became particularly acute in the depression

[1] Alpheus T. Mason, "The Nature of Our Federal Union Reconsidered," 65 *Political Science Quarterly* 502 (1950).

days before World War II and in the years just after, when a great many adjustments to a rapidly changing world had to be made, and it seemed important to decide from what level of government action should be forthcoming. That concern reached a climax in the 1950's when, with the Eisenhower Administration's blessings, the second Hoover Commission, the Commission on Intergovernmental Relations, the House Committee on Government Operations, the Joint Federal-State Action Committee, and the President's Commission on National Goals all devoted at least part of their attention to an examination of the federal system.[2] At the same time, and often in connection with the work of these bodies, an increasing number of scholars and students of government turned their efforts in the same direction.[3] A great addition to the already quite voluminous literature on federalism was thus made, but those who expected to find therein a final resolution of all the questions raised over the years were doomed to disappointment. For the debate still goes on. In discussions in Congress, in Supreme Court opinions, among scholars, and in the press and the public at large, divergent attitudes toward federalism are just as common today as they were at the beginning of the Republic. Nor is an end to the debate in sight. Future generations of Americans will probably find the topic as interesting and compelling as their forebears have.

But all the while the discussion was being carried on and the search for final and definitive answers being conducted, federalism itself was growing into maturity. For some time, its adult nature was not well understood, but thanks to the most recent flurry of attention to the subject, an accurate description of the result of the years of evolution can now be made. Study of the literature yields the conclusion, first of all, that despite continuing debate on such matters as the division of powers and the allocation of functions and responsibilities between the Union and the states, at least with regard to fundamentals there is no longer any real controversy. There was agreement from the outset that government in America should be kept as close to the people as possible and that government at all levels exists at the will of the sovereign people. And through the years agreement has been reached that both the Union and the states are necessary and desirable parts of our system of government. The fears

[2] See for a summary of the first of these activities 104 *Congressional Record* 10112–4 (1957); see also regular and special reports of the House Committee on Government Operations and *Final Report of the Joint Federal-State Action Committee to the President of the United States and to the Chairman of the Governors' Conference* (1960); and see *Goals for Americans,* The Report of the President's Commission on National Goals (1960).

[3] See in particular William Anderson, *The Nation and the States: Rivals or Partners?* (1955) and *Intergovernmental Relations in Review* (1960); Leonard White, *The States and the Nation* (1953); Phillip Montgomery, *The Impact of Federal Grants in Illinois* (1958); Jefferson B. Fordham, *A Larger Concept of Community* (1955).

of those who, from Richard Henry Lee on, have seen the specter of "one consolidated government," [4] have not been realized. The federal government indeed has come, particularly in the twentieth century, to occupy a larger role in managing the affairs of the American nation than it once had. But this was not because the federal government became an aggressor with respect to the powers of the states; rather, it was due to the fact that too often the states failed to take effective action in areas where action had become necessary. By now, a better balance has been struck, and today the states and their local units of government are widely recognized as more important in the scheme of things than they have ever been before. "If one looks closely," Morton Grodzins reports, "there is scant evidence for the fear of the federal octopus, the fear that expansion of central programs and influence threatens to reduce the states and localities to compliant administrative arms of the central government. In fact, state and local governments are touching a larger proportion of the people in more ways than ever before; and they are spending a higher fraction of the total national product" as they do so.[5] Rather than the creation of a federal Leviathan, what happened, William Anderson points out, was the development of a partnership between the nation and the states and their subordinate units of government for the most effective handling of the nation's public business. The end product is a single interwoven fabric of government to perform all the services the American people see fit to entrust to its hands.

The states were among the first to acknowledge this development, their governors adopting the following resolution as early as 1944, at the 36th Annual Governors' Conference:

> . . . the Governors' Conference approves and urges the following principles having to do with the administration of . . . public services, involving the cooperation of national, state, and local governments:
> 1. Policies and programs should be developed cooperatively;
> 2. All levels of government should participate financially;
> 3. . . . the respective parts of [a] program to be performed by the several levels of government [should be] clearly defined and due recognition given to the rights and duties of each. . . .
> 6. Necessary authority should be commensurate with responsibility. . . .[6]

Government, in a federal system, properly conceived, the governors saw, involves interaction between all the units of government at every point in the program process. No longer is it correct to speak of the governments

---

[4] See the full discussion of Lee's position in Alpheus T. Mason and Richard H. Leach, *In Quest of Freedom: American Political Thought and Practice* (1959), pp. 139–141.

[5] Morton Grodzins, in *Goals for Americans*, p. 281.

[6] 17 *State Government* 369 (1944).

of the United States, as if each were separated and aloof from the others. Today, the governmental process is one, carried on at different levels by partners with different personalities, as it were, but who are joined together in a common enterprise and who share the same over-all objective— the welfare of the American people.

Study of the literature on federalism makes it quite clear in the second place that its chief characteristic is its changing nature, the ability it gives the nation to adapt itself to new conditions and new circumstances. As the nation changed from farming to industry, from rural to urban and more recently to metropolitan, and from a minor role in world affairs to the leader of the free world, and as the nature of the problems to be attacked by government changed accordingly, the concept and functioning of federalism underwent continuous evolution as well, until adaptability became its basic principle, flexibility its very core. For the framers of the Constitution failed to cast the American Union into one ineluctable mold, forever to freeze it into a single pattern. Instead, they left it pliable, easy to change with changing times. Thus at the beginning of the Republic, the federal system could be operated for the most part on two distinct levels, that of a weak federal government on the one hand and that of not much stronger state governments on the other. Somewhere between the two was conceived to lie a sort of no man's land, where it was felt that neither government ought to tread. As the years went by, occasional invasions of that no man's land by both governments began to be permitted, and a larger role was assigned to local governments. To some, federalism at this stage resembled "a three-layer cake," [7] government "trifurcated into Federal, State, and local" compartments.[8] By the mid-twentieth century, the image, as we have seen, needed revision again. By then it was appropriate to liken it to "the rainbow or marble cake, characterized by an inseparable mingling of differently colored ingredients," each color representing a different unit or level of government.[9] Before long, still another description will no doubt be required for accuracy. For within "the amplitude of the United States system of government as a whole there is room for many . . . changes," William Anderson has concluded. And we "can safely predict that such will take place, and that they will not mark the end of the federal system." [10] Perhaps Governor Nelson Rockefeller captured the essence of American federalism as well as anyone when he called it an "adaptable and creative" form of government with more "than one center of power, energy, and creativity," a form, moreover, which provides America with diversity while at the same time it preserves unity

[7] Grodzins, *op. cit.*, p. 265.
[8] The phrase of Senator Thomas B. Curtis. 107 *Congressional Record* 16325 (1961).
[9] Grodzins, *op. cit.*
[10] Anderson, *op. cit.*, p. 164.

and encourages "imagination and innovation in meeting the needs of the people." [11] Under such a system, each generation has been able to use government as it has felt was necessary to meet the peculiar needs of the time, sure that the federal fabric of government had stretch and give enough to accommodate the many changes which have taken place in the nation and in the world.

Moreover, careful analysis of the literature on federalism shows that as federalism has developed, theory has been largely unimportant. To be sure, our basic adherence to a multi-level system and to a division of powers among the units of that system is a theoretical position. But any attempt to argue on theoretical grounds for a particular division of powers falls flat for lack of corroboration. Instead, it is clear that American federalism should properly be regarded as a device, a tool, rather than as a rigid set of principles. It is concerned with function, with practice, not with theory. It developed in response to changing needs rather than because of the demands of a universally accepted theory. The "inexorable sweep of scientific and economic events . . . has dictated the readjustment of responsibility and power" in the United States, the Chief Justice of New Jersey noted not long ago. "We may lament the course of history," Chief Justice Weintraub went on, "but let us not suppose that we can . . . stay the current of events." [12] As educational needs developed, for example, to have refused to attempt to meet them out of reverence for some mystical balance of power between federal and state governments would have been untenable. "We cannot turn back the clock in the educational aspect of our national life," Senator Mike Mansfield recently told the Senate. "We can no longer say to the States and localities, as we once did, worry about education by yourselves. The realities of contemporary life do not permit us to do so." [13] Instead, those realities force America to use federalism to facilitate educational progress, not as a bar to frustrate it. It is the same with water pollution. The water pollution control program which has been in effect since 1948 has been an intergovernmental program from the start, in frank recognition of the fact that "in the last half century, this has . . . become a national problem of the first magnitude."

> Individual communities are no longer able to cope with the problem and are not equipped to undertake the large-scale planning necessary to clean up the rivers and streams which have no regard for city or State lines. A concentrated effort by Federal, State, and local governments, and industry itself, is necessary if we are to stop pollution and prevent future pollution of this precious resource.[14]

[11] Quoted in 108 *Congressional Record* A1439 (1962). See his Godkin Lectures delivered at Harvard University, February, 1962.
[12] Quoted in 105 *Congressional Record* A687 (1959).
[13] 107 *Congressional Record* 8159 (1961).
[14] *Ibid.*, 108, 4744 (1962).

Similarly, the famous Hill-Burton hospital construction program is an "example of Federal and State and local government cooperation to meet the needs of the people all levels of government serve." [15] And there is now wide recognition that "the era of building roads on a 'cell' basis is past. No longer can towns, cities, counties, or even States plan their highway networks without regard for each other—and for the nation. The need is for integrated planning. . . ." [16] The same kind of conclusions have been reached in field after field. It has not been the dictates of some abstract federal theory but the needs of the American people which have molded the American federal system. As problems have arisen, a pragmatic solution has been sought for each until the pragmatic approach has become characteristic of government action in virtually every action area.

As the nation developed, in short, the American people came to understand that the services and facilities they needed could not be provided by observing a single set of principles, even if they had been clearly articulated, which indeed they never were. Thus the assumptions behind the resolution passed recently by the Louisiana General Assembly were false from the outset:

> . . . Federal aid to education is another in the current series of insidious measures and actions on the part of the Federal Government which . . . are no more than means by which [it] can further encroach upon the constitutional rights of the States. . . . [17]

For such a resolution suggests that the nation early made a theoretical commitment to the principle of states' rights, a commitment supported by a categorical statement of those rights, which then acquired somehow an aura of sanctity and came to demand absolute respect from all the members of the federal system in the future. In fact, however, and fortunately for the development of the Republic, the framers cast neither the rights of the states nor those of the federal government into a rigid mold. Indeed, they disdained such theoretical excursions and thus freed the nation from the chains of dogma, in the process assuring it the flexibility it needed to meet the exigencies of the times. Consider thus as much more representative of the American tradition the following recent joint resolution of the Assembly and Senate of California:

> Whereas there is in California and the rest of the Nation a continuing and increasing need for research . . . on the causes and effects . . . of air pollution. . . . Now, therefore, be it Resolved . . . That the Legislature of the State of California respectfully memorialize the Congress of the United States to make provision for an increase in the air pollution research program of the U. S. Public Health Service . . . and

[15] *Ibid.*, 107, A2667 (1961).
[16] Automotive Safety Foundation, *Expressway Laws: Are Yours Adequate?* Highway Legal Research Report (n. d.), p. 5.
[17] House Concurrent Resolution 22, 1961, 107 *Congressional Record* A3611 (1961).

specifically to provide . . . research resources to California to assist with the State's program for the control of . . . air pollution. . . .[18]

Particularly since World War II, Congress has been besieged with such petitions, and it has acted in response to them, rather than in response to any abstract commitment to theoretical principles.

But the most important conclusion of all to be derived from the vast literature on federalism—a conclusion that has already been suggested a number of times because it is so intimately a part of the fabric of American government—is that intergovernmental relations are the key to modern federalism. The solution of almost "every new public problem that arises . . . involves government at all levels. . . ." "If we are to meet them with maximum effectiveness," the resources of all governments, used in harmony, not in opposition to each other, must be brought to bear.[19] Intergovernmental cooperation, indeed, must be recognized as the motive force of working federalism. "Instead of viewing Federalism as a political Janus in which the loyalty of the people is divided, as are the governmental powers," it has become clear to the discerning that federalism involves all "levels of government cooperating with or complementing each other in meeting the growing demands" on them all.[20] Federalism in the United States, in sum, is based on an amalgam of interrelationships between the several units of government involved, on shared responsibilities in serving the people of the nation.

If cooperation is the *leit motif* of American federalism, however, no uniform pattern of cooperation has developed. Rather, variation and adaptation to particular needs have been characteristic of intergovernmental relations. In some action areas, atomic energy, for example, no clear pattern of intergovernmental relations has emerged at all. In other fields, joint programs have been carried on long enough to permit fairly well defined sets of relations to have developed. Seldom is the same set employed in two programs. Most often, Brooke Graves tells us, cooperation is achieved in the following ways: through informal arrangements, such as those in use in police and narcotics control activities; through formal agreements and contracts, such as those used by the Veterans Administration with state universities under the G. I. Bill after World War II

[18] Assembly Joint Resolution 32, 1961, 107 *Congressional Record* 5669 (1961). See a similar resolution by the Common Council of South Milwaukee, Wisc., on the very next page of the *Record*, asking for federal help in removing pollution from a municipal beach in its jurisdiction.

[19] Statement of Governor Herschel C. Loveless of Iowa, before a Joint Meeting of the Intergovernmental Relations Subcommittee of the House Committee on Government Operations and the Senate Committee on Government Operations, reported in *To Establish An Advisory Commission on Intergovernmental Relations*, 86th Congress, 1st Session, p. 9.

[20] A. J. Davies, "Federal Relations," in R. N. Spann, ed., *Public Administration in Australia* (n. d.), p. 63.

and the growing number of compacts between two or more states; through the shared use of personnel—the county agent engaged in agricultural extension work is the oldest example of this type of cooperation; through interdependent law and administration, where federal authorities require observance of state laws as a condition to granting federal licenses for power developments and state banking officials accept Federal Deposit Insurance Corporation bank audits in lieu of their own; and through a wide variety of grants-in-aid and other fiscal arrangements.[21] Nor have all the possibilities for cooperation been exhausted yet. In fact, it would appear that the only limitation to the development of cooperative techniques lies in the imagination of the men responsible for taking government action. Working within the existing framework of governments and recognizing that governments at all levels must be supported and strengthened, the possibilities for cooperative action are legion. Indeed, the surface has hardly been scratched.[22]

But to say all this barely begins to suggest the difficulties of federalism as a working system of government. Developed as it has been with no foreordained plan, no clearly defined guidelines to help it on its way, trial and error, experimentation, advance and retreat have marked its progress, and overlapping, duplication of effort, conflict and waste have been frequent by-products of its development. Cities, states, and Washington too, have revealed all the sensitivities that plague individuals striving for cooperation, and progress has not been easy. Moreover, lacking moves dictated by the demands of theory, federalism has become problem-oriented. By and large, all levels of government react to problems after they have developed rather than seeking to take cooperative action to prevent their emergence in the first place. Thus, although great strides have been made in achieving cooperative solutions to problems in such functional areas as agriculture, education, highway construction, airport development, housing, public health, and welfare,[23] relatively little progress has been made in attacking a number of other problems which are equally serious, if of a somewhat different nature. The problem of accretion of power at the federal level, for example, and the companion problem of apathy and inaction at the state and local level, have neither been tackled head on, although both are being exacerbated by the greater tax advantages of the federal government. Nor has the problem of how to define properly the national objectives toward which governments on all levels should direct their joint efforts been approached. Problems of lack of coordination be-

[21] W. Brooke Graves, *American State Government* (4th ed., 1953), pp. 902–903.
[22] See for example the *Proceedings of the American Municipal Congress, 1961* (1961), which is entirely devoted to the theme "Intergovernmental Cooperation."
[23] It is instructive to note that most of the attention of the Commission on Intergovernmental Relations was devoted to functional programs. See *Report of the Commission on Intergovernmental Relations to the President* (1955), *passim.*

tween levels and of conflict of laws both remain unsolved. So too to a large extent do problems arising out of competition for revenues and problems resulting from the presence of property of one unit of government in the jurisdiction of another. The whole question of payments in lieu of taxes is still unresolved, as is the matter of the jurisdiction over federal areas within the states.

The newest and potentially the most explosive problem yet to test the viability of intergovernmental cooperation is that arising in the nation's vast and rapidly growing metropolitan areas. The 1960 census showed that about two-thirds of the American people live in something over 200 metropolitan areas, many of which have grown together until they form great metropolitan clusters. Such clusters jump city, county, and state lines with happy abandon, thus making accommodation and adjustment to the changes within them even more difficult than rapid population changes have already made them. As those areas developed, particularly since 1900, the states and local governments moved slowly to solve the problems arising in them. The result was the creation of a kind of vacuum, into which almost inevitably and without any preconceived plan or direction the federal government began to move. Where once it had no connection at all with metropolitan development, today the federal government finds itself, through its fiscal policies, grants-in-aid, subsidies, regulations, research activities, and redevelopment programs, heavily involved in metropolitan growth.[24] And, given the problems still emerging in those areas, further involvement will probably be necessary. Yet to date far too little attention has been devoted to the impact of this involvement on any of the partners in the federal system.

Still other problems of this magnitude, so far unseen, can be expected to develop on the federal stage in the years ahead. For can "there be any doubt that the chores of government will be greater and that the division of labors among the three levels of government will be different [then] than they are today. . . ? How do we make sure that the powers of government continue to be diffused while at the same time the chores of government are effectively performed? This is the great dilemma which faces us with increasing urgency."[25]

For a long time no answer to this dilemma suggested itself. Through the crisis years of depression and war, when swift and effective governmental action became imperative, the number of intergovernmental programs was allowed to grow in virtually geometric proportions, until a near chaotic situation was the result. It was this near-chaos in intergovernmental relations, threatening as it did the very roots of cooperation, that

[24] See Robert H. Connery and Richard H. Leach, *The Federal Government and Metropolitan Areas* (1960), *passim*.
[25] Senator Edmund S. Muskie of Maine, quoted in *Proceedings, op. cit.*, p. 18.

led after World War II to turning the strong spotlight of research on federalism and to the resultant conclusion that perhaps the main barrier in the way of its future development was the lack of a systematic method of bringing problems arising between governments out into the open and of providing a regular forum for their discussion and resolution.[26] As Meyer Kestnbaum put it, gradually it came to be understood that problems of intergovernmental cooperation were "not isolated problems to be completely surveyed or solved at one point in time. They are part and parcel of evolving public policy, requiring continuous study. . . ." "There is a basic and permanent obligation," therefore, to give attention to intergovernmental relations, an obligation which has primarily to be met by the federal government.[27] For only it has the resources to do the job the way it needs to be done.

Acting chiefly upon the Kestnbaum Commission's recommendation, such a continuing agency for study, information, and guidance in the field of intergovernmental relations was established as an arm of the federal government in 1959. Indeed, the creation of the permanent Advisory Commission on Intergovernmental Relations is perhaps the most important development in American federalism in its long and turbulent history. For although "created by an act of Congress and although deriving . . . practically all of its financial support from Federal appropriations, the Commission functions as a national body responsive to the needs of all three major levels of government" [28] and provides for the first time an impartial agency to study trouble spots in intergovernmental relations and to make recommendations for their removal as well as a sort of clearing-house for information between the several levels of government. Its creation gives the United States, in short, a steady force at work, dedicated to the improvement and development of effective working relations between its several units of government and thus greater assurance than ever before of the continued strength and utility of the federal system.

The Commission is a bipartisan body of twenty-six. Its members, as required by the statute which created it, consist of governors, mayors, county officials, members of state legislatures and of the Congress, representatives of the federal executive branch, and members of the public at large—all the parties involved in modern functional federalism. It has a small professional staff and makes occasional use of consultants. The Commission has made it clear from the beginning that it will work within the pragmatic context which is characteristic of American federalism. It

---

[26] See the statement of Mayor Frank P. Zeidler of Milwaukee, in *To Establish an Advisory Commission, op. cit.,* p. 44.

[27] Meyer Kestnbaum to author, September 11, 1958, p. 4.

[28] Advisory Commission on Intergovernmental Relations. *Third Annual Report* (1962), p. 2.

will concentrate, in the words of its staff director, on the production of "practical recommendations with a reasonable degree of political feasibility." [29] For it recognizes that the need it was designed to meet was a practical one and that "its own value and place in the federal system will be determined by its ability to make constructive contributions" to the operation of the over-all governmental system.[30] So far it has turned its attention to the problems involved in the coordination of state and federal inheritance, estate and gift taxes; the investment of idle cash balances by state and local units of government; governmental structure, organization and planning in metropolitan areas; intergovernmental cooperation in tax administration; state and local taxation of private property in federally controlled areas; and tax overlapping in the United States. It has listed for future study and recommendation a number of other similarly practical problems. But the Commission is "not content with merely making studies and recommendations. Commission members want to see the recommendations put into effect and have devoted considerable attention to following through in behalf of their recommendations in terms of legislative or administrative action." [31] Of thirteen recommendations made in 1961 requiring congressional action, six were promptly enacted into law and one received administrative implementation, and of twenty-one recommendations for state legislative action, nine were accepted by the Council of State Governments and included in its 1963 legislation program.[32]

Although these are impressive results, the Commission has not been at work long enough to permit a meaningful assessment of its contribution to be made. A number of conclusions can be drawn from its work thus far, however. The Commission seems to see, for one thing, that intergovernmental cooperation involves far more than federal-state relations alone. "Consequently, the Commission is concerned with State-local and inter-local problems just as much as with Federal-State problems." [33] It also has concluded that in order to achieve the most effective balance in American government, it is the state and local units which are most in need of being strengthened. Thus it is particularly concerned to do what it can to enable state and local governments to play their full part in the partnership. Finally, it has realized that its greatest contribution will result from approaching "its work selectively and . . . consider[ing] problems in depth." [34] It is just this kind of approach which has always been lacking, and its adoption by the Commission is a most heartening sign.

[29] The phrase of William Colman, Executive Director, Advisory Commission on Intergovernmental Relations, 107 *Congressional Record* A5671 (1961).
[30] Advisory Commission on Intergovernmental Relations, *op. cit.*
[31] Senator Edmund Muskie, 109 *Congressional Record* 6129 (1963).
[32] *Ibid.*
[33] Advisory Commission on Intergovernmental Relations, *op. cit.*
[34] *Ibid.*

But even with the Advisory Commission at work, the problems of operating a governmental system on the basis of cooperative effort will not all be solved. Just as much depends upon the creation in the public at large of an image of federalism to match the facts of the case. Intergovernmental cooperation is not a competitive symbol that attracts public attention. Although they have lost much of their meaning in terms of reality, city boundaries, county lines, and state borders are still full of significance to the average citizen. Ever since the days of ancient Greece, men's loyalties have been to single units of government—cities, towns, states—and American public education has done little to bring about an awareness of the changes that have taken place on the American scene. There is great need to educate the American people, both to bring them an understanding of the present situation in America and to prepare them for further changes yet to come. As one of the members of the Kestnbaum Commission pointed out, we must educate "the people in the reality of governmental operations." "We have given so much of our intellectual energies in America to other fields, . . . business, . . . education, . . . religious institutionalism . . . . If we could relate these energies to . . . getting the people to recognize their mutual interests and to be less rigid in their loyalties" to single units of government, if we could get them "to take the broader view through imaginative eyes," the last barrier to a sound and enduring federal system would be removed.[35]

And the time to do so is growing short. Changes of tremendous importance are in the process of taking place in the United States. The population explosion since the end of the war, rapidly increasing urbanization, technological advances in many fields, and the ever-growing "nationalization" of business, labor, and agriculture, to say nothing of the cold war and its attendant problems, are all combining to produce greater challenges to American federalism than it has yet had to withstand. Take the challenge of population pressure alone. At present rates of growth, the population of the United States will more than double in the next hundred years. "Will the lines of jurisdiction of towns and counties have any meaning [then] at all as appropriate divisions of responsibility for providing local services? What will have happened to the great open spaces America has always known? What will be the source of our water supply, and at what level of government will responsibility for it lie? How will people move about? Where will they find their recreation?"[36] What adjustments in government structure will be necessary to meet needs in these and other areas? Only a people alert to the nature of the changes themselves on the one hand and to the way government operates in

[35] Brooks Hays, in *To Establish an Advisory Commission, op. cit.*, p. 71.
[36] Muskie, *op. cit.*

reaction to them on the other will assure that those changes will be efficiently met.

Challenges exist not only in the future, however. They exist as well in the present. On neither the federal nor the state level, for example, have all the alterations yet been made that are necessary to bring laws and constitutions fully into the era of cooperation. Both federal and state laws need to be examined to assure that they do not contain provisions which inadvertently hinder the development of effective intergovernmental cooperation by requiring the use of outmoded forms or procedures. Many state constitutions in particular are full of clauses that inhibit cooperation. In the words of Albert L. Sturm, "The familiar principle of limited government written into state constitutions has been a source of restrictions on the scope of cooperative federalism." [37] Too often, the way of constitutional amendment and revision is hard, but recently movements have been made to remove those impediments. The constitutions of Alaska and Hawaii, and the Model State Constitution, provide guidance to states wishing to take remedial action.

Nor have administrators yet paid sufficient attention to the difficulties they place in the way of cooperation. It should surely not be necessary at this late date for the Governors' Conference to have to deplore officially "the tendency of Federal agencies to dictate the organizational form and structure through which the States carry out federally supported programs." [38] Nor should complaints about delays caused by unreasonable federal administrative requirements and red tape still be too numerous to count. The Subcommittee on Intergovernmental Relations of the House Committee on Government Operations found not long ago that "Federal supervision of the public housing and urban renewal program was strongly and almost universally criticized for hampering local effort . . . [by] (1) detailed and cumbersome . . . procedures and requirements for obtaining project approval, (2) tight centralization of administrative authority in Washington, and (3) inadequate staffing of field offices." [39] "The greatest single weakness in the Federal Government's activities in the field of water resources development," said a recent cabinet committee report on that problem, "is lack of cooperation and coordination of Federal agencies with each other and with the States and local interests." [40] The same weakness has been noticed in connection with other federal programs. Nor is the fault all on the federal side. State and local officials can be just as obstructive as their federal fellows. But the states, which

[37] Albert L. Sturm, *Major Constitutional Issues in West Virginia* (1961), p. 109.
[38] Resolution of the 53rd Annual Meeting of the Governors' Conference, July, 1961, 107 *Congressional Record* 11639 (1961).
[39] Connery and Leach, *op. cit.*, p. 18.
[40] *Ibid.*, p. 22.

have long been laggard in this respect, have begun to devote attention to removing some of these difficulties. "Little Hoover Commissions" have been at work in a number of the states, and as a result, the states are rapidly developing their administrative strength. This "trend . . . toward increased technical competence in state government will in due course permit a fundamental transformation of federal-state relations in many fields." [41] The federal government too must begin to attack the problem, for every effort to simplify procedures and to coordinate programs must be made by administrators all along the line if the way to intergovernmental cooperation is to be made smooth.

More than anything else, the lessons of the past teach that federalism, like any other partnership, requires mutual forbearance. It will not work if any of the partners push their own interests too hard. The federal government for its part must learn to resist the temptation to be the rich and overbearing senior partner and the states and local governments to resist the equally strong temptation to accept the role of subsidized junior partners. Cooperation—partnership—implies the full joint efforts of two or more principals. To assure that such efforts will be forthcoming, all the partners must be continually alert to their roles in the governing process and to the need regularly to assess their own institutions to assure that they are carrying their full share of the burden of government. Federalism will always be in flux, and effective action will be possible only if care is devoted by every partner to facilitating the adjustments among them which changes in circumstances will continually require.

American federalism has come a long way since the framers of the Constitution set it in motion more than 175 years ago. Despite the many changes it has undergone, it remains a powerful element in the American way of life today. The years have proved that it provides a democratic people with the best instrument yet devised to work for their own betterment in a changing and uncertain world. In the years ahead, as the increased attention lately being paid to its functioning bears fruit, federalism can be expected not only to remain at the center of American life but to make an even greater contribution than it has in the past to the development of "one Nation, indivisible, with liberty and justice for all."

[41] Emil J. Sady, *Research in Federal-State Relations* (1957), p. 4.

8

Stateways Versus Folkways:
Critical Factors in Southern Reactions to
Brown v. Board of Education

Donald R. Matthews
James W. Prothro

The Supreme Court's historic decision in the school desegregation cases[1] on May 17, 1954, has had many far-reaching implications. One of these is that it has forced academic as well as lay observers to recognize that, contrary to Chief Justice Hughes, the Constitution is *not* necessarily what the Supreme Court says it is—if by the Constitution we mean the organic law that is actually applied by officials and observed by citizens on pain of punishment. While close observers of government have always known that Supreme Court decisions are not self-enforcing, the great prestige of the Court has led political scientists to concentrate largely on the logic of the decisions themselves—and on their relationship to other decisions rather than on their relationship to antecedent or subsequent political situations and behaviors.

Researchers have recently tried to fill the gap left by the traditional neglect of Supreme Court decisions as political acts influenced by and influencing other political conditions. But this effort is not as new as some of those committed to it assume; Professor Mason's work has long

---

[1] *Brown v. Board of Education*, 347 U.S. 483 (1954).

moved beyond the exegesis of official decisions. In research of this sort, one may focus either on the antecedent or the subsequent factors related to Supreme Court decisions, *i.e.*, if court decisions are viewed as political acts in a continuing struggle to influence policy, one may profitably examine both the independent and the dependent variables associated with those acts. Professor Mason has explored the former with such thoroughness as to evoke pained protests from law professors who feel that the justices should not be exposed to the analytical eye of the political scientist.[2]

In this essay, we shall follow Mason's lead in placing the *Brown* v. *Board of Education* decision in a setting broader than that offered by other decisions alone. Rather than analyzing antecedent factors, however, we shall focus on behaviors that stemmed from the decision. Except for our reliance on UNIVAC technology, then, our effort represents a continuation of at least one facet of Mason's approach to the work of the Court. As Professor Mason himself has said, "It should not be assumed that these legal solutions have meant the abolition of segregated schools and other public facilities throughout the South." [3] We shall identify some of the critical factors that appear to account for variations in compliance.

A recurrent problem in political science is that of "stateways" versus "folkways." Perhaps the generally accepted point of view among academicians has been that of William Graham Sumner: stateways merely reflect folkways; should the two come into conflict, the folkways would inevitably prove to be the dominant force.[4] Robert MacIver has more recently expressed the same general idea in less extreme terms:

> Wherever technology advances, wherever private business extends its range, wherever the cultural life becomes more complex, new tasks are imposed on government. This happens apart from, or in spite of, the particular philosophies that governments cherish. . . . In the longer run the tasks undertaken by governments are dictated by changing conditions, and governments on the whole are more responsive than creative in fulfilling them.[5]

[2] Edmond Cahn, "Eavesdropping on Justice," *Nation*, Vol. 184 (January 5, 1957), 14–16. An excellent example of Professor Mason's rigorous examination of the broad social and political forces that shape Supreme Court decisions is "The Conservative World of Mr. Justice Sutherland, 1883–1910," 32 *American Political Science Review* 443–447 (1938).

[3] Alpheus Thomas Mason and William M. Beaney, *The Supreme Court in a Free Society* (1959), p. 264.

[4] See William Graham Sumner, *Folkways* (1906).

[5] *The Web of Government* (1947), pp. 314–315. Also see Talcott Parsons, *The Structure of Social Action* (1949). One of the most familiar arguments to the effect that government represents mere "superstructure" rather than an autonomous force in society is, of course, that of Karl Marx. Unlike Spencer, MacIver, and Parsons, however, Marx elevated economic forces to the status of a single determinant.

Since this interpretation appears to denigrate the importance of the political process, political scientists have been somewhat reluctant to accept it. Nor have the academic dissenters been without support in the general public. The reformist strain of the American tradition emphasizes the idea that evils can be cured merely by "passing a law." Conservatives scoff at such reliance on government power and argue, like the Supreme Court in *Plessey* v. *Ferguson*,[6] that "you can't change human nature by law." The reformer's retort is that laws and court decisions attempt to regulate behaviors rather than beliefs, and that the former are subject to governmental control.

Both the academic and the popular aspects of this dispute may be elucidated by an analysis of reactions to *Brown* v. *Board of Education*, the decision that ruled state-enforced segregation in public schools to be unconstitutional. Here we have an official act of the national government that ran counter to the most deeply set folkways of an entire section of the country. What were the reactions? Our first task in this essay will be to consider the extent and the distribution of school desegregation in the South[7] in response to the decision. This examination of similarities and contrasts among the southern states will place in sharper focus the question of stateways versus folkways. Second, we shall analyze the relationship between a battery of demographic variables—taken as reflecting the varying folkways of the region—and school desegregation in the South in order to determine the extent to which the former are predictive of the latter. Third, we shall attempt to determine whether a battery of political variables—taken as reflecting the varying stateways of the region—add significantly to the explanatory power of the demographic variables. Finally, we shall undertake an explanation of our over-all findings and an interpretation of their significance for political science.

SCHOOL DESEGREGATION IN THE SOUTH, 1954–62

On "Black Monday"—as May 17, 1954, is still bitterly called by some white southerners—17 states and the District of Columbia required racial segregation in public schools by law. In the border states of Delaware, Kentucky, Maryland, Missouri, Oklahoma, and West Virginia and in the District of Columbia, school authorities now have completed, or are in the process of completing, the desegregation of the schools. Of the 756 biracial school districts in these states, 642 were desegregated by May,

---

[6] 163 U.S. 537 (1896).

[7] In this study, the South is defined as the eleven former Confederate states: Alabama, Arkansas, Florida, Georgia, Louisiana, Mississippi, North Carolina, South Carolina, Tennessee, Texas, Virginia.

1960.[8] This desegregation, very largely accomplished without prodding from the federal courts, has not been of the token variety. In the 1961–62 school year, eighty-six per cent of the Negro school children in the District of Columbia were attending schools with whites. In West Virginia, 62 per cent of the Negro school children were attending desegregated schools; in Delaware, 53 per cent; Kentucky, 49 per cent; Missouri, 41 per cent; Maryland, 33 per cent; and in Oklahoma, 26 per cent.[9]

In the 11 states of the former Confederacy, however, the story has been different. Reactions to *Brown* v. *Board of Education* have been legion, but almost all have been negative. Two hundred and twenty-eight new laws and resolutions designed to prevent, restrict, or control desegregation have been adopted by southern legislatures—pupil assignment laws, repeal of compulsory attendance laws, provisions for the closing of public schools, tuition grants to private schools, resolutions of interposition, and the like.[10] All but a handful of the region's congressmen and senators joined in promulgating the "Southern Manifesto." Southern school boards moved with more "deliberation" than "speed."

The overall picture from 1954 to 1962 is set forth in Table 1. Not one southern school district was integrated during the 1954–55 or 1955–56 academic years. In 1956–57, 108 school districts, about 5 per cent of the biracial districts in the region, opened their doors to one or more Negro children. Five years later the number of desegregated school districts had risen to 208, or approximately 10 per cent of all biracial districts.

The compliance with the court ruling has not only been slow, but it has also been uneven (Table 2). Texas, Arkansas, and Tennessee admitted the first Negro students during 1956–57; only in Texas was this more than a gesture. North Carolina began desegregation in 1957–58; Virginia, in 1958–59; Florida, in 1959–60; and Louisiana and Georgia, in 1961–62. In none of these states did the proportion of school districts initially desegregated exceed 2 per cent. The deep southern states of Mississippi, Alabama, and South Carolina have yet to integrate a school district.

By 1962, 23 per cent of Texas' biracial school districts were desegregated. Virginia, the initial proponent of "massive resistance" to the decision, was next with about 15 per cent of her biracial districts accepting Negro students. Tennessee, Florida, and North Carolina followed, with from 6 to 9 per cent of their districts accepting Negro students. Arkansas, one of the region's leaders before Little Rock, had dropped to sixth place, with only about 4 per cent of her biracial districts integrated. Louisiana and Georgia followed well behind.

[8] Southern Education Reporting Service, *Status of Segregation-Desegregation in the Southern and Border States*, Nashville, Tenn., 1960.

[9] *Southern School News*, Dec. 1961, p. 7.

[10] Southern Education Reporting Service, *op. cit.*

Few Negro children are typically involved in a formally "desegregated" district. The actual numbers of Negro students in white schools, by state, are presented in Table 3. In 1956, there were 3,440 Negro children attending school with whites in the 11 former Confederate states and all but 40 of these were in Texas. The number has inched upward since then, hitting 4,275 in 1960–61. Six thousand nine hundred Negro children were

Table 1

NUMBER AND PERCENTAGE OF BIRACIAL SCHOOL
DISTRICTS DESEGREGATED IN 11 SOUTHERN STATES, 1954–62

Academic year	No. of districts desegregated	Per cent of biracial districts desegregated
1954–55	0	0
1955–56	0	0
1956–57	108	4.9%
1957–58	135	6.1
1958–59	141	6.7
1959–60	153	7.3
1960–61	169	8.4
1961–62	208	10.3

Sources: Derived from statistics in Southern Education Reporting Service, *Status of School Segregation-Desegregation in the Southern and Border States*, Nashville, Tenn., 1960; *Southern School News*, December 1960, p. 1; *ibid.*, December 1961, p. 1; Southern Regional Council, *School Desegregation: The First Six Years*, Atlanta, Ga., 1960.

Table 2

PERCENTAGE OF BIRACIAL SCHOOL DISTRICTS
DESEGREGATED IN 11 SOUTHERN STATES, 1956–62

State	Academic year					
	1956–57	1957–58	1958–59	1959–60	1960–61	1961–62
Mississippi	0	0	0	0	0	0
Alabama	0	0	0	0	0	0
South Carolina	0	0	0	0	0	0
Georgia	0	0	0	0	0	0.5%
Louisiana	0	0	0	0	0	1.5
Florida	0	0	0	0.5%	0.5%	7.5
Virginia	0	0	2.3%	4.7	8.6	14.7
North Carolina	0	1.7%	2.3	4.0	5.8	6.4
Tennessee	0.7%	1.4	2.1	2.8	4.2	9.1
Arkansas	1.8	3.1	2.6	3.5	4.4	4.4
Texas	12.3	14.6	17.3	17.6	18.1	23.0

Sources: Same as for Table 1.

Table 3

ESTIMATED NUMBER OF NEGROES IN PUBLIC SCHOOLS
WITH WHITES IN 11 SOUTHERN STATES, 1956–62

State	Academic year					
	1956–57	1957–58	1958–59	1959–60	1960–61	1961–62
Mississippi	0	0	0	0	0	0
Alabama	0	0	0	0	0	0
South Carolina	0	0	0	0	0	0
Georgia	0	0	0	0	0	9
Louisiana	0	0	0	0	4	12
Florida	0	0	0	22 *	27	552
Virginia	0	0	30	103	208	533
North Carolina	0	11	14	34	82	203
Tennessee	6 **	19 **	82	169	342	1,142
Arkansas	34	91	73	94	113	152
Texas ***	3,400	3,600	3,250	3,300	3,500	4,300
Totals	3,440	3,721	3,449	3,722	4,276	6,903

* These 22 Negroes were attending the Homestead Air Force Base school with 745 whites. In Orchard Villa (Dade County) school 8 whites also attended classes with 490 Negroes; these are omitted from the table.

** These figures exclude Negroes attending school in Oak Ridge, which was operated during these years by the federal government on a desegregated basis.

*** Texas figures are estimates. The decline between 1958 and 1961 is apparently the result of more accurate estimates in recent times.

Sources: Same as for Table 1.

enrolled in white schools during 1961–62, a 50 per cent increase over the previous year. Even so, two-thirds of these were found in the state of Texas.

The microscopic number of Negro children involved in this historic "movement," or lack thereof, is underscored by the figures in Table 4. One and one-half per cent of the Negro school children in Texas, the undisputed leader of school desegregation in the region, were enrolled in "white" schools! Enlightened Tennessee had 0.7 per cent; progressive Florida, 0.3 per cent; reluctant Virginia, 0.2 per cent. In no other state in the South did the proportion of Negro children in white schools significantly exceed one tenth of one per cent!

At the rate of desegregation established since 1954, the last southern school district will have token integration in the year 2030. And assuming that Negro students enter white schools at the same rate that they have since the *Brown* decision, it would take 3,180 years to desegregate the present student population of the South.

Table 4

PER CENT OF NEGRO SCHOOL CHILDREN IN PUBLIC
SCHOOL WITH WHITES, DECEMBER 1961

State	Per cent
Mississippi	0
Alabama	0
South Carolina	0
Georgia	0.003%
Louisiana	0.004
Florida	0.258
Virginia	0.246
North Carolina	0.061
Tennessee	0.734
Arkansas	0.142
Texas	1.420

Source: *Southern School News,* Dec. 1961, p. 7.

DEMOGRAPHIC FACTORS AND COUNTY RESPONSES TO THE SCHOOL DESEGREGATION DECISION

Southern school districts have, on the whole, responded to *Brown* v. *Board of Education* with glacial slowness. When one examines the distribution of the relatively few districts that have obeyed the decision, however, he finds that they are most unevenly distributed among the states. Moreover, considerable variation is found within states—the fact that one district in a state desegregates does not mean that the entire state is ready to accept school desegregation.

What accounts for this pattern of general segregation with pockets of desegregation? The great contrast between the eleven states we refer to as "the South" and other states sometimes thought of as southern suggests part of the answer. The socio-political systems of the eleven states of the former Confederacy mark them off as a relatively homogeneous section quite different from border states in their dedication to segregation. But the homogeneity of the South is only relative. Despite the slow movement toward desegregation, the variations we have noted both among and within the southern states remain to be explained.

The most commonly accepted explanation is that desegregation varies inversely with the proportion of Negroes in the population, but a number of other influences have also been identified. The Southern Regional Council sums up a number of these influences in a report on the first six years of response to the desegregation decision: "The density of Negro population is no absolute yardstick of racial attitudes. Many other factors are important: urbanization, the quality of local leadership, economic and political arrangements, and the mixture of memory and habit which gives a community its unique traditions. But the Negro-white ratio is the best single index to the adjustment . . . required by the Supreme Court's decision." [11] Here we find six independent variables against which to examine the pattern of school desegregation. Four of these are clearly demographic variables on which it is possible to collect data for all the counties in the South: (1) proportion of population Negro, (2) per cent of population urban, (3) leadership potential, and (4) the nature of the economy. The first two factors can be expressed by county data taken directly from the census. The last two can be expressed less directly through data on several county attributes: leadership potential through data on education and income levels; the nature of the economy through data on per cent of labor force in agriculture and in manufacturing. Of the two additional influences cited by the Southern Regional Council— political arrangements and the community's mixture of memory and habit —the first is clearly a combination of political variables and the second is ambiguous, a result of both demographic and political influences. We shall reserve consideration of purely political factors for the next section, but we have collected one demographic item relevant to a community's memory and past habits—the per cent of population Negro in 1900.

The emphasis by the Southern Regional Council on the percentage of Negroes in the population as the most critical factor in school desegregation is found in a number of other studies.[12] Jack Peltason gives greater emphasis, however, to urbanism. "Token integration is winning in large southern cities . . . because such a program marks the terms on which the dominant groups can agree. Urban white citizens are not unwilling to accept limited integration. . . . In the rural South no school integration is in sight. Here the Negro is still economically depressed; he has no vote, and the white community is opposed even to symbolic integration." [13] In addition to giving greater weight to urbanism than to the percentage of Negroes in the population, Peltason calls attention to still another demographic factor: the degree to which the Negro is economically depressed. As measures of this variable, we collected data for each county on nonwhite

---

[11] *School Desegregation: The First Six Years* (1960), p. 19.

[12] See *e.g.*, A. Stephen Stephan, "Integration and Sparse Negro Populations," 81 *School and Society* 133–135 (1955), and the same author's "Population Ratios, Racial Attitudes, and Desegregation," paper presented at the annual meeting of the Southwestern Social Science Association, Sociology Section, San Antonio, March 30, 1956.

[13] *Fifty-Eight Lonely Men: Southern Federal Judges and School Desegregation* (1961), pp. 249–250.

median income and on the per cent of the nonwhite labor force in white-collar occupations.[14] Other studies have identified levels of education and industrialization [15] and church membership [16] as factors associated with desegregation.

Whatever their particular emphases, all studies of southern responses to *Brown* v. *Board of Education* stress social and economic variables in accounting for differences from one area to another. In a state-by-state analysis of "The Demography of Desegregation," Thomas F. Pettigrew and M. Richard Cramer emphasize "The demographic consistency of such southern racial phenomena as lynching, segregationist voting, and school desegregation . . . it is the poor, traditional, rural areas with large percentages of uneducated Negroes that form the core of racial conflict." [17] In order to ascertain how much explanatory power demographic variables have for the South as a whole, we collected data on twenty-one social and economic attributes of 997 southern counties.[18] These attributes include measures of all of the demographic influences suggested by the literature (see Table 5). With the presence or absence of some school desegregation in each county in 1960 as the dependent variable,[19] we carried out a correlation analysis to determine the influence of the 21 variables on school desegregation.

As a first step, simple correlations were computed for each of the independent variables and school desegregation. The coefficient of correlation (r) varies from zero (no association between the independent and dependent variables) to 1.0 (one variable perfectly predicts the other). A positive correlation indicates that as one variable increases the other also increases; a negative correlation indicates an inverse relationship—as one variable increases, the other decreases. The simple correlations are pre-

---

[14] Nonwhite median income could be taken directly from the census, on a county basis. Per cent of employed Negroes in white-collar occupations is not reported as such by the census. This figure was derived by totaling the number of nonwhites (both male and female) employed as professional, technical, and kindred workers; managers, officials, and proprietors (except farm); clerical and kindred workers; sales workers; craftsmen, foremen, and kindred workers; and dividing by the total nonwhite labor force in each county. Source: U.S. Census of Population: 1950, Vol. II, *Characteristics of the Population*, Parts 2, 4, 10, 11, 18, 24, 33, 40, 42, 43, 46, Table 44 "Characteristics of the Nonwhite Population, for Counties: 1950."

[15] James M. Nabrit, Jr., "Legal Inventions and the Desegregation Process," 304 *The Annals* 35–43 (1956).

[16] Southern Regional Council, *op. cit.*, pp. 19–22.

[17] 15 *The Journal of Social Issues* 70 (1959).

[18] The total number of counties in the eleven southern states is 1136; 108 are excluded because their populations contain less than 1 per cent Negroes, and an additional 31 are excluded because of incomplete data.

[19] Desegregation of any school district in a county suffices to classify the county as desegregated. Data on segregation were taken from *Southern School News* through Vol. 7, No. 3 (September 1960).

sented in Table 5, with the variables ranked by the strength of their association with school desegregation.[20]

Table 5

SIMPLE CORRELATIONS BETWEEN COUNTY DEMOGRAPHIC VARIABLES
AND STATUS OF SCHOOL DESEGREGATION IN 11 SOUTHERN STATES

Rank	Variable	r
1	Per cent of population urban	+.30
2	Nonwhite median income	+.29
3	Nonwhite median school years completed	+.28
4	White median income	+.28
5	Per cent of population Negro in 1900	−.26
6	Per cent of population Negro in 1950	−.26
7	Per cent population increase, 1940–50	+.24
8	Per cent of church members Roman Catholic	+.23
9	Per cent of church members Baptist	−.19
10	Per cent of nonwhite labor force in white-collar occupations	+.18
11	Per cent of labor force in agriculture	−.18
12	Per cent of labor force in manufacturing	−.16
13	Difference in white-nonwhite median income	+.16
14	White median school years completed	+.11
15	Percentage point difference in Negro population, 1900–1950	+.08
16	Per cent of church membership Jewish	+.07
17	Presence/absence of Negro college	+.07
18	Per cent of farms operated by tenants	−.04
19	Per cent of population belonging to a church	−.03
20	Difference in white and nonwhite median school years completed	−.02

No tests of statistical significance of correlations are reported in this essay because the correlations are based upon a complete enumeration rather than a sample.

A complete list of sources for these data would be too lengthy to reproduce here; such a list (for this table and for Table 6) may be secured from the authors at the University of North Carolina, Chapel Hill, N.C.

The largest simple correlation is not contributed, as anticipated from some of the literature, by per cent of population Negro. Rather, Peltason's emphasis on urbanism and lack of economic depression among Negroes is supported by the first and second ranking of per cent of population urban and nonwhite median income. Going beyond the first two items to include the four variables most positively associated with school desegregation, we

[20] No simple correlation can be obtained for one qualitative variable—size of Standard Metropolitan Area, if any, in which the county is located—used in computing the multiple correlation between demographic variables and county school desegregation.

may say that desegregation is most likely in an urban environment in which Negroes and whites receive relatively high incomes and Negroes are relatively well educated. But the emphasis on the proportion of Negroes in the population is not inappropriate—per cent of population Negro in 1900 and 1950 have the strongest negative correlations with school desegregation. One of the reasons why an urban environment is more conducive to desegregation is that it includes a smaller percentage of Negroes than a rural environment.[21]

Among the other positive correlations, we find that an expanding population (item 7), a relatively large number of Roman Catholics (item 8), and a large white-collar class among Negroes (item 10) are strongly associated with desegregation. In negative terms, a relatively large number of Baptists (item 9) and an agricultural economy (item 11) are strongly related to continued segregation. Perhaps the most surprising negative correlation is contributed by per cent of labor force in manufacturing (item 12). One would expect employment in manufacturing to be strongly associated with urbanism, even if it did not itself facilitate desegregation. In fact, however, per cent of labor force in manufacturing in the South has a negligible relationship to urbanism (+.08) and to per cent of population Negro (+.001).

Each of the factors we have discussed is significantly related to school desegregation. The findings might appear, then, to support the theory of social determinism—and, inferentially, the idea that folkways outweigh stateways. To see just how far one can go with this theory, however, we must look at the combined effect of all 21 variables. A multiple correlation coefficient of .50 was obtained when all 21 demographic variables were together correlated with presence or absence of school desegregation in southern counties. This means that 21 demographic variables account for about 25 per cent (R^2) of the variation in school desegregation in the South.

POLITICAL FACTORS AND COUNTY RESPONSES TO THE SCHOOL DESEGREGATION DECISION

The multiple correlation of demographic factors and school desegregation in the South is of rather impressive magnitude. On the basis of a multiple correlation of identical strength in another area of political behavior—voting preference—Paul Lazarsfeld and his associates concluded that "social characteristics determine political preference." [22] While the

[21] Per cent of population urban and per cent of population Negro have a —.18 correlation.
[22] Paul Lazarsfeld, Bernard Berelson, and Hazel Gaudet, *The People's Choice: How the Voter Makes Up His Mind in a Presidential Campaign* (1948), p. 27.

data do not seem to call for quite so strong a statement, we may conservatively conclude that demographic characteristics are critically important—although not wholly determinant—in southern responses to *Brown v. Board of Education.* Moreover, we propose, rather than stopping with this conclusion, to go further and discover whether political factors add substantially to the explanatory power of demographic variables. Our underlying hypothesis in this undertaking is that state political systems not only vary with demographic factors but that they also exert an independent influence on school desegregation.

The literature we summarized on demography and school desegregation also contained references to political influences. The Southern Regional Council speaks in general of the importance of "political arrangements" in school desegregation.[23] Although different political arrangements cannot easily be expressed as measurable characteristics of counties, we can record county data that will tend to vary with different political systems, *e.g.*, strength of States' Rights vote in the 1948 presidential election, Republican voting strength in presidential and state elections, and the presence or absence of Negro and white race organizations such as an NAACP chapter or a White Citizens Council. We have accordingly collected information on all of these political attributes of southern counties (see Table 6).

An additional political factor that is thought to be of prime importance in the Negroes' efforts toward desegregation is the rate of Negro voting. As Peltason puts it, "One of the decisive factors in determining the outcome [of desegregation efforts] will be the ability of Negroes to translate their potential voting power into actual ballots."[24] Congress, the U.S. Civil Rights Commission, the press, and Negro leaders all seem to agree wholeheartedly with this view. The Civil Rights Acts of 1957 and 1960 both deal primarily with the right to vote.[25] The Civil Rights Commission created by the 1957 Act has invested a heavy share of its limited resources in the voting area.[26] Both Attorney General Robert F. Kennedy and his predecessor, Herbert Brownell, are reported to believe that the vote provides the southern Negro with his most effective means of advancing toward equality, and recent actions of the Justice Department reflect this view.[27] The press argues that "political rights pave the way to all others."[28]

[23] *Op. cit.*, p. 19.
[24] *Op. cit.*, p. 250.
[25] 71 *Stat.* 635; 74 *Stat.* 86.
[26] Cf. U.S. Commission on Civil Rights, *Report of the U.S. Commission on Civil Rights, 1959* (1959); *1961 Commission on Civil Rights Report*, Vol. I, "Voting" (1961).
[27] *The New York Times*, January 7, 1962.
[28] *Ibid.* See also the editorial entitled "The Ballot-Box Method," *The New York Times*, September 28, 1961.

Negro organizations have concentrated on voter registration efforts in the belief expressed by Martin Luther King that the most significant step Negroes can take is in the "direction of the voting booths." [29] Although information on the number of Negroes actually voting in southern counties cannot be secured, we did collect estimates of the number of Negroes registered to vote in each county.[30]

The simple correlations between all of these political variables and school desegregation are presented in Table 6.[31] The highest correlation (−.24) demonstrates a strong negative relationship between States' Rights voting and school desegregation; the cluster of variables on Republicanism (items 2, 3, 4, and 5) reveals a positive relationship between Republican strength and school desegregation. As one would expect, a political environment marked by some degree of party competition is more conducive to permissive racial attitudes whereas areas of overt states' rights sentiment are most repressive. Although our data on political organizations are very crude—indicating merely the presence or absence of white and Negro race organizations [32]—they show the expected influence: counties with Negro race organizations are more likely to have desegregated schools, while counties with white race organizations are more likely to maintain segregated schools.

The most unexpected finding reported in Table 6 is the low order of relationship (+.03) between Negro voter registration and school desegregation. Although greater numbers of Negro voters may be expected eventually to promote greater local response to Negro demands, the proportion of Negroes registered as of 1960 would be the poorest of political variables for predicting the presence or absence of school desegregation. Negro registration seems currently to be more closely associated with the proportion of Negroes in the population than with urbanism, the most critical demographic variable for desegregation.[33]

All of the political variables show some relationship to school desegre-

---

[29] Baltimore *Afro-American*, October 7, 1961; *The New York Times*, July 10, 1961.

[30] These estimates are from the reports of the Civil Rights Commission cited in note 26.

[31] Simple correlations could not be obtained for two qualitative variables included in the computation of the multiple correlation between political factors and county school desegregation. These variables are: the states as political units; the presence or absence of acts of racial violence in each county.

[32] "Race organizations" include groups arising in either race to oppose practices considered inimical to its interests by the other race. Sources: *The New York Times Index*, January, 1945-February, 1961. Southern Educational Reporting Service, "Facts on Film," Rolls 1–40 (May, 1954-June, 1958); first supplement, Rolls 1–13 (July, 1958-June, 1959); second supplement, Rolls 1–11 (July, 1959-June, 1960). Letters of inquiry to statewide race organizations and to known local influentials and knowledgeable persons requesting information on such organizations in their areas.

[33] The simple correlation of Negro registration with per cent of population urban is +.07; the correlation with per cent of population Negro is −.46.

Table 6

SIMPLE CORRELATIONS BETWEEN COUNTY POLITICAL VARIABLES
AND STATUS OF SCHOOL DESEGREGATION IN 11 SOUTHERN STATES

Rank	Variable	r
1	Per cent States' Rights, presidential vote in 1948	−.24
2	Per cent Republican, presidential vote in 1928	+.20
3	Per cent Republican, presidential vote in 1956	+.18
4	Highest per cent Republican in race for statewide office, 1950–59	+.16
5	Per cent Republican, presidential vote in 1948	+.16
6	Presence/absence of Negro race organization	+.10
7	Presence/absence of white race organization	−.04
8	Per cent of voting age Negroes registered to vote	+.03

Sources: Same as for Table 5.

gation but these simple correlations cannot demonstrate, by themselves, that political factors have an *independent* influence. In other words, the strong relationship between States' Rights voting and resistance to school desegregation may exist simply because States' Rights voting is influenced by the same demographic factors that influence school desegregation. Do the political factors have an independent influence or are they related to school desegregation merely as intervening variables?

We can answer this question by determining the combined impact of all of the variables introduced to this point, demographic and political. This will demonstrate the extent to which our political variables add to the explanatory power already discovered—through multiple regression analysis—for the complete array of demographic variables. Taken together, the demographic variables yielded a multiple correlation of .50, which indicates that they account for about 25 per cent of the variation in school desegregation. A multiple correlation of the same 21 demographic variables *plus* the 10 political variables yields an R of .55, which explains slightly more than 30 per cent (R^2) of the variation in school desegregation.[34] Contrary to our hypothesis, demographic factors are of far greater importance than political factors in accounting for variations in southern responses to *Brown* v. *Board of Education*. While the addition of 10 political variables adds less than anticipated to the explanation of the pattern of school desegregation in the South, it does increase the explanatory power of the demographic variables by about one-fifth.

[34] It should be noted that, in this multiple regression analysis, we are able to include the qualitative variables omitted in the discussion of simple correlations. See notes 20 and 31.

SUMMARY AND CONCLUSIONS

In this essay we have attempted to account for some of the critical factors in southern responses to the Supreme Court's ruling that state-enforced segregation in public schools is unconstitutional. By examining the influence of demographic and political variables, we hoped to throw some light on the old problem of stateways versus folkways as influences on public behavior.

First we found that, in contrast to the large-scale desegregation of Border States, the South as a whole has been characterized by only token desegregation. The proportion of Negro children attending schools with whites in 1961 ranged from 26 per cent (Oklahoma) to 62 per cent (West Virginia) in the Border States. In the South, the range was from zero per cent in Mississippi, Alabama, and South Carolina to 1.4 per cent in Texas. While the number of children attending integrated schools in the South is very small, it is not so small as to preclude analysis. Looking at the school districts with some desegregation, we find that desegregation is distributed most unevenly within and among southern states. The proportion of biracial school districts with some desegregation varies from zero in Mississippi, Alabama, and South Carolina to 14.7 per cent in Virginia, and on up to 23.0 per cent in Texas.

Demographic factors—especially urbanism, Negro and white income, and Negro education—help account for a great deal of the variation in school desegregation in the South. The multiple R obtained from correlating 21 social and economic factors with school desegregation was .50, which means that this combination of factors accounts for about 25 per cent of the county-by-county variation. When political variables were brought into the analysis, we found that a "Dixiecratic" political climate decreases the chances of obtaining desegregation and that Republicanism increases the probability of desegregation. Negro voter registration, on the other hand, had a surprisingly low relationship to desegregation. When all 10 political factors were added to the multiple regression equation, the multiple R rose to .55, which means that demographic and political variables together account for about 30 per cent of the variation in desegregation. While political factors have an effect, then, they raise the explanatory power of demographic variables by only one-fifth.

At the most general level, these findings indicate that Supreme Court decisions do not have a uniform effect. In reference to state-enforced segregation in public schools, the Constitution is generally what the Supreme Court says it is in the Border States but not in the South. A second general conclusion is that neither demographic nor political factors alone can account for public responses to official government acts; at least as regards reactions to the desegregation decision, both have an impact. Third, demographic factors heavily outweigh political factors in explaining different rates of desegregation within the South. Does this mean that William Graham Sumner was correct in the assertion that folkways must always outweigh stateways? Before accepting such a broad conclusion, we need to look closely at the scope and the special characteristics of the data employed in this study.

Although the detailed analysis was confined to the South (the eleven former Confederate states), state-wide data on the six Border States with officially enforced segregation before *Brown* v. *Board of Education* are highly suggestive. In these states, desegregation has been substantially achieved; in the southern states, segregation has been substantially maintained. The demographic differences between these states—*e.g.*, Oklahoma and Texas, Missouri and Arkansas, Kentucky and Tennessee, West Virginia and Virginia—are hardly great enough to account for such extreme contrasts in responses to the desegregation decision. We think it safe to assume that political factors would have appeared as major variables had the detailed analysis been between the South and the Border States.

The scope of our detailed analysis was limited, however, to variations in school desegregation *within* the South. This had the effect of stacking the cards against the significance of political variables. Although the South is not truly "solid," the superordinate (white) elements do approach solidarity on sensitive racial issues like school segregation—as the official efforts of every southern state to forestall integration have so loudly attested. In view of the unanimous opposition of southern states to school desegregation, perhaps our surprise should have been that the political variables had *any* effect on school desegregation rather than that they were less powerful than demographic factors.

To conclude that southern school desegregation in 1960 was more responsive to demographic than to political forces is not to say that the former always outweigh the latter. We have carried out a similar demographic and political analysis of Negro voter registration in the South that permits us to put our findings on school desegregation in better perspective.[35] When correlated with Negro registration, the same 21 demographic variables we considered in this essay yielded a multiple correlation of .53, almost identical to their correlation with county school desegregation. In the case of Negro voter registration, however, the addition of political variables to the analysis raised the multiple correlation to .70, a

---

[35] See "Social and Economic Factors and Negro Voter Registration in the South," and "Political Factors and Negro Voter Registration in the South," 57 *American Political Science Review* 24, 355 (1963); also see "Negro Voter Registration in the South," in Allan P. Sindler, ed., *Change in the Contemporary South* (1963), pp. 119–149.

tremendous increase which means that political variables doubled the explanatory power afforded by demographic variables alone.[36]

Why do we find such a sharp decrease in the impact of political variables when we shift our focus from Negro voter registration to school desegregation? And what does the difference imply for political science and for the American constitutional system? The answer to the first question appears to be that there *is* less variation in the political systems of the southern states so far as policy on school desegregation is concerned. Negro voting is an integral part of the political system in almost all southern states, but it is strongly discouraged in a few and it varies widely within all states.[37] School desegregation is a much more sensitive issue, so strongly opposed throughout the South that demographic forces operate with only modest influences by the varying political characteristics that so strongly affect Negro voter registration.

For political science (and for other social sciences that have neglected the autonomous influence of political systems), our findings suggest that the old problem of stateways versus folkways is too general to receive any meaningful answer. *The relative importance of demographic and political factors varies from one issue to another;* neither set of forces can be neglected if we are to comprehend a wide range of political phenomena. Rather than a simple answer that one or another is more powerful, we face the more complicated task of determining the varying impact of each as we move from one policy area to another.

Once we recognize that the roles of demography and politics vary from issue to issue, we are led to ask whether they may not also vary from one time to another. The picture we have presented here is static. On the basis of 1960 data, we found political variables to be of great importance in accounting for variations in Negro voter registration but not in accounting for variations in school desegregation. But what would a similar analysis have demonstrated twenty years ago? The political systems of southern states differed then as they do today, but not substantially as regards Negro voting—all southern states had "white primary" laws and other devices to discourage Negro voting. We surmise that the low level of Negro registration varied then according to demographic but not political factors. By the same token, we may infer that the modest effect of political variables on school desegregation in 1960 may appear as a major effect twenty years from now.

As school desegregation passes the threshold of legitimacy in the South, it will become more and more responsive to political manipulation. In-

---

[36] A multiple R of .70 accounts for 49 per cent of the variance (R^2) in the variable under consideration; a multiple R of .53 accounts for 27 per cent of the variance.

[37] In addition to the items cited in note 35, see U.S. Commission on Civil Rights, *1961 Report*, Vol. I, "Voting."

deed, while we would argue that the question of stateways versus folk-ways cannot be answered except in reference to specific issues, we suggest that the proportion of issues in a society in which stateways outweigh folkways is one indication of the degree to which it has attained democracy. As more issues are subject to solution through the political process, rather than being bound by folkways, we may say that the Constitution is—if not exactly what the Supreme Court says it is—at least what the Supreme Court and other political leaders say it is.

IV

Foreign Policy

9

Constitutional Limitation

and American Foreign Policy

Woodford Howard

Few constitutional problems
have produced more discourse, with less result, than the scope of constitutional limitation on foreign policy-making. While challenges to the
constitutional capacity of the government have flourished throughout
American diplomatic history, we have relied more on Holmes' chief guide,
experience, than on the native talent at converting policy distastes into
constitutional dogmas. The fact is that the nation's rise to giant power
status has been accompanied by ever-increasing discretion on the part of
its authorities and only passing regard to self-limitation. Constitutional
theorizing, in the main, has been fruitless in the face of necessity.

Yet tenaciously we cling to a philosophy of limitation, some mechanical
means of control beyond the ballot box. A sadder, but wiser John Foster
Dulles recognized this trait a decade ago when he retracted his statement
that treaties could "override the Constitution." [1] So did a closeted Princeton seminar when Alpheus T. Mason shook it with a typical query: "What
is the future of our subject, constitutionalism, in an age of prolonged
Cold War?" Certainly no student dared take up the whole challenge, nor
do I. But in belated and partial response to one of those lingering questions which mark the gifted teacher, this essay attempts a general critique
of constitutional limitation affecting American foreign policy, with special
reference to the role of the judiciary.

[1] U.S. Senate, Committee on the Judiciary, Hearing on S. J. Res. 1 & 43, "Treaties
and Executive Agreements," 83rd Congress, 1st Session, pp. 862, 866–870 (1953).

At the outset, the main argument should be stated. First—and a truism today—it is illusory to expect judges to control foreign policy-makers in any but circumspect ways. Reliance against abuse must be placed largely on political and institutional restraints. Second—and not a truism—even these checks provide no greater assurance of responsible control than do parliamentary governments, and probably less. In an era in which inefficiency itself is unsafe, it is a fair question whether constitutional restrictions have backfired.

Has limitation achieved its major purpose of restraining government without enfeebling it? Before answering, it is necessary to reach some understanding of the disputed restraints involved.

THE CONSTITUTIONAL SYSTEM

What controls did the Constitution actually impose over the conduct of foreign policy? Political life in this country would be simpler were the answer clear; but the range of intended controls, even if now relevant, is not easily discovered under the gloss of interpretation made by successive generations (and the Framers themselves) when facing different problems.[2] Do executive overseas commitments bind the nation? May Congress "direct" the executive to spend appropriated funds against his military judgment as commander-in-chief? Do individual rights limit national authority or vice versa? Are foreign policy powers delegated, resultant, or inherent? One can scan the original handwork *ad infinitum* and find little light on such unforeseen questions. Indeed, one can find little conclusive evidence that the Framers even had an explicit theory of foreign policy-making, much less the inherent power and executive primacy principles now favored by the Supreme Court. The delegates at Philadelphia no doubt understood the sovereignty theory which rationalized the nation-state system. Many probably knew that Locke, Montesquieu, and Blackstone had treated foreign policy as a special function partaking of sovereign prerogative.[3] The critical problem of fashioning a government that would be internationally adequate yet internally free loomed larger, and received a greater consensus, in 1789 than historians concerned with domestic economic battles are inclined to stress. Nonetheless, too many wayward facts warn against imputing broad theoretical significance to consti-

---

[2] Throwing the Constitution at a partisan problem is an old tradition. Compare, for example, the shifting views of Hamilton and Madison regarding executive power. Hamilton, *The Federalist*, Nos. 69 and 75 (Modern Library ed.); "Pacificus" debate, *Works* (Lodge ed., 1904), IV, 432; Madison, *Elliot's Debates on the Federal Constitution* (2nd rev. ed., 1941), III, 514–516; "Helvidius," *Writings* (Hunt ed., 1906), VI, 138.

[3] Quincy Wright, *The Control of American Foreign Relations* (1922), pp. 141–147, 363.

tutional provisions that rested on eighteenth century conditions and compromises. Interpretation is difficult enough without the spirit of an *ex post facto* Clio.

That warning applies particularly to the inherent power principles which Mr. Justice Sutherland installed into Supreme Court Reports.[4] Despite the nationalistic ring of an organic Union under executive leadership, these ideas are organic themselves and are troublesome, factually and conceptually. When asserting that authority over foreign relations was inherent rather than enumerated, Justice Sutherland argued that *external* sovereignty flowed directly from Great Britain to the Union, whereas *internal* powers lodged in the thirteen states. In fact, the *ad hoc* Continental Congress did not conceive of itself as having received sovereign international capacity from Britain, yet the state governments did. In theory, the division of sovereignty into external and internal compartments conflicts with the basic constitutional postulate that *all* governmental power derived from the "sovereign people" and was subject to the limits imposed by them. The broad phrases of Article VI, distinguishing treaties made "under the authority of the United States" from laws made "in pursuance" of the Constitution, do not support a contrary inference. Quite clearly, that linguistic device aimed at covering existing agreements under the supremacy clause and not at freeing treaties from the principle that power must be deduced from a written instrument, be it express, implied or, in a pinch, "resultant." While treaty power was considered plenary and intentionally left undefined in scope, no one suggested that it was exempt from constitutional control, even if the enforcement mechanism was far from clear.[5] How foreign policy power thus could be "independent" of the Constitution and yet subject to its prohibitions, Justice Sutherland never explained. The essential difficulty is that governments are considered to be empowered differently in international law and American constitutional thought. Justice Sutherland's undifferentiated conception mixed the two with a contradictory dash of dual sovereignty theory as well. For all its organic realism, his version of inherent power rests on shaky foundations.

[4] See, *United States* v. *Curtiss-Wright Export Corp.*, 299 U.S. 304, 315–320 (1936), which embraced Sutherland's view as a Senator that to match national power with international responsibility, it would be necessary "to *find*—though not to *make*—new meanings . . . in light of what the Constitution permits from failure to deny." David M. Levitan, "The Foreign Relations Power: An Analysis of Mr. Justice Sutherland's Theory," 55 *Yale Law Journal* 476 (1946). For support of inherent power theory, see McDougal and Lans, "Treaties and Congressional-Executive or Presidential Agreements: Interchangeable Instruments of National Policy," 54 *Yale Law Journal* 255–261 (1945), and sources there cited.

[5] Levitan, *op. cit.*, pp. 478–490; Max Farrand, *The Records of the Federal Convention* (1911), I, 54, 61; II, 417. Cf. *Missouri* v. *Holland*, 252 U.S. 416, 433–434 (1922) and *Curtiss-Wright* case, 299 U.S. 304, 318. Edward S. Corwin, *National Supremacy: Treaty Power vs. State Power* (1913), pp. 64–74.

Similar hazards face popular myths that the Framers inspired perpetual warfare for congressional-executive relations in foreign affairs. Too much has been read into pragmatic bargains that were not founded in principle at all. Senate participation in treaty-making, for instance, though popularly viewed as part of a grand design to balance authority, resulted only after great flux, if not weariness, in the Convention and was sought to protect sectional commercial interests plainly as much as to guard against Presidents.[6] Modern interpretation may be sound, as a general proposition, that separation of powers was intended to supply an in-built inefficiency for sake of safety against arbitrary government; but in foreign policy, safety against whom?[7] The Framers faced a situation in which foreign relations had been conducted in theory by Congress in the name of the thirteen states, in fact by a cumbersome legislative committee, and occasionally by states themselves. And in 1787, there the primary focus remained—on the relationship between Congress and runaway state governments, not the potential erosion of power to the Presidency. Even Hamilton, arch proponent of executive authority, dismissed the power to command the armed services as purely military and to receive foreign emissaries as *pro forma*. It took two post-constitutional generations to affirm that the executive was the sole official spokesman of the United States internationally and four to accept the nonmilitary aspects of his power as commander-in-chief. While executive leadership is easily inferred from the Constitution, the notion that checks and balances were designed primarily for legislative protection is a distinctly modern concept. What learning there is suggests that the controls imposed were designed to work at least equally the other way around. Foreign affairs, in fact, may well have been thought of as exempt altogether from the countervailing power principle. Judging by Washington's disappointment over the failure of Senate "advice," the Framers appear to have assumed that cooperation, not conflict, would govern.[8] It scarcely exaggerates truth to say that between 1789 and the present, our frame of reference has totally changed.

Thus, in searching for constitutional meaning, we would do well to avoid projecting contemporary assumptions backwards and to heed, in-

---

[6] Farrand, *op. cit.*, II, 143, 169, 183, 392–394; *Elliot's Debates*, III, 499–501; Charles Warren, "The Mississippi River and the Treaty Clause of the Constitution," 2 *George Washington Law Review* 271 (1934); McDougal and Lans, *op. cit.*, pp. 541–544.

[7] Mr. Justice Brandeis gave the theory classic statement in *Myers* v. *United States*, 272 U.S. 52, 293–295 (1926).

[8] Wright, *op. cit.*, pp. 21–35, 250, 360–361; Edward S. Corwin, *The President: Office and Powers* (4th rev. ed., 1957), pp. 228–233; *The Federalist*, No. 69. Also, Charles Warren, *The Making of the Constitution* (1928), pp. 651–658, 657; and Wilfred E. Binkley, *President and Congress* (3rd rev. ed., 1962), p. 28.

stead, Madison's advice: "The best keys to the true objects of all laws and constitutions are furnished by the evils which were to be cured or the benefits to be obtained." [9] To the extent that the Constitution rested on conscious theory of international politics, the only safe conclusion is that foreign policy power, like all power, was granted by a sovereign people to eliminate clear-cut evils—Congress' dependency on the states for enforcement of international engagements and the disadvantages of legislative administration of foreign relations. For sake of a single national voice in the international arena, the Constitution monopolized foreign affairs power in a national government operating on individuals; created federal courts to enforce the supremacy of national acts and international law over the states; and then distributed centralized national authority among the political branches for administrative convenience as well as control. It was generally assumed: (1) that the powers conferred were necessarily exclusive, plenary, and flexible, but not beyond constitutional regulation; (2) that clear distinctions existed between war and peace, internal and external affairs, and civil and military authority, which would serve to delimit the legitimacy of necessarily elastic powers; (3) that foreign policy-making would be a collaborative effort of the executive and a genuinely "advising" Senate, both of which would function as a council of wise men without reference to party, organized pressure groups, or spoils; (4) that ordinary legislative powers were sufficient to keep ambitious executives in rein, though the reverse might not be true; (5) that the fledgling nation should, and would, exercise its treaty power sparingly; and (6) that, in any case, the political process rather than litigation was the primary mechanism of restraint.[10]

In assessing constitutional limitations, therefore, we assume that the Constitution's goal was a national government adequate to international exigencies, but itself internally controlled. The primary restraints were thought to be patriotism and representative government by a pluralistic people, but "auxillary precautions," as Madison called them, also were provided in the form of institutional divisions of authority—federalism, separation of powers, and guaranteed individual rights.[11] Each method depends on both judicial and political processes for enforcement. Since practice rather than theory has determined their force, the real question is: how effective are these controls at a time when many assumptions on which they were based have collapsed?

[9] Corwin, *National Supremacy*, p. 21.
[10] Willoughby, *The Constitutional Law of the United States* (2nd ed., 1929), I, 91–93; *Elliot's Debates*, III, 499–516; Hamilton *Works*, V, 158–159; *The Federalist*, Nos. 69 and 75; Farrand, *op. cit.*, II, 52–55; *The Federalist*, No. 48, p. 322; No. 49, p. 330; No. 51, p. 338. Wright, *op. cit.*, p. 246.
[11] *The Federalist*, No. 51, p. 337.

JUDICIAL RESTRAINTS

Federalism

No one familiar with the New Orleans Mafia riots, the troubles of foreign corporations seeking state licenses, or more recently, Birmingham and segregation on Route 40, can doubt the impact of state conduct on American foreign relations. But it is ironic that, as a constitutional restriction, the one safeguard which the Framers excluded from foreign policy has given rise to the greatest dispute. From the time of the ratifying conventions to the recent rumblings of the American Bar, the familiar argument has run that state reserved powers limit national treaty-making authority. Otherwise, it is said, treaty power plus implied power plus federal supremacy could wither away state authority and leave the people, in Jefferson's words, with "no Constitution." [12]

Whatever havoc the exclusive state power doctrine has played with domestic social legislation, in foreign affairs the short answer is Mr. Justice Gray's: "The Constitution of the United States speaks with no uncertain sound upon this subject." [13] Nearly every conceivable power necessary for international politics was conferred on the national government; the same powers were expressly withheld from the states. Since any sovereignty states once possessed was surrendered in full, by its own terms the Tenth Amendment does not apply.

These principles did not creep into the Constitution by stealth. The very purpose of federal union, as Jefferson declared after the British peace-treaty fiasco, was to make the states "one as to all foreign, and several as to all domestic matters." [14] However treacherous the line between these two domains, federal supremacy was plainly necessary to prevent the nation from being subject to embarrassment or retaliation by its inability to enforce obligations incurred for sake of reciprocal advantages abroad. Logically, supreme treaty power might imply national capacity to pre-empt states out of existence; but that horrendum was conceivable for all authority conferred, and the Federalists met it with a lasting reply—in practice there was no cause for alarm. The political representation of states in Congress afforded ample protection of their interests.

Apart from a few dicta in the Taney era, the courts have consistently hewed the Federalist party line. Repeatedly, they have upheld treaties regulating subjects, *e.g.*, inheritance rights, treatment of aliens, extradition,

---

[12] Quoted in George A. Finch, "The Need to Restrain the Treaty-Making Power of the United States within Constitutional Limits," 48 *Am. J. Int'l. Law* 69 (1954).

[13] *Fong Yue Ting* v. *United States*, 149 U.S. 698, 711 (1893).

[14] Quoted in Warren, *The Making of the Constitution*, p. 451; Farrand, *op. cit.*, I, 164, 316; III, 113, 342.

and wildlife, over which Congress was delegated no independent power.[15] If recently the Supreme Court has been more lenient toward state taxation of foreign commerce than formerly, it has been less so in fields thought to lie within Congress' dominant interest in national security affairs.[16] Whether rationalized by resultant or inherent power theory, the Justices have not flinched from the implications of national supremacy, which received classic expression in the first Chinese Exclusion case:

> The United States, in their relation to foreign countries and their subjects or citizens are one nation, invested with powers which belong to independent nations. . . . For local interests the several States of the Union exist, but for national purposes, embracing our relations with foreign nations, we are but one people, one nation, one power.

Significantly, none has been more vocal in sustaining that principle than the very Justices most eager to restrict it internally. "In respect of all international negotiations and compacts, and in respect of our foreign relations generally," Justice Sutherland declared, "state lines disappear. As to such purposes the State of New York does not exist." [17]

Are the states then at the mercy of boundless discretion and indefinite federal power? The Court's vigorous rhetoric has fanned this fear, but the logic of supremacy has always been qualified in theory and in practice. Commentators and court dicta traditionally have assumed that two sets of legal principles limit the treaty power: (1) specific prohibitions of the Constitution, and (2) restrictions implied by the general purpose of the treaty power grant. In other words, treaties cannot do what the Constitution expressly forbids; and since treaty power was conferred only for "proper subjects of negotiation," it cannot be used to alter the structure of government, to alienate state territory without consent, or to regulate domestic matters of no *bona fide* international interest.[18]

Though rarely present in litigation, these implied restrictions have been the subject of occasional controversy. Prior to World War I, some Sena-

---

[15] For dicta, see *Prevost* v. *Greneaux*, 60 U.S. (19 How.) 1 (1856); *License cases,* 46 U.S. (5 How.) 504 (1847); *The Passenger* cases, 48 U.S. (7 How.) 283 (1849). Cf. *Ware* v. *Hylton*, 3 U.S. (3 Dall.) 199 (1796); *Fairfax's Devisee* v. *Hunter's Lessee,* 11 U.S. (7 Cranch) 603 (1813); *Chirac* v. *Chirac*, 15 U.S. (2 Wheat.) 259 (1817); *Hauenstein* v. *Lynham*, 100 U.S. 483 (1880); *Missouri* v. *Holland*, 252 U.S. 416 (1920). For a "representative list" of these treaties, see "Treaties and Executive Agreements," (note 1), pp. 843–847.

[16] *Youngstown Sheet and Tube Co.* v. *Bowers*, 358 U.S. 534 (1959); *Hines* v. *Davidowitz*, 312 U.S. 52 (1941); *Pennsylvania* v. *Nelson*, 350 U.S. 497 (1956).

[17] *Chae Chan Ping* v. *United States*, 130 U.S. 581, 604, 606 (1889); *United States* v. *Belmont*, 301 U.S. 324, 331 (1937).

[18] See, *e.g.*, *Holden* v. *Joy*, 84 U.S. (17 Wall.) 211, 243 (1872); *DeGeofroy* v. *Riggs*, 133 U.S. 258, 266 (1890); Hamilton *Works*, IV, 158; *Elliot's Debates*, III, 514; Charles Evans Hughes, 23 *Proc. Am. Soc. Int'l. Law* 196 (1929); and cases cited in Note, "Matters of Domestic Concern: A Potential Judicial Limitation on the Treaty-Making Power?" 34 *Indiana Law Journal* 66, note 45 (1958).

tors objected to United States participation in arbitration agreements on the ground that they constituted unconstitutional delegations of judicial power.[19] Consent by Maine (for a price) to the cession of territory in the Canadian boundary settlement of 1842 forestalled the only test of the alienation question.[20] And in 1957, Judge Bazelon intimated that a Senate reservation to a treaty concerning Niagara River development, if part of the treaty, would be invalid because it touched matters of purely domestic concern.[21]

Presumably, the judiciary could void a colorable exercise of treaty power. Yet it is important to recognize that no treaty has ever been invalidated by the Supreme Court.[22] Nor in face of political safeguards in Congress is a judicial veto likely. While state lines may be said to disappear in logic, they have rarely done so in anyone's mind. Federal courts frequently have avoided conflict by state power-saving construction of treaties. The Senate has protected state interests so vigorously as to make most legal issues academic.[23] And if worse came to worst, Congress has undoubted power to repeal the domestic effect of treaties affecting matters within its large area of competence.[24] For all these reasons, the case against the treaty power is still, practically speaking, a phantom.

A subtler issue is presented by agreements which require no advance Senate approval. Controversial secret agreements during World War II, current status of forces agreements with allies abroad, and sweeping judicial language equating executive agreements with supreme law have aggravated fears that Presidents may mount a new Trojan Horse to subvert state powers and individual rights. Even if it is assumed that Presidents are less sensitive to civil liberty than state officials, few issues afford better illustration of the futility of indulging constitutional possibilities without regard to political reality. The great proportion of executive agreements are made pursuant to congressional authorization or to treaties already approved. The utility of the device in modern international practice is so apparent that even the Bricker Amendment advocates conceded the impossibility of distinguishing proper from improper occasions for its

---

[19] Wright, *op. cit.*, pp. 103–118.

[20] Corwin, *National Supremacy*, pp. 129–133. Corwin argues cogently that the assumed restriction against alienation of state territory without its consent is unsupportable dictum. Also, see Warren, *The Making of the Constitution*, p. 656.

[21] *Power Authority of New York* v. *Federal Power Commission*, 247 F. 2d 538 (D. C. Cir. 1957), *vacated as moot*, 355 U.S. 64 (1957).

[22] John B. Whitton and J. Edward Fowler, "Bricker Amendment—Fallacies and Dangers," 48 *Am. J. Int'l. Law* 52 (1954).

[23] Wright, *op. cit.*, p. 75; note, "Matters of Domestic Concern," (note 18), p. 60.

[24] See, *The Cherokee Tobacco* case, 78 U.S. (11 Wall.) 616 (1871); *Edye* v. *Robertson*, 112 U.S. 580 (1884); *Whitney* v. *Robertson*, 124 U.S. 190 (1888); *Chae Chan Ping* v. *United States*, 130 U.S. 581 (1889); *Fong Yue Ting* v. *United States*, 149 U.S. 698 (1893); *Moser* v. *United States*, 341 U.S. 41, 45 (1951).

use. It is hard to imagine Presidents courting political disaster by a rampage of unpopular agreements, but if they did, Congress has formidable means of obstruction and correction.[25]

Judicial review of executive agreements, for that matter, is available. The equation of agreements with treaties as supreme law settled only their supremacy over the states, not over Congress or individual rights. It is by no means certain that even self-executing treaties may override traditional limitations or acts of Congress, not to speak of executive agreements.[26] All that the celebrated Litvinov Assignment cases decided was that state interests must bow to national policy as determined by those on whom the Constitution entrusted responsibility for the centralized direction of foreign affairs.[27] The question whether other constitutional interests may defeat those policies illustrates an important characteristic of the American constitutional system, the fact that major questions are often left unsettled.

Subordination of state to national policy, however, is as clear as constitutional interpretation can make it. In theory, federalism was never meant to bar national authority in international politics, and for their part courts have not permitted it to in practice. From the start, the chief role of the judiciary has been to fulfill the purpose of its creation, namely, defending national supremacy. Rather than state power limiting national power, the reverse is therefore true. As Marshall once remarked, the Constitution created a nation "susceptible of no limitation not imposed by itself"; for protection against abuse, the people and the courts must look to the controls it actually provided—separation of powers, guaranteed private rights, and ballots.[28]

Separation of powers

The complex system of power distribution within the national government was assumed to be the major institutional control over foreign policy-making. Although the assumption of easy interbranch collaboration collapsed at its first trial, the crucial nexus has always been the political relations among the Presidency and houses of Congress, and not the courts. The few *causes célèbres* in which the Justices asserted their ad-

[25] McDougal and Lans, *op. cit., passim;* Arthur E. Sutherland, Jr., "Restricting The Treaty Power," 65 *Harvard Law Review* 1324 (1952).

[26] See, *United States* v. *Guy W. Capps, Inc.,* 204 F. 2d 655 (4th Cir. 1953); 348 U.S. 296 (1955); *Power Authority of New York* v. *F. P. C.,* 247 F. 2d 538 (D. C. Cir. 1957); 355 U.S. 64 (1957). Doubt exists whether even treaties may supersede an act of Congress. See Willoughby, *op. cit.,* I, 548–560; Corwin, *Total War and the Constitution* (1947), p. 153. Cf. *Cook* v. *United States,* 288 U.S. 102 (1933); and *Clark* v. *Allen,* 331 U.S. 503 (1947).

[27] *United States* v. *Belmont,* 301 U.S. 324 (1937); *United States* v. *Pink,* 315 U.S. 203 (1942).

[28] *The Schooner Exchange* v. *McFaddon,* 11 U.S. (7 Cranch) 116, 136 (1812).

mitted supervisory function over separation of powers have obscured the small part they have actually played in shaping those relations respecting foreign policy. To be sure, resolution of what was once a great issue—whether the House was legally bound to execute treaties made by President and Senate—was aided by the judicial distinction between self-executing and non–self-executing treaties and by the principle of equality between treaties and statutes, which makes the later in time govern. Both principles enhance the political check by affirming the power of Congress to refuse treaty execution or to repeal the domestic effect of treaties already in force. The result is that international commitments "in no wise diminish Congress' constitutional powers," however infrequently Congress has chosen to use them.[29]

Beyond its impact as an ultimate threat, nonetheless, judicial review has had little to do with the evolution of American foreign policy or the machinery of making it. In no area of public law has judicial self-restraint been more marked. As a matter of history, courts have interpreted treaties in a manner avoiding constitutional conflict; they have refused to subject Congress' "plenary" power over aliens, immigration, and acquisition of territory to more than the barest procedural requirements; they have graced the fusion of Presidential powers with approving references to executive prerogative; and they have explicitly held that the restraints of separation of powers have less force in foreign as distinct from domestic affairs. By recognizing "the very delicate, plenary and exclusive power of the President as the sole organ of the federal government in the field of international relations," the Justices have converted a fact of life into constitutional principle.[30]

Perhaps the clearest manifestation of judicial withdrawal is the broad application of the "political question" doctrine to foreign policy issues. No one knows exactly what a political question is or when it will apply. But the Court recently indicated that it is "primarily a function of the separation of powers." Numerous cases have been dismissed as "nonjusticiable" when the following elements appeared—the Constitution conferred exclusive discretion on political branches, the issues turned on "standards that defy judicial application," or the situation demanded a "single-voiced statement" and finality of the government's position.[31] Whether or not the doctrine itself is a constitutional command, its fullest coverage has been in foreign affairs. Recognition and nonrecognition of states and governments, diplomatic immunities, abrogation of treaties,

---

[29] See *supra* Notes 24 and 26. Corwin, *The Constitution of the United States, annotated* (1953), p. 420.

[30] For example, *Harisiades v. Shaughnessy*, 342 U.S. 580 (1952). Clinton Rossiter, *The Supreme Court and the Commander in Chief* (1951), pp. 122–123. *United States v. Curtiss-Wright Export Corp.*, 299 U.S. 304, 320 (1936).

[31] *Baker v. Carr*, 369 U.S. 186, 210–214 (1962).

duration of war, reprisals, the conduct of military government, and the like, all are matters thought to lie within the exclusive domain of the political branches, whose decisions are considered binding on courts.[32] The list doubtless would be longer but for the reinforcing lack of standing of parties to challenge broad classes of executive discretion. Political scientists may quarrel that the legal distinction between discretionary and ministerial duties is unreal, but it, too, has been a useful judicial tool to avoid involvement in delicate matters of statecraft.[33]

These devices of judicial avoidance are not simply a matter of courts, being "powerless in fact," declaring themselves to be "powerless in law." [34] They rest on recognition of the inherent limitations of adjudication in the governing process as well as the necessity of concerted—and often unprincipled—policy *vis à vis* nations abroad. When judges have followed, and occasionally compelled, State Department determination of the jural status of foreign parties even in private suits, they have merely applied the same considerations foreclosing state participation in international politics to themselves.[35] Of all public agencies, none has been quicker than the judiciary to perceive that foreign policy requires centralized direction by agencies capable of speed, secrecy, and ample authority. As the Justices declared in *MacKenzie* v. *Hare*, "We should hesitate long before limiting or embarrassing such powers." [36] The upshot is that, as a legally enforceable restriction, separation of powers has functioned most to remove the judiciary from the foreign policy realm.

Doctrines of deference, of course, have not always been applied consistently nor without judicial discomfort. Supreme Court Justices have not scrapped constitutional distinctions between war and peace, or between military and civil authority, as easily as have other sectors of the government. Obviously, they have been troubled by the legal implications of the nation's far-flung foreign policy activities, especially those which call into question individual liberty or structural distribution of power. Is it still true, as men thought fifty years ago, that all agreements must rest on consent of Congress, express or implied? Is there no specific time limit to

---

[32] *Oetjen* v. *Central Leather Co.*, 246 U.S. 297 (1918); *United States* v. *Pink*, 315 U.S. 203 (1942); *Kennett* v. *Chambers*, 55 U.S. (14 How.) 38 (1852); *Martin* v. *Mott*, 25 U.S. (12 Wheat.) 19 (1827); *Doe* v. *Braden*, 57 U.S. (16 How.) 635 (1854); *Clark* v. *Allen*, 331 U.S. 503 (1947); *Commercial Trust* v. *Miller*, 262 U.S. 51 (1923); *Ludecke* v. *Watkins*, 335 U.S. 160 (1948); *Neely* v. *Henkel*, 180 U.S. 109 (1901). Also, *Chicago & Southern Airlines, Inc.* v. *Waterman S. S. Corp.*, 333 U.S. 103 (1948).

[33] In another connection, see *Mississippi* v. *Johnson*, 71 U.S. (4 Wall.) 475 (1867).

[34] Rossiter, *op. cit.*, p. 17.

[35] *Guaranty Trust Co.* v. *United States*, 304 U.S. 126 (1938); *National City Bank of New York* v. *Republic of China*, 348 U.S. 356 (1955). See, Thomas M. Franck, "The Courts, The State Department and National Policy: A Criterion for Judicial Abdication," 44 *Minnesota Law Review* 1101 (1960).

[36] 239 U.S. 299, 311 (1915).

domestic regulation under color of delegated war power? Short of specific prohibitions, does the executive possess an inherent aggregate of power to handle emergencies without legislative approval or by means otherwise regulated by Congress? [37] Sufficient doubts have been expressed in court to leave these matters open for future judicial intervention. And intervention is amply precedented. With forceful rhetoric in defense of liberty, Supreme Court Justices have proclaimed again and again that even "the war power . . . is subject to applicable constitutional limitations." [38] Yet the fact remains that with rare exceptions the declaration has been followed by exceptions so wide as to admit the opposite. World War II plainly consolidated a pattern of transferring responsibility from Congress to President, and thence to civilian and military bureaucracies, with full judicial approval. In the Japanese Relocation cases, not only were some Justices eager to join the buck-passing which characterized that sad operation, but the Court affirmed both Charles Evans Hughes' dictum that the war power is "the power to wage war successfully" and Chief Justice Stone's significant addition: "it is not for any court to sit in review of the wisdom" of action taken by "those branches of the Government on which the Constitution has placed the responsibility of war-making." [39] Despite the return from relativism toward emergency power after the war, the hard lessons of the OPA and military jurisdiction cases appear the same. Events have vastly increased national authority and the Presidency's share of it. If judicial supervision of separation of powers means the maintenance of a relatively fixed equilibrium of authority, the force of that principle has long been lost.

As a question of constitutional allocation, the drift of power into executive hands must be resisted primarily by Congress itself. For all practical purposes, the judge-made barrier against congressional delegation of power appears to have been shelved in foreign affairs. Judicial supervision of executive removals, at best, amounts to little more than a slight rebuff and a wounded Presidential "image." [40] Notwithstanding their boldness, the Steel Seizure case and the recent denial of military jurisdiction over civilian dependents abroad hardly repudiate Theodore Roosevelt's stewardship

[37] Chandler P. Anderson, "The Extent and Limitations of the Treaty-Making Power under the Constitution," 1 *Am. J. Int'l. L.* 645 (1907). *Woods* v. *Miller Co.,* 333 U.S. 138 (1948); *Youngstown Sheet and Tube Co.* v. *Sawyer,* 343 U.S. 579 (1952).

[38] *Hamilton* v. *Kentucky Distilleries Co.,* 251 U.S. 146, 156 (1919).

[39] *Yakus* v. *United States,* 321 U.S. 414 (1944); *Bowles* v. *Willingham,* 321 U.S. 503 (1944); *Korematsu* v. *United States,* 323 U.S. 214 (1944); *Hirabayashi* v. *United States,* 320 U.S. 81, 93 (1943).

[40] Cf. Chief Justice Taft's legerdemain justifying tariff delegation in *Hampton & Co.* v. *United States,* 276 U.S. 394 (1928) with Justice Sutherland's removal of the restriction in the *Curtiss-Wright* case, 299 U.S. 304, 319–22 (1936). *Wiener* v. *United States,* 357 U.S. 349 (1958).

theory that Presidents may do anything that the Constitution or laws do not forbid.[41] Indeed, the weight of opinion in *Youngstown Sheet and Tube* confirms it. Seven out of nine Justices in that case refused to deny ultimate executive capacity to explore unoccupied frontiers of power and hinged the decision instead on President Truman's refusal to follow procedures prescribed in advance by Congress.

The same infirmity was the basis of Judge Parker's initial invalidation of an executive agreement in the *Capps* case. A parallel infirmity underlay the Warren Court's insistence that the passport and industrial security programs must be based on actual rather than assumed delegations of power.[42] However unsung, these decisions may point to the only tenable strategy for judicial review in a Cold War world. On the one hand, only for the most "essential liberties" will judges deny in advance broad substantive powers on which survival itself may depend. On the other hand, they may routinely insist that claimed authority be founded on the express approval and prescribed procedures of the constitutionally responsible agency. Procedural requirements and administrative standards, in short, may regulate the exercise of admittedly plenary power without seriously diminishing national capacity to deal with international crisis. And a salutary by-product is the enhanced political responsibility which stems from the requirement that decisions be made in places where they belong.[43]

Such a gingerly approach to separation of powers has not been free from logical difficulty in particular cases. Nor will it ever satisfy those who seek constitutional restriction against every conceivable abuse. Though the fate of cases attempting broad constitutional limitation is even less happy, one must express a certain sympathy for the frustrated expectations aroused by the historic weakening of the separation principle. For the primary impact of judicial review has been the "legitimation" rather than the restriction of expanding national and executive authority in foreign and national security affairs. Here, as elsewhere, courts have worked on the unstated principle that Cardozo expressed for commerce—the "power is as broad as the need that evokes it." [44] The result is that *constitutional limitation* is explicitly less stringent in foreign as distinct from domestic

---

[41] 343 U.S. 579 (1952).

[42] 204 F. 2d 655 (4th Cir. 1953); *Kent v. Dulles,* 357 U.S. 116 (1958); *Greene v. McElroy,* 360 U.S. 474 (1959).

[43] For suggestive discussion, see Alexander Bickel, "Forward: The Passive Virtues," 75 *Harvard Law Review* 64–79 (1961); Willard Hurst, "Review and the Distribution of National Powers," in Edmond Cahn, ed., *Supreme Court and Supreme Law* (1954), pp. 146–149; and C. Herman Pritchett, *The Political Offender and the Warren Court* (1958).

[44] *Carter v. Carter Coal Co.,* 298 U.S. 238, 328 (1936).

policy, at the very time when that distinction itself is increasingly unreal. Hence, the effectiveness of separation of powers as a restraining principle is to be found largely in political rather than in judicial sectors. Rather than by constitutional regulation, the courts have contributed to the control of foreign policy-making machinery mainly through the interstitial, undramatic, and often misunderstood modes of procedural and administrative review.[45] Perhaps the realistic Federalists who wrote the Constitution would have expected even less from judges, but when the final cause of limitation is considered in light of modern conditions, that is by no means an inglorious task.

Private rights

Closely associated with the debate over federalism and separation of powers has been the great goal of individual liberty. May foreign policy needs override constitutional rights? Except for occasional aberrations like John Foster Dulles' celebrated Louisville speech, it has been seldom admitted that foreign policy decisions may abridge express constitutional prohibitions; and since Madison's day, a system of expectations has flourished that the defense of liberty is the peculiar province of courts.[46] While few would argue that judges *cannot* review invasions of private guarantees, however, in the twentieth century fears have multiplied that in practice the judiciary *will not* interfere.

Despite the continuing disclaimers from the Supreme Court, these fears are not altogether groundless. On the few past occasions in which the Justices faced the issue squarely, means were usually found to uphold the government. The *Ross* case, though now discarded as a "relic from a different era," found no deprivation when American seamen were tried without jury by our consuls abroad.[47] Dialectical distinctions between types of territory and types of fundamental rights also made it possible for Congress to withhold certain glories of Anglo-American law from colonial dependencies unaccustomed to them.[48] Whether the Constitution "follows the flag" has been a baffling issue for decades. If a general principle can be deduced from the cases, it appears to be that overseas operations must conform to the fundamental decencies of due process, at least where civilians are concerned. Yet, until recently, the test of "fundamental" was

---

[45] Hurst, *op. cit.*, pp. 151–58.

[46] See *supra* Note 1. Alpheus T. Mason, *The Supreme Court from Taft to Warren* (1958), p. 141.

[47] 140 U.S. 453 (1891); *Reid v. Covert*, 354 U.S. 1, 8–12 (1957).

[48] The distinction is that constitutional limitations do not apply *ex propio vigore* until Congress "incorporates" territory, although due process does apply to "unincorporated" territory. *Downes v. Bidwell*, 182 U.S. 244 (1901); *Hawaii v. Mankichi*, 190 U.S. 197 (1903); *Dorr v. United States*, 195 U.S. 138 (1904); *Rassmussen v. United States*, 197 U.S. 516 (1905); *Balzac v. Porto Rico*, 259 U.S. 298 (1922).

below the Bill of Rights.[49] Even when a specific guarantee has been held applicable, the case of Fifth Amendment property rights illustrates how different standards may prevail. Apart from the respect shown to property in treaty-making and interpretation, the relevant portions of the Amendment seldom, if ever, have been successfully invoked. Even Chief Justice Marshall expressed his misgivings about the force of vested rights in collision with the "sovereign's" international acts.[50]

Mr. Justice Holmes, and more recently, Mr. Justice Black, it is true, took pains to assert that the government cannot barter away the Bill of Rights.[51] The paucity of decisions on the subject may indicate that few officials are disposed to. Yet Congress can qualify severely the rights of three million soldiers, especially those overseas. Subject to certain "procedural observances," it has virtually absolute power over aliens. Under the war power, Congress and its agents can make serious inroads on economic liberty as well as access to judical relief. In World War II, the government did jail over 5,000 conscientious objectors and incarcerate 70,000 Nisei citizens under pleas of necessity held to be plausible.[52] Should these cases be dismissed as extremities of total war, the Court recently upheld power to curtail the activities of domestic communists and to strip native-born individuals of citizenship by presuming voluntary expatriation from conduct though embarrassing to foreign policy goals—*e.g.*, voting in foreign countries that permit aliens to do so. Although no such embarrassing connection was found in the companion case of desertion during wartime, and though the Court in 1963 found a new and possibly determinative restriction in the due process clause, the measure of Congress' discretion in these sharply divided decisions seemed the same—some rational nexus between individual behavior and "the successful conduct of international relations. . . ." If that is all the Fourteenth Amendment achieved in defining citizenship, which Chief Justice Warren described as "nothing less than the right to have rights," the comment of one fair-minded critic is

---

[49] *Ibid.* Cf. *Wade* v. *Hunter*, 336 U.S. 684 (1949); *Johnson* v. *Eisentrager*, 339 U.S. 763 (1950). See Arthur E. Sutherland, Jr., "The Flag, the Constitution, and International Agreements," 68 *Harvard Law Review* 1374 (1955); and Robert A. Horn, "The Warren Court and the Discretionary Power of the Executive," 44 *Minnesota Law Review* 669 (1960).

[50] *United States* v. *Pink*, 315 U.S. 203, 228 (1942); Willard B. Cowles, *Treaties and Constitutional Law: Property Interferences and Due Process of Law* (1941); *United States* v. *Caltex, Inc.*, 344 U.S. 149 (1952). *The Schooner Exchange* v. *Mc-Faddon*, 11 U.S. (7 Cranch) 116, 146 (1812).

[51] *Missouri* v. *Holland*, 252 U.S. 416, 433 (1922); *Reid* v. *Covert*, 354 U.S. 1, 17–18 (1957).

[52] See, *ex parte Milligan*, 71 U.S. (4 Wall.) 2, 123, 137–139 (1866); "Criminal Jurisdiction over American Forces Abroad," 70 *Harvard Law Review* 1043 (1957). *Fong Yue Ting* v. *United States*, 149 U.S. 698 (1893); *Carlson* v. *Landon*, 342 U.S. 524 (1952); *Galvan* v. *Press*, 347 U.S. 522 (1954); Robert E. Cushman, *Civil Liberties in the United States* (1956), p. 96; and cases cited in note 39.

well taken: "The philosophy of deference to the legislature as the primary judicial duty . . . has seldom yielded a more pernicious result." [53]

It should be recalled, of course, that the tension between the needs of power and guaranteed rights is embedded in the constitutional system itself. After all, it is the Fifth Amendment that exempts the armed forces from the full range of the Bill of Rights, even if what remains is complex and unsettled.[54] The Constitution also empowers Congress to regulate both appellate judisdiction of federal courts and naturalization, however much some Justices might denounce deportation as "pure, simple, undisguised despotism and tyranny," or concede that immigration policy has been cruel, offensive to American traditions, and at times a threat to the peace.[55] Accustomed to think of the paramount law more as a system of limits rather than as a source of power, later generations chafe more readily than former ones to reminders that the Constitution created vast reservoirs of power to be controlled solely by elections and the processes of representative government. Nonetheless, if *Perez* v. *Brownell* is any guide, judicial abstinence involves more than recognizing power "when it exists." [56] The extreme language of deference to the foreign policy discretion of Congress, coupled with the balancing interest rubric of the communist control cases, clearly indicates a continuing relativism toward individual rights that run afoul of Congress' choice of means in national self-defense. Given the needs of power, the sheer physical limitations of judicial review, and the real possibility of retaliation against the Court, the fears which Justice Black sought to dispel can be erased only by erasing memory itself. The fact is that few agencies have been more solicitous of the power of Congress in this area than the Supreme Court.

At first glance, the Warren Court's expansion of review regarding military jurisdiction over civilians may refute the foregoing. The invalidation of acts assigning to the military criminal jurisdiction over civilian dependents and employees abroad, despite the inconvenience of the alternatives, was surely a reminder that the Justices have not abdicated. At least for certain rights in semi-peace, *Reid* v. *Covert, United States ex rel. Toth* v. *Quarles, Trop* v. *Dulles, Harmon* v. *Brucker,* and their offspring, all form an impressive stance against the erosion of constitutional limits in a cold war environment.[57] Yet, for all their revealed distrust of military justice and

[53] *Scales* v. *United States,* 367 U.S. 203 (1961); *Communist Party* v. *Subversive Activities Control Board,* 367 U.S. 1 (1961). *Perez* v. *Brownell,* 356 U.S. 44, 58–59, 64 (1958); and *Kennedy* v. *Mendoza-Martinez,* 372 U.S. 144 (1963). *Trop* v. *Dulles,* 356 U.S. 86, 105 (1958); Pritchett, *The American Constitution* (1959), p. 640.

[54] See *Wilson* v. *Girard,* 354 U.S. 524 (1957); Horn, *op. cit.,* pp. 661–663.

[55] Justice Field in *Fong Yue Ting* v. *United States,* 149 U.S. 698, 755 (1893); and Justice Frankfurter in *Harisiades* v. *Shaughnessy,* 342 U.S. 580, 597 (1952).

[56] 356 U.S. 44 (1958). Justice Holmes, *Tyson* v. *Banton,* 273 U.S. 418, 445 (1927).

[57] 354 U.S. 1 (1957); 350 U.S. 11 (1955); 356 U.S. 86 (1958); 355 U.S. 579 (1958); and *McElroy* v. *United States ex rel. Guagliardo,* 361 U.S. 281 (1960).

perhaps hindsight regrets about the Court's own past tolerance of it, these cases are confined to drawing the jurisdictional line between civilian and military authority, which is otherwise left untouched. Neither has the Court denied the government's ultimate power to expatriate draft-dodging citizens. In face of the post-1957 retreat across a broad spectrum of civil liberties issues, the cases hardly signal a bold new era of judicial supremacy for sake of individual freedom. The Court is on record that invasions of the Bill of Rights will not be tolerated, and perhaps in flatfooted instances that is the law. To date, however, the contrasts and complexities of the military jurisdiction, expatriation, and communism cases support no more generality than that the extent of judicial protection of individual guarantees is circumstantial and in flux. Not least in explaining that flux are shifting Court personnel and cold war tempos.

All the more important, therefore, is the strategic distinction between constitutional limitation and lesser interference containing threats of sterner stuff. While cautious on constitutional questions, the Warren Court's sensitivity to the civil liberties implications of Cold War measures has carried the techniques of nonconstitutional intervention to a new level of art. Whether craft or merely internal struggle is the cause, no court has given fuller demonstration that protection of liberty need not require the ultimate axe of constitutional adjudication. Softer blows, in a wide variety of cases, have achieved similar results without reaching the grave constitutional issues lurking beneath. By insisting on procedural safeguards of confrontation and notice and by holding governmental agencies to their own announced procedures, the federal judiciary has removed some of the sting from passport regulation, security dismissals, and investigations.[58] By reading a standard of action into the Smith Act and denaturalization statutes, the frightening implications of the *Dennis* doctrine were reduced, and self-incrimination may well do the same for the Subversive Activities Control Act.[59] By requiring express rather than assumed delegation of authority in passport regulation, industrial security programs, and at least once in congressional investigations, the Court not only secured relief for particular individuals, but forced the responsible

[58] For passport regulation: *Service* v. *Dulles*, 354 U.S. 363 (1957); *Kent* v. *Dulles*, 357 U.S. 116 (1958); *Bauer* v. *Acheson*, 106 F. Supp. 445 (1952); *Boudin* v. *Dulles*, 136 F. Supp. 218 (1955); and *The New York Times*, January 12, 1962, p. 1, col. 6. Security dismissals: *Vitarelli* v. *Seaton*, 359 U.S. 535 (1959); *Greene* v. *McElroy*, 360 U.S. 474 (1959); cf. *Cafeteria & Restaurant Workers Union, Local 473* v. *McElroy*, 367 U.S. 886 (1961). Investigations: *Watkins* v. *United States*, 354 U.S. 178 (1957); and *Yellin* v. *United States*, 374 U.S. 109 (1963).

[59] *Yates* v. *United States*, 355 U.S. 66 (1957); cf. *Scales* v. *United States*, 367 U.S. 203 (1961). *Nowak* v. *United States*, 356 U.S. 660 (1958); *Nishikawa* v. *Dulles*, 356 U.S. 129 (1958); and *Communist Party* v. *Subversive Activities Control Board*, 367 U.S. 1 (1961).

agencies to re-examine policies made in their name that bordered closely on constitutional danger zones.[60]

These techniques of circumspect intervention are neither new nor without their costs. In some instances procedural requirements can shackle effective power; in others the search for nonconstitutional grounds has produced some rather grossly distorted statutes. The want of delegated authority in *Kent v. Dulles*, especially, "taxed credulity." More difficult is an intellectually satisfying explanation of the source of reviewing power. No one has yet answered Mr. Justice Reed's complaint that judicial authority to supervise delegation differs between branches and within them.[61] And even if the long-winded explanations of pertinence following the *Watkins* ruling are more than perfunctory rituals in legislative hearings, the Court has been far more successful in regulating conduct in the executive branch than in Congress. When the judicial invitation to closer scrutiny over policy goes unheeded, or when the Court itself applies more lenient standards to the legislature, the tactics of delay invite the very constitutional in-fighting the Justices seek to avoid.

Still, the advantages of "avoidance and admonition" would seem to outweigh the disadvantages.[62] The trouble with constitutional adjudication of ultimates is that the odds usually favor power rather than restriction. Regulation of how admittedly plenary power may be exercised, especially in areas of traditional judicial competence like fair procedure, may be the most that circumstances allow. Futhermore, narrower regulation comports more with the realities of American decision-making than do the dramatics of constitutional conflict. In concrete situations, the effectiveness of the checks and balances system is found less in broad, substantive divisions of authority than in the narrower and more informal administrative and political relationships that surround constitutional structures. By procedural and statutory review, courts not only may enter the field where the decisive activity often lies, but they can soften the impact on individuals of necessarily generous powers without denying political branches the ultimate capacity to govern. Where constitutional issues are proximate, it is not too much to ask, as the Court did in *Rumely*, that judicial judgment be suspended until "Congress has demonstrated its full awareness of what is at stake. . . ."[63] Such manuevers tend to regularize democratic processes

---

[60] See note 58. *United States v. Rumely*, 345 U.S. 41 (1953). Cf. *Wilkinson v. United States*, 365 U.S. 399 (1961); and *Braden v. United States*, 365 U.S. 431 (1961).

[61] *Peters v. Hobby*, 349 U.S. 331, 354 (1955); 357 U.S. 116 (1958). Horn, *op. cit.*, pp. 668–672. Cf. Bickel, *op. cit.*, pp. 64–74.

[62] *Ibid.*, p. 67. For examples of the untoward results reached by precipitate constitutional litigation, see *Adler v. Board of Education*, 342 U.S. 485 (1952); *Dennis v. United States*, 341 U.S. 494 (1951); and *Times Film Corp. v. Chicago*, 365 U.S. 43 (1961).

[63] 345 U.S. 41, 46 **(1953).**

and, incidentally, to curtail the buck-passing that all too frequently has occurred in this field. Finally, as one of the multiple balances in American politics, the judiciary's postponement and preachment may assist the political forces arrayed against a particular encroachment on liberty to the point of policy reversal. Industrial security illustrates neatly how the limited move can checkmate a program until sober second thoughts prevail.

As Alpheus T. Mason has reminded us, little more should reasonably be expected from the judiciary. Even the most "activist" court can do no more than to soften, to suspend, and to teach toward the end that the democratic process will right itself.[64] In the daily life of an increasingly regimented society, that role is not to be minimized. Besides legitimizing authority, the judiciary's greatest impact on foreign affairs may well lie in its contribution to the over-all quality of American democracy as projected to the world at large. The very generosity of power which judges must protect calls for some process of moderating its harsh individual applications, while leaving governmental discretion essentially unimpaired. Where there are alternative paths available, in short, the judiciary may induce other officials to take the less destructive route. But those who yearn for more could profit from the lecture of a Justice who was seldom accused of excessive modesty concerning the power and influence of his calling. Wrote Justice Story:

> . . . if the whole society is not to be revolutionized at every critical period, and remodelled in every generation, there must be left to those, who administer the government, a very large mass of discretionary powers, capable of greater or less actual expansion according to circumstances, and sufficiently flexible not to involve the nation in utter destruction from the rigid limitations imposed upon it by an improvident jealousy. Every power, however limited, as well as broad, is in its own nature susceptible of abuse. No constitution can provide perfect guards against it. Confidence must be reposed somewhere; and in free governments, the ordinary securities against abuse are found in the responsibility of rulers to the people, and in the just exercise of their elective franchise; and ultimately in the sovereign power of change belonging to them, in cases requiring extraordinary remedies.[65]

POLITICAL RESTRAINTS

If it is a cruel delusion to expect the judiciary to serve as the mainspring of foreign policy control, what judges do is not the end of the matter.[66] Both Constitution and practice entrust the safety of the Republic primarily to the wisdom of the people's representatives, as tempered by elections and by institutional distribution of power. Do these politically enforced

[64] Mason, *op. cit.*, pp. 183–187.
[65] *Commentaries on the Constitution* (3rd ed., 1858), pp. 301–302.
[66] Clinton Rossiter, *The American Presidency* (2nd ed., 1960), p. 58.

precautions of the Constitution achieve their larger purpose of controlling, without weakening, government?

There was a time when the mere recital of the numerous checks available, not to speak of elections and rebellion, supplied a ready answer to that imponderable. Today, unfortunately, the stresses felt by every major government have shaken easy confidence in the capacity of institutional controls to restrain abuse. For one thing, safeguards are hardly available for the kind of situation most likely to be feared. Yalta, Suez, and Cuba have taught us what the Framers already knew—that no constitutional system can prevent rash error without imposing fatal impotence. Experience also suggests that, even when safeguards are available, the Constitution's alternative of restraining authority by dispersing it exacts a heavier price than is commonly assumed. Although few modern critics have accepted Walter Lippmann's challenge to the very concept of popular control over foreign policy, the perennial professional criticism of structural checks and balances has begun to win new adherents.[67] The concern is not that these devices fail to restrict authority, which no one denies, nor merely that they obstruct efficient operations, which was the essence of past complaints. Criticism has mounted because of evidence that division of power encumbers both effective policy formation *and* democratic accountability. While reserving our faith in the adaptability of the American scheme, so strong a case can be made that mechanical controls do not achieve their larger purpose that the once fashionable habit of assessing constitutional adequacy could stand revival. Dangerous inefficiencies exist side by side with dangerous irresponsibilities.

The case against present arrangements has been so well stated elsewhere that only a summary need be provided here.[68] Formal division of power has always been an open invitation to conflict over national policy. Whether institutional friction was meant to extend to foreign affairs, American folklore lauds it as a benign slowdown, in both the Aristotelian sense that two heads are better than one and the old Southern sense that consensus rests on offending the vital interests of none. Although it is doubtful that the Senate's conduct in treaty-making has veered seriously from popular thought at any given time, every schoolboy is familiar with

[67] Walter Lippmann, *Essays in the Public Philosophy* (1955), pp. 24–25. Bertram Gross, *The Legislative Struggle: A Study in Social Combat* (1953), pp. 121–122. Cf. Justice Frankfurter's characterization of this criticism as "too easy." *Youngstown Sheet & Tube Co.* v. *Sawyer*, 343 U.S. 579, 593–94 (1952). It should be noted that the Justice does not refer to the criticism of democratic responsibility, although it closely resembles his own interest in curtailing judicial power for the same purpose.

[68] Robert A. Dahl, *Congress and Foreign Policy* (1950); Daniel S. Cheever and H. Field Haviland, *American Foreign Policy and the Separation of Powers* (1952); William Y. Elliott, *United States Foreign Policy*, Report of a Study Group for the Woodrow Wilson Foundation (1952). Doubtless the move "toward a more responsible party system" stems from similar concern. Cf. Wright, *op. cit.*, pp. 99–100.

the formal need of collaboration and how it can be exacerbated by division of offices between parties and among them, by institutional jealousies, and the like.[69] When one considers the less familiar, but pervasive informal arrangements of day-to-day policy-making, however, the whole issue of limitation takes on a radically different complexion. To settle broad outlines of constitutional authority is not to dispose of the issue of foreign policy control. To set formal blocs of power against others is not to dispose of it either. *Ad hoc* coalitions of power have so complicated the formal apparatus of government that constitutional questions are normally irrelevant and the effectiveness of policy formation and popular control may still be in doubt.

The most obvious formal change in the American government, for example, is the enormous growth of Presidential power at the expense of Congress. Nowadays it is commonplace to assign the Presidency a multitude of roles ranging from chief executive, legislator, and diplomat to chief economist and patron of certain sports and arts. Equally commonplace is the recognized switch of functions in which routinely, the President proposes while the Congress vetoes and in which, exceptionally, the President gets us into wars and then becomes a "constitutional dictator" to end them.[70] Many view these developments with alarm, particularly when the Presidency's advantages in information, secrecy, and staff are contrasted with Congress' waning power to resist. No doubt, technology has reduced the "declaration of war" to a mere formality and well-nigh obliterated the distinction between military and civilian affairs. Mere semantic change from "treaty" to "agreement," or from "war" to "police action," permits evasion of once potent constitutional limits. In the sense of establishing priorities through systematic budgetary review, the legislature's power of the purse is overrated. And apart from making noise, what can Congress or the electorate do when confronted with a *fait accompli* like Korea or the Cuban blockade? Events confirm Hamilton's observation that hard times will cause dominance of executive process over legislative process, and we have not escaped.[71]

Were executive-legislative relationships a see-saw battle between two monoliths, the concentration of executive power might well menace the already strained capacity of Congress to serve as watchdog over the Presi-

---

[69] Harold J. Laski, *The American Democracy* (1948), pp. 518–520. A decade before his own trial-by-combat, Woodrow Wilson wrote of President and Congress: "Their cooperation is indispensable, their warfare fatal." *Constitutional Government in the United States* (1908), p. 57.

[70] See Corwin, *Total War and the Constitution* and Clinton Rossiter, *Constitutional Dictatorship* (1948).

[71] *The Federalist*, No. 22, p. 139. For an attempt to strengthen budgetary review in military affairs, see Raymond H. Dawson, "Congressional Innovation and Intervention," 66 *Am. Pol. Sci. Rev.* 42 (1962).

dency. Yet close observers of the political scene have long noted that the dominant characteristic, if not weakness, of American policy-making is the wide dispersion of authority that exists in practice.[72] It is a fiction to say that foreign policy requires the collaboration of chief executive and Congress; rather, it requires the synchronization of Presidency, Congressmen, and their respective political allies, which is a far different matter. The President's will, as two Hoover Commissions and the CIA remind us, is not necessarily his bureaucracy's command. Sheer physical size, the creation of independent agencies, and the manifold alliances among administrators, private groups, and legislators, all have magnified the universal problem of bureaucratic control.

Similarly, the localistic roots of Congress, which compel diffuse organization, and prevent its reform, have aggravated the common problem of legislative decline. Even assuming that such a thing as a national majority exists, one of the easiest generalizations in American politics is the absence of a genuinely national legislature capable of internal self-control.[73] Congressional leadership is so decentralized that outside direction, either executive or private, is indispensable for positive action. Whether greater party discipline is a desirable or even a possible remedy, fragmentation of authority is so prevalent that effective powers and limits are to be found only by analysis of the most intricate and shifting, official and unofficial relationships throughout the total governing process. Government in the United States may be based on an explicit constitutional framework, but its actual character varies according to issue. Diffusion of power may be a precondition of limited government, but it prevails so widely that Bertram Gross' dismissal of the phantom of a monolithic bureaucracy applies to the whole:

> As a result of these diverse and often conflicting allegiances, there are more checks and balances within the executive branch itself than the Founding Fathers ever dreamed of when they wrote the Constitution.[74]

Whatever comfort this added dimension of informal power fragmentation may provide against arbitrary action, the phenomenon is disturbing because it impedes both efficiency and accountability, while fostering its own kind of abuse. The same inability of the chief executive to master his administration means that the burden of generating concerted policy

---

[72] The leading work is David B. Truman, *The Governmental Process* (1951). For a provocative plea that constitutional theory take account of the informal governing process, see Arthur S. Miller, "The Constitutional Law of the 'Security State,'" 10 *Stanford Law Review* 620 (1958).

[73] Robert A. Dahl and Charles E. Lindblom, *Politics, Economics, and Welfare* (1953), pp. 336, 324–365; George B. Galloway, *The Legislative Process in Congress* (1953), p. 352.

[74] Gross, *op. cit.*, pp. 104–105. For the effects of pluralism on defense policy, see Samuel P. Huntington, *The Common Defense* (1961).

within the executive branch is multiplied. It also means that some agencies like the State Department during the McCarthy era are subject to massive outside interference while others like the CIA are beyond effective control from any visible source. Despite the increasing importance of administrative review and Congress' legitimate supervisory function over the administrative process, a dependable system of controls has yet to be developed over the bureaucracy. Apart from a few "great debates" and certain semipermanent suzerainties in immigration, foreign aid, and military procurement, the typical legislative intervention appears to be concerned more with constituency-inspired details—who gets this contract, that peril point —than with the larger policy alternatives being pursued. While any distinction between policy formation and execution is risky, and while a certain amount of friction is healthy, it is difficult to avoid the impression that legislative oversight at best is sporadic and at worst excessively concerned with detail.

Although a decentralized legislature is not necessarily incapable of swift action, the issue of accountability is more serious within Congress. For all the impressive competence of the Foreign Relations committees, power is so amorphous in the legislature that pinpointing responsibility is difficult and public retaliation often impossible. Even if it was known that Representative Walter was lord and master of immigration in this country, for example, how could voters and organized interests outside the 15th District of Pennsylvania have responded if they disagreed with his version of the national interest? In Congress' defense, it should be recognized, as Madison did, that legislators are but "advocates and parties to the causes which they determine." [75] Pressures which Presidents do not share invite the administrative forays, the domestic orientation, and indeed the simplistic world view to which Congress is prone. For good reason members of Congress are more expert with the intricacies of parity prices and unemployment than with trade balances and overseas underdevelopment. Yet to admit that the political system generates these disparities in outlook is to admit that legislative competence in foreign policy is achieved in spite of the system rather than because of it. That complaint has been levied against the government as a whole by men as experienced as Henry Cabot Lodge.[76] And the admission points to the manifold perils involved.

In the first place, the weakness of one branch does not necessarily strengthen the other. Just as commonly, it invites dual irresponsibility— excessive executive secrecy and the executive by-pass on the one hand and the "grand inquest" on the other. The profusion of conflicting official voices also creates confusion abroad which, needless to say, is "a grave

[75] *The Federalist*, No. 10, p. 56.
[76] *Christian Science Monitor*, August 16, 1961, p. 3, col. 2.

danger in the field of foreign affairs." [77] Second, assuming that the public sets the limits of action, albeit in uncharted ways, the difficulties of harmonizing a multitude of decision-makers tempt officialdom to oversimplification and overselling in their appeals within and without the government. The dangers here are not merely the questionable dissimulation introduced into public debate, but also the prospect of self-deception which mistakes rhetoric for policy and which lays the groundwork for the future inflexibilities and disillusionment that inhibit action far more than constitutions ever could. Arguably, these were the fruits of the hard-sell that occurred with respect to China, the UN, and perhaps even NATO. When a policy is oversold, what happens if the situation that called it into being has changed? Our wooing of Germany and Japan demonstrates that international politics creates strange bedfellows. Are we equipped to change partners fast enough? Finally, and perhaps most serious, so much time and effort is spent collaborating, in overcoming structural encumbrances and their progeny, that attention is deflected from the agonizing task of policy formation and thought. For all the pains taken in interbranch coordination, the result may still be an "irrelevant equilibrium," a phenomenon akin to the party platform which strikes a splendid balance among contending internal forces, but perforce is out of touch with a revolutionary world.[78]

In reciting these rather commonplace criticisms of American foreign policy-making, the point is not that the Constitution is a positive hindrance in foreign affairs. For certainly the generalizations themselves are debatable value judgments, and much is beyond our control. Though we are inclined to forget that on one unromantic occasion the system did collapse, numerous examples can be cited where the nation's "inevitable frictions," including Senate treaty-power, served it well.[79] The point is merely that the Constitution did not fix the aims of effectiveness and limitation in perpetual counterpoise. Each generation must strike that balance for itself. The courts, as we have seen, perform a dual function of blessing power while imposing partial restraints, at a cost of chronic doubts about the propriety of judicial review in a democratic order. Structural limitations in the political sector, on the other hand, foster such fragmentation of power that they exact a heavy price in efficiency and responsibility for the dubious securities gained. The case against mechanical controls is not closed.

In posing the alternatives as popular control versus institutional checks,

---

[77] Secretary of Defense McNamara, quoted in Jack Raymond, "Mr. McNamara Remodels the Pentagon," *The Reporter*, Vol. 26 (January 18, 1962), 33.

[78] Robert Bendiner, "Pennsylvania Avenue Gets Longer and Longer," *The Reporter*, Vol. 18 (February 20, 1958), 25–27. Hamilton sounded similar warnings, *The Federalist*, No. 22, pp. 136–137.

[79] See Laski, *The American Democracy*, pp. 518–520.

Americans habitually overstate the problem. The issue is not whether institutional controls are safer than popular democracy, but whether at any given time we can afford and achieve a workable blend. Institutional safeguards, in design and in operation, can provide at best only imperfect security. Indeed, it is doubtful that they could work at all without basis in the permeating "social pluralism" of a free society or without the pervasive "constitutional understandings" that fill the lacunae of an eighteenth century instrument.[80] Could judicial review, for example, long exist without "sustained public confidence in its moral sanction"?[81] Could a "chaotic situation," in President Kennedy's words, be avoided if the executive and the legislature each pushed power to "its logical, or . . . possible conclusion"?[82] The cease-fire in the B-70 controversy, established during a stroll in the White House garden, demonstrates how deeply understood is the necessity of restraint by those who practice constitutional government. Senator Dirksen revealed no less during the UN bond issue debate when he led his colleagues to accept another inroad on their power of the purse with the remark: "I am willing, as always, to trust my President, because he is my President."[83] Of such sentiments constitutional limitations are never built, but who can deny that they are the foundation on which free government ultimately rests?

"While the Constitution diffuses power the better to secure liberty," Justice Jackson once wrote, "it also contemplates that practice will integrate the dispersed powers into a workable government."[84] Through practice an eighteenth century Constitution has been made to survive. But in the process we have moved closer to British notions of responsibility in foreign affairs than men would have dreamed possible even thirty years ago. Like the British, we are thrown back to Locke's profound insight that, in the last analysis, protection rests on good faith among free men and personal responsibility among those who wield power for the public good.[85] That faith in reasonableness has always been thought inadequate by those who assume that every power must, and can, have its counterpart check. But if it is true that mechanical contrivances offer only partial pro-

---

[80] Dahl and Lindblom, *op. cit.*, p. 308. Wright, *op. cit.*, pp. 7–8, 368–369.

[81] Justice Frankfurter, *Baker v. Carr*, 369 U.S. 186, 267 (1962).

[82] *The New York Times*, March 22, 1962, p. 16, col. 8.

[83] *The New York Times*, March 23, 1962, p. 5, col. 4; and April 8, 1962, Sec. 4, p. 1, col. 8.

[84] *Youngstown Sheet & Tube Co. v. Sawyer*, 343 U.S. 579, 635 (1952).

[85] *Two Treatises of Civil Government* (Everyman's Library ed., 1924), p. 160. Justice Johnson agreed: "The idea is utopian, that government can exist without leaving the exercise of discretion somewhere. Public security against the abuse of such discretion must rest on responsibility, and stated appeals to public approbation. Where all power is derived from the people, and public functionaries, at short intervals, deposit it at the feet of the people, to be resumed again only at their will, individual fears may be alarmed by the monsters of imagination, but individual liberty can be in little danger." *Anderson v. Dunn*, 19 U.S. (6 Wheat.) 204, 226 (1821).

tection and rest on community restraint anyway, one may reasonably question whether they are necessary or worth their toll. Certainly one may oppose their enlargement. For the lesson of history is surely that constitutions cannot save us, either from our enemies or from ourselves. To think otherwise is to invite the peril of a mental Maginot line.

V

The Constitution Abroad

10

Robert von Mohl,
Germany's de Tocqueville *

Gottfried Dietze

I

In an attempt to protect the rights of the individual, the Bonn Basic
Law does not only provide for a far-reaching bill of rights, but also for
three major aspects of constitutional government, namely, federalism,
representative democracy, and judicial review.[1] The presence of all these
features perhaps makes that Law the most "constitutionalist" German
constitution. For whereas the Imperial constitution provided for federalism,
it hardly established democracy; whereas the Weimar constitution was
democratic, it hardly was federal. And neither one of these constitutions
accepted judicial review.[2]

The presence in the Basic Law of the characteristic features of American constitutionalism suggests an inquiry into the degree to which that
Law was influenced from the other side of the Atlantic, or even the broader
question about the general impact of American constitutional law upon
Germany. In view of the fact that the United States military government

* The author wishes to express his thanks to the Relm Foundation for a research and
travel grant which facilitated the writing of this article.

[1] A discussion of federalism, democracy, and judicial review as aspects of constitutionalism under the Basic Law can be found in the author's "The Federal Republic
of Germany: An Evaluation After Ten Years," 22 *Journal of Politics* 121–135 (1960).

[2] For the Imperial constitution, see Georg Meyer and Gerhard Anschütz, *Lehrbuch
des deutschen Staatsrechts* (7th ed., 1919), pp. 743–744. The absence of judicial review under the Weimar constitution is discussed by Gerhard Anschütz, *Die Verfassung
des deutschen Reichs* (4th ed., 1932), pp. 370–374, 401.

made its desires known to the Parliamentary Council that drafted the new fundamental law at Bonn, it is not surprising that American concepts of government became reflected in the Basic Law.[3] However, the assertion that the Germans themselves had a strong inclination toward adopting major features of American constitutionalism is also justified. This desire was not so much due to some sudden awareness of American values, brought about by the contact with the occupation power, but, rather, to an influence which had existed ever since the nineteenth century.

Whereas American students during that century flocked to Germany for graduate work in the sciences, philology, and political economy, they hardly came in order to study law. In that field, German jurists often looked for guidance to the New World. The student of German literature on government cannot but be impressed by the many references to American constitutional theory and practice. While these references prevail in writings on federalism, they can also be found in discussions of democracy and judicial review. To many, this will come as a surprise in view of the fact that they probably never heard of a German who introduced American constitutional ideas to his countrymen. Or was there perhaps a German counterpart to de Tocqueville and James Bryce?

The man who takes the lion's share in acquainting Germans with American concepts of government is Robert von Mohl. One of the most influential *Staatsrechtler* of his time, he was perhaps the greatest German political scientist of his age.[4] Born in 1799, the year Friedrich Gentz probably wrote his essay on *The Origin and Principles of the American Revolution, as Compared to the Origin and Principles of the French Revolution,*[5] he died in 1875, ten years after American unity had been reconfirmed, the year the Constitutional Laws of the Third Republic were adopted. Mohl's life is thus framed by events which show both the value and danger of democracy. This is, in a way, symbolic of his thought. A nineteenth century

---

[3] See Doemming, Füsslein, and Matz, "Entstehungsgeschichte der Artikel des Grundgesetzes," 1 *Jahrbuch des öffentlichen Rechts der Gegenwart* (N.F.), 1 (1951); Edward H. Lichfield, ed., *Governing Postwar Germany* (1953); John F. Golay, *The Founding of the Federal Republic of Germany* (1958).

[4] The combination of *Staatsrechtler* and political scientist was not unusual in Germany at that time. Only with the advance of legal positivism in the latter part of the nineteenth century did there come about an increasing separation of political science from *Staatsrecht*, resulting in the neglect and academic discredit of the former. It is the merit of Carl J. Friedrich to have fought from the United States for a reintegration of the two disciplines and thus to have helped to bring about a new recognition of political science in Germany. For Friedrich's indebtedness to Mohl, see his *Der Verfassungsstaat der Neuzeit* (1953), p. vii. Cf. also Hans Huber's review of that work in 81 *Archiv des öffentlichen Rechts* 495 (1956).

[5] Gentz' "Der Ursprung und die Grundsätze der amerikanischen Revolution, verglichen mit dem Ursprunge und den Grundsätzen der französischen," was published in 1800 in the *Historisches Journal*, edited by Gentz. Translated by the then U.S. ambassador to Berlin, John Quincy Adams, it was published the same year in Philadelphia. That translation was, with an introduction by Russell Kirk, republished in 1955.

liberal, Mohl was, while favoring popular government, highly sceptical of "ultrademocratic" tendencies.[6] One of the first advocates of the *Rechts-staat*, he favored the rule of law, characteristic of the American tradition, over the rule of men who make the law, specific to the *gouvernement d'assemblée*.

His career was that of a scholar-statesman.[7] From 1824 to 1845 he was a professor at Tübingen, losing his position because of some frank criticisms of the authorities of Württemberg. As Schiller before him, Mohl found refuge in Baden, where in 1845 he was appointed professor of law at Heidelberg. In 1848, he was a member of the German parliament in Frankfurt. From 1867 to 1871, he served as ambassador of the Grand-Duke of Baden at Munich. After German unification, Mohl became a member of the *Reichstag*. In spite of his activities in the public service, Mohl was a productive scholar throughout his life. His writings, beginning with a dissertation on representative constitutionalism, published in 1821, and ending with a critical discussion of conditions in the *Reich* a few weeks before his death, are impressive from a qualitative as well as quantitative point of view.[8] From among four distinguished brothers, his countrymen seem to consider him the greatest.[9]

Strangely enough, the man who wrote more than any of his compatriots on American government is hardly known in the United States. Even encyclopaedias are silent about him. The 1911 edition of the *Encyclopaedia Britannica*, widely read in the United States, contains articles on his brothers Hugo, a botanist, and Julius, an orientalist, but mentions Robert only in passing. The edition of 1959, while devoting several lines to trivial remarks on Julius's wife, omits a reference to Robert altogether, as does the *Encyclopaedia Americana*.

An omission of Mohl the *Staatsrechtler* and political scientist by an American encyclopaedia is, in view of the recognition in his native land, strange, but understandable. However, an omission of Mohl the commentator on America must appear peculiar. What are the reasons for this

[6] Erich Angermann, *Robert von Mohl* (1962), gave that work the subtitle, "Leben und Werk eines altliberalen Staatsgelehrten." Mohl refers to himself as an English Whig, a member of the French left center, an American Federalist. *Lebenserinnerungen* (1902), I, 139f.

[7] See Mohl, *Lebenserinnerungen* (1902); Ernst Meier, "Robert von Mohl," 34 *Zeitschrift für die gesamte Staatswissenschaft* 431 (1878); Hermann Schulze, *Robert von Mohl* (1886); Kurt Landsberg, *Geschichte der deutschen Rechtswissenschaft*, III (2nd part, 1910), 401–411; Erich Angermann, *Robert von Mohl* (1962). The last work is the most comprehensive work on Mohl.

[8] For a complete bibliography, combined with a discussion of Mohl's major works, see Meier, *op. cit.* Angermann, *op. cit.*, pp. 451–456, contains a list of Mohl's writings, as well as a list of literature on Mohl.

[9] *Der Grosse Brockhaus*, outstanding German encyclopaedia, in its edition of 1955 only mentions two of the brothers, Hugo, a botanist, and Robert, devoting considerably more space to the latter.

neglect? Was Mohl's expertise doubted because he had never been to America? Was it because his writings on the United States were, in distinction to those of de Tocqueville and Bryce, scattered over a period of fifty years, and thus probably never had as compact an impact? Or because his writings on America were never translated? [10] Or was it the fact that his first study and only book on America, *Das Bundes-Staatsrecht der Vereinigten Staaten von Nord-Amerika*, published in 1824, being rather short and never complemented by the planned second volume,[11] was of mediocre quality? We are able only to provide some answer to the last question.

Mohl himself, writing more than thirty years after the publication of the book, referred to it as a "work of youth" and disclaimed any intention to consider it a masterpiece. He admitted that a satisfactory study could hardly have been written owing to the want of experience and source material, as well as to the fact that the development of American federal law had not yet progressed too far. Furthermore, he admitted that at the time of writing he did not yet possess the training which would have given him a commanding view of the importance of the federal state for world history and law and a precise understanding of the basic principles and different conceptions of federalism. Consequently, his exposition had to be confined to the obvious and to strictly legal matter, and many important questions were omitted. Mohl also mentioned that his book might have found more recognition had it been the work of a well-known author.[12] After Mohl's death, a colleague at the University of Halle gave his own explanation of the absence of interest in Mohl's study. According to him, the work was not published at the right time. In the eighteen-twenties, it was of no interest to the German public or German scholars. "At that time, people were exclusively concerned with . . . constitutional monarchy. Consequently, they were attracted by the French Charter of 1814 and perhaps by the Spanish Cortes constitution of 1812. On the other hand, there was no understanding for problems of representative democracy. Also, there was yet little talk of plans for a federal state. . . . The success of this book would have been quite different had it been published a whole generation later." [13]

Recognizing the shortcomings of the work as set forth by the author

[10] The only exception being a review of Story's *Commentaries on the Constitution of the United States.*

[11] That volume, concerned with administrative law, was already outlined in the table of contents of the first volume. However, in spite of its completion in draft, it was never published, owing to Mohl's premature transfer from Paris to Tübingen. See Meier, *op. cit.,* p. 447; the remark of the editors, 14 *American Jurist* 331 (1835); Angermann, *op. cit.,* p. 27.

[12] Mohl, *Die Geschichte und Literatur der Staatswissenschaften* (1855), I, 575–576.

[13] Meier, *op. cit.,* pp. 446–447. See also Landsberg, *loc. cit.,* p. 404; Angermann, *op. cit.,* p. 27.

himself, we are inclined to attribute the want of attention accorded to it mainly to the fact that a rather unknown author wrote on an obscure subject for a disinterested audience. It would seem unfair, however, to ignore the merits of the book. We tend to agree with Mohl's statement that his study, written in the German tradition, is more systematic than any other work published on the same subject before or thereafter, and that its presentation is both simple and clear.[14] We also tend to agree with Ernst Meier's opinion that Mohl's presentation "must be called truly classic because it connects the clearest discussion of existing law with the deepest penetration into the innermost spirit of that law," as well as with his praise of Mohl's discussion of the federal state, popular sovereignty, the relation of the President to Congress, the importance of judicial review, and the separation of powers.[15] The outstanding work on German legal history called Mohl's book "an achievement which displays a very unusual understanding of the strange and complicated nature of American *Staatsrecht;* combining a remarkable skill in its approach and organization with a diligent perception of numerous hidden details." [16]

Clearly, Mohl's first—and major—publication on the United States, whatever its shortcomings may have been, can hardly account for his being forgotten in America. As a matter of fact, it seems to have earned him a reputation in this country shortly after publication.[17] Furthermore, that treatise was followed by many other writings on the United States, which, from a qualitative as well as quantitative point of view, are at least on a par with the book discussed.

We shall now be concerned with his various studies on the United States. Roughly speaking, these studies can be divided into two groups, containing respectively, treatises in *Staatsrecht,* and political writings.[18] We shall first discuss the former.

[14] Mohl, *Die Geschichte und Literatur der Staatswissenschaften,* I, 575–576.

[15] Meier, *op. cit.,* p. 446.

[16] Landsberg, *loc. cit.,* p. 404. Schulze, *op. cit.,* p. 17, writes that the book "demonstrated, for the first time, the federal principle upon which the Union was based and, with a clear view, penetrated into the nature of North American political institutions." See also Angermann, *op. cit.,* pp. 26–27.

[17] The great American jurist Joseph Story congratulated Mohl on that book in two letters which are in the library of the University of Tübingen. Collection Md. 613, No. 864. See Angermann, *op. cit.,* p. 26. Accepting an invitation to dine with Chevalier and Mohl, Charles Sumner wrote Chevalier in 1858: "I am not a stranger to the writings of Professor Mohl. . . . His appreciation of the history and institutions of my country is marvelous, beginning with his labors twenty years ago, and showing itself in his late masterly work on public law, which I trust soon to see finished." Edward L. Pierce, *Memoir and Letters of Charles Sumner* (1893–94), III, 532. (I am indebted for the latter information to Professor David Donald.)

[18] Landsberg, *loc. cit.,* distinguishes between *positiv-rechtlichen* and *politischen sowie allgemein-staatsrechtlichen* writings, being aware of the difficulties involved in separating the two.

II

Mohl collected some of his source material for his book of 1824 on a trip through Europe. In Paris, where he was employed in the diplomatic service, he profited from a collection of American documents and from the advice and counsel of Americans.[19] His study was mainly prompted by the consideration that there existed no systematic study on the Constitution of the United States, and by his interest in federalism and democracy as aspects of constitutionalism, and keeps within the bounds of *Staatsrecht*.[20] It is based upon the text of the Constitution and only occasionally draws upon such sources as the debates of the Federal Convention, the French translation of the *Federalist*, and a few other writings. The study is divided into six chapters, dealing with the member states of the Union, the Constitution, the three branches of government, the relation of the nation to the states, the relations among the states, and the rights of the inhabitants. It contains many interesting statements, especially with respect to federalism, democracy, and judicial review.

The text is preceded by a quotation from Milton's *On the Liberty of the Press*: "Methinks I see in my mind a noble and puissant nation, rousing herself as a strong man after sleep, and shaking her invincible locks; methinks I see her as an eagle, mewing her mighty mouth, and kindling her endazzled eyes at the full mid-day beam." [21] In tune with this quotation, the foreword is full of admiration for America and foresees a great future for the United States. Mohl refers to the United States as the "miracle of our time," expressing doubts as to whether any nation would more merit the reflection by statesmen and whether any federal constitution had ever been more remarkable than that of the United States. The remarkable thing about that Constitution is that it does not just establish a *Staatenbund*, but a *Bundesstaat*, i.e., the rarer and more complicated of the two federal species.[22] The adoption of that form of government has proved that "at least sometimes man, even in a great mass, can overcome himself and sacrifice lesser interests to the attainment of higher ends." Apart from the "disgrace of slavery," Mohl praises the United States for having most unequivocally realized political principles, the division of

---

[19] Mohl, "Nordamerikanisches Staatsrecht," 7 *Kritische Zeitschrift für Rechtswissenschaft und Gesetzgebung des Auslandes* (hereafter *Kritische Zeitschrift*) 5 (1835). (Translation, "German Criticism of Mr. Justice Story's Commentaries on the Constitution of the United States," 14 *American Jurist* 335–336 (1835).) *Geschichte und Literatur der Staatswissenschaften*, I, 575. Comp. Meier, *op. cit.*, pp. 444–445.

[20] Mohl, *Geschichte und Literatur der Staatswissenschaften*, I, 575–576.

[21] Mohl, *Das Bundes-Staatsrecht der Vereinigten Staaten von Nord-Amerika* (1824), p. ii.

[22] *Ibid.*, pp. vii–viii.

powers, and the rights and duties of the state.[23] "There is no government in the world today which would as much refrain from burdening the people for the blessing of being governed, be it by means of enormous taxes, too much administration and unnecessary interference into the affairs of civil life, or by an accumulation of debts which cannot be paid off and prevents all prosperity," he says of the United States government, adding that "there is no country which, protected by its geographic position, would suffer as little from the unavoidable necessity of standing armies, no country in which an equal amount of truly useful knowledge would be spread to the whole mass of inhabitants, even though for the time being the top of the education-pyramid is still missing." [24] Stressing the need for proving the validity of "metaphysical fantasies" on the actual functioning of institutions, Mohl writes that a description of the United States must be especially desirable in view of the fact "that the ideas which are so enormously revolutionizing our time have been perceived and presented by her in the purest fashion, with the result that the consequences of these ideas, be they good or bad, had to develop most clearly in that country." [25] He expresses a desire to demonstrate that American principles of government are justified only under American conditions and more or less harmful under different circumstances.[26]

The text of the book, containing a long description of the member states of the Union and a discussion of constitutional history prior to the adoption of the Constitution, mainly consists in descriptions of and comments upon various constitutional provisions. Although Mohl's remarks on some specific aspects of the Constitution are not without interest,[27] the following will be restricted chiefly to examining his comments upon the general nature of the American system.

Describing the *staatsrechtliche Charakter* of the Constitution, Mohl

---

[23] *Ibid.*, p. ix.

[24] *Ibid.*, pp. ix–x.

[25] *Ibid.*, p. xii.

[26] *Ibid.*, pp. xii–xiii.

[27] According to Mohl, the terms for Representatives, Senators, and the President are "perhaps" too short; the right of revolution, though existing under the Constitution, is a "highly dangerous" right; the want of a fixed period within which a State must ratify a constitutional amendment is a "gap" in legislation; it is regrettable that the separation of powers has "sneaked into" American law, and the judicial power constitutes nothing but a power that is subordinated to the executive; the prohibition to admit public officials as legislators has definite disadvantages, as does the regulation of suffrage by the States; the status of the slaves, as defined by the Constitution, is "childish"; attainder is sentencing for high treason, a bill of attainder is a law made *pro re nata*; the President's right of pardon includes the right to pardon himself; it is regrettable that no constitutional provisions exist as to who shall administer the national government when a President is being impeached; Article IV, section 2, clause 1, in connection with the provision that no titles of nobility shall be granted, is "one of the fundaments" of the American system. *Ibid.*, pp. 128, 130 n., 137, 142 n., 149 n., 150 n., 190 n., 268 n., 374.

considers federalism and popular sovereignty as the basic features of American government. He sees the difference between *Staatenbund* and *Bundesstaat* in the fact that the latter is formally a state and not just a treaty among states that remain independent or, at best, form a defensive alliance. A *Bundesstaat* possesses all the attributes of an ordinary state, such as its own legislation, directly binding upon individuals, a government equipped with the means required for the execution of the constitution and the laws, and courts of law. It is distinguished from an ordinary state only in so far as it is divided into different, separate "provinces" which are free to handle their own internal affairs. However, no trace of this division is supposed to be seen from the outside as well as, in the most important cases, from the inside. Only the government common to and standing above the whole is supposed to appear and to act. Mohl asserts that the *Bund* forming the United States fully corresponds to a *Bundesstaat.* In support of his assertion, he enumerates constitutional limitations upon the states and aspects of national sovereignty.[28]

Mohl then proceeds "to look for the principle upon which the American *Bundesstaat* is based, in order to determine to what category of states it belongs." Not having in mind the orthodox distinction between monarchy, aristocracy, and democracy, Mohl the Liberal thinks of categories which are determined by the relation between the individual and the government, by the "*staatsrechtliche* character of the Constitution." Under that criterion, he distinguishes between a "patriarchic state" (based upon family ties), "hierarchy" (based upon the relationship of men to God and his servants), "despoty" (based upon the relationship of master and slave, of person and matter). "Finally, where the relationship between government and citizen is that of two equally entitled subjects, where there is a relationship between rightful claim and obligation, there exists a *Rechtsstaat.*" [29]

By this definition, the United States is a *Rechtsstaat,* a "representative democracy, where general legal equality of the citizens and freedom from any other kind of rule constitute the first principles of the Constitution, and where, generally speaking, the people are the rightful owner of governmental power." The United States, "(as, by the way, any moderate and constitutional monarchy)," is a state whose members consider justice, peace, and security from oppression as the ends of their unification. She is "a state whose citizens have the right to demand the fulfillment of these ends in all respects from the state and all its servants. On the other hand, like citizens of other states, they have the obligation to obey all measures, whatever they may be." Commenting upon the source of power, Mohl

28 *Ibid.,* pp. 121–124.
29 *Ibid.,* pp. 124–125.

writes that "this federal state exists by virtue of the free consensus of all its citizens. This consensus is also the basis for the Constitution. The latter was adopted by the people themselves. Therefore, only the people can make and sanction future laws." [30] In view of the great number of people and the extension of territory, the people have to delegate their power to representatives. In his description of constitutional provisions on representative democracy, Mohl is happy to note that all those affairs that require "unity of counsel, secrecy of decision, and speedy and uncompromising execution have been delegated to one man." [31] Frequent elections (in his opinion they are too frequent) protect the people from their delegates' abuse of power. In order that the representatives may know the limits of their power, and the people their rights and duties, "the people, when founding the federal state, put down in a written document the principles which ought to govern the administration of the state." [32]

Exhorting the importance of the Constitution, Mohl goes so far as to claim a right of revolution under the supreme law. "This instrument, called Constitutional Document, is the supreme law. . . . No later decree of any kind, be it emanating from a federal power or a member state, may contravene it; each act incompatible with it is invalid, and its originator punishable . . . ; a specific provision even prohibits the representatives of the people to exercise a right that has not expressly been delegated to them by the Constitutional Document. If, however, the provisions of the Constitution are transgressed by whoever it may be, and if all means provided by it for the restitution of lawful conditions are exhausted and of no use, then the sovereign people need not at all suffer such a formal interference with their will, but have the right to resist with force and to suppress this usurpation by the highest authority." [33] Although Mohl considers the right of revolution "a highly dangerous right which, for that reason, is not expressly laid down in the constitutional document," he stresses that, owing to the principle of popular sovereignty, there can be no doubt that the people of the United States possess that right, a right he considers "an unhappy attribute" of the American set-up only because of the difficulty of determining "measure and purpose" of revolution.[34]

In view of Mohl's emphasis upon restrictions of popular representatives through a written constitution, it is hardly surprising that in his opinion laws and decrees incompatible with the Constitution must be void. Although Article VI, section 2 of the Constitution does not expressly limit

[30] *Ibid.*, pp. 125–126.
[31] *Ibid.*, p. 127.
[32] *Ibid.*, pp. 128–129.
[33] *Ibid.*, pp. 129–130.
[34] *Ibid.*, p. 132.

Congress in the same manner in which it limits state legislative bodies, the fact that the Constitution takes precedence over acts of Congress follows "from the nature of things." For "the federal authorities exist only by virtue of the federal constitution, and possess authority only in so far as it has been granted to them by the Constitution. However, the right to infringe upon the Constitution cannot have and has not been granted to them. Therefore, they cannot take any steps against the Constitution, and such steps are null and not binding. They must be considered a violation of popular sovereignty. . . . No inhabitant of the United States is bound to obey laws or other decrees which are incompatible with the federal Constitution, or to see to it that they are being obeyed." [35]

In tune with this line of thought, Mohl, in a later chapter, writes that under the Constitution the judges have the right to test laws for their constitutionality. Having discussed the independence of the judiciary, he states his reasons for judicial review. In view of the importance of that institution for American constitutionalism, the relevant passage shall be quoted in full:

> From this independence of the judicial power, combined with the existence of a written constitutional document which, being the expressly and definitely announced will of the sovereign people, exactly allots to every part of the federal authority the rights it must exercise and cannot transgress without committing an act that is void and need not be obeyed by anyone, there follows the important power of the federal courts to decide upon the constitutionality, and thus validity, of acts of Congress. The people of the United States are the unlimited sovereign; in order to form a federal state, they established three branches of government independent of one another, and provided them with a written constitution as a rule from which they must not swerve. Therefore, should one of the three deviate from this basic rule, the other powers have no reason whatsoever to commit the same mistake. On the contrary, they have the duty to prevent the execution of such an unconstitutional act if they can. The judicial power is supposed to execute the valid laws made by the other two powers. However, if the legislature, be it through transgressing its authority, be it through neglecting a principle under which it operates, takes the liberty of passing a law which is incompatible with the Constitution, then the judges are not bound to execute it, although they have no right to declare a law they consider unconstitutional invalid and abolished, for this would be an assumption of legislative power. Formally, the law continues to exist as such as long as it has not been revoked by the legislative power itself. However, the federal courts do not at all contribute to its execution and thus, in reality, destroy it. As if it were legally nonexistent, they do not consider it for their decisions. They rather apply earlier federal laws, which perhaps were supposed to be changed by such a law, as if they were fully valid; they do not punish any act committed by a citizen in violation of such a law as a violation of a valid law. By the way, on these occasions, in the absence of any provision to the

[35] *Ibid.*, pp. 133–134.

contrary, the majority cannot bind the minority. The higher court cannot bind the lower courts. Each individual court is its own judge as to the constitutionality of a law.[36]

In a footnote, Mohl adds that while judicial review is not expressly provided for by the Constitution or the laws, its existence "follows so naturally from the principles, that never, even in the most violent party disputes, has there been any doubt about it." Judicial review is also justified by analogy, due to its exercise in several member states of the Union. Also, under section 25 of the Judiciary Act of 1789, 'the Supreme Court can, on appeal from state courts, decide whether these courts have justly declared a federal law unconstitutional. Furthermore, "if . . . the courts of the individual members of the Union have the right to declare a law of the United States invalid, the more must the judicial power of the federation possess this right." [37]

Mohl's conception of judicial review as a means for the protection of the people from illegitimate acts of their representatives lets that institution appear as a means for the protection of the individual. Indeed, Mohl advocates the individual's rights. As if he wanted to emphasize their fundamental importance, he reserved their discussion till the end of his book. His high opinion of these rights can be gathered from a remark at the beginning of the chapter entitled "The Personal Rights of the Inhabitants." After having discussed institutions and forms which were established by the sovereign American people, Mohl writes that it remains to discuss rights Americans can claim as "obeyors," as "their own subjects." "Whereas so far rights which the whole people possess against the individual were dealt with," he states, "now those which the community has granted to the particular individuals will be examined." [38]

Mohl distinguishes political from civil (*bürgerliche*) rights. From among the former, he mentions the right to vote, to occupy public office, the right of assembly and petition. Civil rights are divided into two groups, namely, the rights of personal freedom (such as freedom of religion, of speech, protection from judicial oppression) and property rights.[39] Both groups seem to him to be of equal value.

Mohl's main criticism of the protection of the individual is want of equality. Unlike the Declaration of Independence, he complains, positive constitutional law does not cherish the idea of equality. It divides the population into different classes, the least fortunate being the slaves. This discrimination is "incompatible with the motive for the United States' . . . separation from England, and thus with the justification for their existence,

---

[36] *Ibid.*, pp. 298–300.
[37] *Ibid.*, pp. 300–301.
[38] *Ibid.*, p. 376.
[39] *Ibid.*, pp. 388–393.

incompatible with the principles upon which the constitutional structure of the member states as well as of the federal state are based . . . , incompatible with justice," a result of "prejudice and rapacity." [40] Mohl feels that an enumeration of the rights of the individual in a constitution is harmful rather than a blessing. He refers to the "dry and unfriendly, but invincible logic" of Bentham's remarks on the disadvantages of bills of rights.[41]

In summary, it can be said that, aside from being a "pioneering work" on the United States,[42] Mohl's *Bundes-Staatsrecht der Vereinigten Staaten von Nord-Amerika* is a systematic treatise on American constitutionalism which reveals a good grasp of the essential.[43] And although the work was not a smashing success, it seems to have made him known as an expert on American government.[44] At any rate, in 1835 Mohl, now a well-known *Staatsrechtler*,[45] was asked to review Story's *Commentaries on the Constitution of the United States* in a leading journal, where his remarks appeared as a leading article.[46] This review impressed the editors of *The American Jurist* so much that they translated part of it.[47] "We hardly know which most to admire, the deep insight into our institutions, which is so rare a quality to find in a foreigner, or the intimate acquaintance with the work reviewed, or the high tone of criticism, which are displayed by the learned reviewer," they wrote, continuing, "we do not remember ever to have read a criticism, which impressed our mind with a higher opinion of the learning and talents of its author, than the present." [48] The response

[40] *Ibid.*, pp. 377–378.

[41] *Ibid.*, p. 109. Although Mohl had read a French translation of the Federalist Papers, he does not mention that Hamilton took a similar position in essay 84.

[42] Landsberg, *loc. cit.*, p. 404.

[43] Cf. Friedrich Kapp, "Zur deutschen wissenschaftlichen Literatur über die Vereinigten Staaten von Amerika," 31 *Historische Zeitschrift* 247 ff. (1874); Meier, *op. cit.*, pp. 444–446; Schulze, *op. cit.*, p. 17; Marquardsen, "Mohl," *Allgemeine Deutsche Biographie* (edited by Kommission bei der Bayerischen Akademie der Wissenschaften, 1875–1910), XXII, 746; Eckhardt G. Franz, *Das Amerikabild der deutschen Revolution von 1848–49* (1958), pp. 77 ff.

[44] See F. A. Hayek, *The Constitution of Liberty* (1960), p. 482, note 26.

[45] For the importance of his major works, *Das Staatsrecht des Königreichs Württemberg* (1829–1831, 2nd ed. 1840), and *Die Polizeiwissenschaft nach den Grundsätzen des Rechtsstaates* (1832, 2nd ed. 1844, 3rd ed. 1866), see Meier, *op. cit.*, pp. 448–449, 490–493; Schulze, *op. cit.*, pp. 20–30; Landsberg, *loc. cit.*, pp. 405–408; Angermann, *op. cit.*, pp. 35–37, 95 ff.

[46] Mohl, "Nordamerikanisches Staatsrecht," 7 *Kritische Zeitschrift* 1 (1835).

[47] "German Criticism of Mr. Justice Story's Commentaries on the Constitution of the United States," 14 *American Jurist* 330 (1835); *ibid.*, XV, 1 (1836).

[48] *Ibid.*, XIV, 331. The editors continue: "The subject of our constitutional law—one which foreigners have not hitherto deigned to touch, or, if they have turned their attention to it for a moment, have very imperfectly treated—is handled with great ability, and the work of Mr. Justice Story is praised with a discrimination which gives the opinion of the reviewer the highest value, and cannot fail to make it deeply appreciated by the distinguished author and by the public. But this criticism is not

to the translation was so favorable that the editors of the *American Jurist* decided, against their original intention, to publish a full translation.[49]

Mohl's review, written a decade after publication of his *Bundes-Staatsrecht der Vereinigten Staaten*, again stresses the importance of studying the American Constitution for "all who desire to have an opinion of their own on the great political questions of today." America is considered a "remarkable nation" in which "the fundamental principles of government, first set up in the struggles with the Stuarts, and since become the pivot upon which the popular government in more than one part of the world is turning, are . . . carried out to their utmost extent in their practical results." America appears as "a vast field of experiment, upon which the collective advantages and disadvantages of theoretical principles are developing and may be observed in gigantic proportions." In the Constitution there was solved, "in a perfectly satisfactory manner, the double problem, first, the establishment of a democracy in a territory of great extent; and, secondly, the reconciling of the necessary participation of all the citizens, in the conduct of public affairs, with the modern passive notions of freedom, to wit, with the requisition, that the pursuit of private purposes shall be as little as possible impeded or interfered with by the state." [50] Judicial review is considered "as one of the boldest and most interesting experiments in modern public law." [51] Questioning the idea that the happiness of the Americans is due mainly to favorable physical conditions, Mohl asserts that it largely derives from the federal form of government which enables the people to make full use of their country's natural assets.[52]

In Mohl's opinion, the American Constitution is ideally suited to American conditions and circumstances.[53] Still, being the work of man, it is not perfect.[54] In his enumeration of its shortcomings, Mohl, who was

---

simply an instance of the *laudari a viro laudato*. Written, as it is, by a foreigner, in a distant land, in a language addressed to his countrymen—and far removed from all those disturbing influences, growing out of friendship, social and party connections, or the ties of a common country, which too often come, with more than the weight of Brennus' sword, into the scales which the critic holds aloft, it seems, not as the voice of a single individual, but as the impartial judgment of posterity." *Ibid.,* XIV, 331–332.

[49] *Ibid.,* XIV, 344; XV, 1.

[50] *Ibid.,* XIV, 332–333.

[51] *Ibid.,* XV, 11. The whole passage reads: "Dr. Story mentions several interesting cases which . . . resulted in a declaration of the unconstitutionality of the law in question. Notwithstanding the highly successful exposition of the author, we are far from regarding this provision as the necessary, and, in its consequences, just, result of the independent character of the judicial power . . . ;—nor would we, by any means, advise to its imitation: we can only look upon it as one of the boldest and most interesting experiments in modern public law."

[52] *Ibid.,* XV, 3.

[53] *Ibid.,* XV, 5.

[54] *Ibid.,* XV, 12–13.

one of the great authors on the *Rechtsstaat*,[55] significantly mentions first and last aspects that are concerned with the protection of the individual from the government, namely, "the fundamental principle that legal proceedings cannot be instituted, in favor of an individual, against the government, without its consent," and "the possibility that a defendant in a State court may be arraigned before a second court, on account of the same transaction." [56] The greatest fault of the Constitution is its permission of slavery, that "blot and cancer upon the United States." [57] Due to conditions existing at the time of the adoption of the Constitution, however, slavery is a "heavy misfortune" rather than a "fault." [58]

The review of Story's book was followed five years later by another comment on American constitutional law, a review of *The Writings of John Marshall, late Chief Justice of the United States* (1839).[59] These writings, containing decisions on constitutional law, reminded Mohl, who doubted whether a higher praise was possible, "on every page of Story's Commentaries." Marshall's decisions are characterized by a "clear, strict logic, the constant awareness of the main purpose and all subsidiary questions and analogous provisions which are relevant for the decision, the so-to-speak naïve sagacity, and, finally, by the serene constitutional atmosphere, which impress us so much in the writings of good North American jurists." Mohl feels that the work is of great importance not only for Americans, but also for Europeans and the evalution of European conditions and problems.[60]

In this review, Mohl reveals himself as a follower of Marshall when he writes that the Constitution was freely adopted by the American people as a whole, that national power rests on the will of the people and not upon concessions made by the States, when he favors the doctrine of implied powers. National power is necessary to prevent a petty adherence to states' rights ("*Kantönli-Geist*"), a destruction of the federal government, general anarchy, and a "*bellum omnium contra omnes*" which would surely result in the destruction of the "fabulous material progress of the United States" and perhaps in things worse. Mohl does not consider the federal government dangerous. For like the governments of the States, it rests upon the consent of the people, and pursues the same ends as the States. It is not selfishly abused for aims which are not in the interest of

---

[55] For a comprehensive discussion of Mohl's concept of *Rechtsstaat*, see Angermann, *op. cit.*, p. 95. A change in that concept is discussed in Dietze, *In Defense of Property* (1963), p. 246, note 69.

[56] "German Criticism of Mr. Justice Story's Commentaries on the Constitution of the United States," 15 *American Jurist* 5–6 (1836).

[57] *Ibid.*, XV, 8; XIV, 332.

[58] *Ibid.*, XV, 8–9.

[59] "Nordamerikanisches Staatsrecht," 12 *Kritische Zeitschrift* 161 (1840).

[60] *Ibid.*, XII, 163–164.

the federation. It is a guardian of the law and the general welfare rather than a tool of restriction and oppression.[61]

Mohl emphasizes the importance of the American judiciary, an institution which, due to the separation of powers, he considers to be co-ordinate with the other two branches of government. He speaks of "the great *staatsrechtliche* importance" of the federal courts, especially that of the Supreme Court. These courts cannot only, "upon the first best litigation," make null and void encroachments by state legislatures upon the rights of the federation, but also national legislation. "Thus the government of the Union is strictly confined to within the bounds of constitutionality, for its departures would soon dash to pieces at those inexorable barriers." Mohl also praises the fact that "doubtful provisions of the fundamental law will receive . . . an immutable interpretation which is based upon strict legal rules." [62]

In the end, Mohl discusses the political wisdom of "strictly juristic and processual" uses of the Constitution. He states that in general a constitution does not depend upon a narrow technical interpretation. A constitution does not win the people's affection "if each particular provision is carried out conscientiously and perhaps even pedantically." New developments and the realization that the achievement of desirable ends is frustrated by constitutional provisions, prevent the desire for change from being suppressed. "The more exact the execution of existing provisions, the more it will hurt." While Mohl admits that disregard for constitutions often resulted in dissatisfaction and violent disturbances, he states that "a rigid adherence to institutions that have become inadequate and detrimental had the same result." "Even in a *Rechtsstaat*, civil society does not only have a legal aspect," he writes, fearing that "emphasis upon that aspect leads to one-sidedness, neglect of real needs, and pedantry." [63]

However, Mohl disclaims any assertion that a strict legal application of a constitution would be absolutely unwise or disadvantageous. He entertains no doubt that such application has "essential advantages": "Above all, people will generally confide in the Constitution's provisions, for the Constitution becomes, in the most scrupulous way, truth. Thus people can rely upon what exists. Secondly, such a strict application of the law even *vis-à-vis* the highest authorities in the state must . . . spread the sense of strict legality to the people. . . . Such a spirit of legality is highly valuable if only because it saves material means for the maintenance of order within the state. Its blessings are reflected in lower taxes as well as in the individual's greater freedom of movement. . . . A very strict interpretation of the laws requires a good framing of the latter, from which

[61] *Ibid.*, XII, 165–166.
[62] *Ibid.*, XII, 162.
[63] *Ibid.*, XII, 182–183.

. . . citizens and authorities will profit. Finally, it can hardly be denied that this strictness eliminates both cause of and pretense for criticism of the authorities; for not only will the latter think twice before they act contrary to the law if their acts can easily be revoked to their own disadvantage, but also the citizen, when he is of the opinion to have been treated unfairly, will soon desire strict law. No matter whether the court's decision is to his advantage or disadvantage, he can and will accept it." [64]

Conditions in the United States prove the correctness of the foregoing statements. "The strict juristic interpretation of the federal constitution (as well as of the constitutions of the member states) . . . does not permit the thought of an attack upon the fundamental law by federal authorities. Therefore, there does not exist uneasiness, but, rather, firm confidence." "However," Mohl adds, "no one in his good senses can overlook the dangers which threaten this whole situation, if only at a distant time and perhaps also vincible." He fears that due to their number, extension, and population, the member states will become unruleable by the "after all, always weak federal government." "Is not the terrible ghost of slavery threatening . . . to bring about the end of the Union and . . . many other, still unthought of, evils? Does not the hyperdemocratic sentiment expand more and more, attacking and eliminating the aristocracy of the mind, of education, and of merits, opening up unpleasant prospects for the true welfare of the people? No one will deny that the Supreme Court is no protection, and that the technically most exact interpretation of the constitutional document is no tool against these evils and dangers." [65]

Mohl's comments in his earlier works on American constitutionalism, discussed in the preceding pages, mainly reflect him as a *Staatsrechtler*. Only seldom does one come across remarks of a political nature. However, it would be wrong to assume that his writings on the United States are confined to strictly legal commentaries. His enthusiasm for America, reflected in repeated admonitions about the importance of the American experience for the development in Europe, was likely to let him see not only the formal framework of American constitutionalism, but also the way it functioned. His inclinations toward politics, evident in many of his works, were unlikely to be absent from his remarks on the United States. Thus Mohl appears as the "political professor," as one author has called him,[66] also in his writings on the United States, especially in those written at a later date. And whereas Mohl the *Staatsrechtler* impresses by his systematic juristic examination of American constitutional law, Mohl the political scientist is remarkable for his acute evaluation of the American political scene, for his penetrating analysis of democratic problems, as

[64] *Ibid.*, XII, 183–184.
[65] *Ibid.*, XII, 184–185.
[66] Angermann, *op. cit.*, p. 16.

well as for his truly prophetic prognoses. This is especially evident in reviews of de Tocqueville's *De la Démocratie en Amérique,* and the reports of the constitutional conventions of California and Massachusetts of 1849 and 1853, respectively.[67]

III

In his book of 1824, Mohl had written that the consequences of democratic ideas, "be they good or bad," developed most clearly in the United States.[68] And while in the works discussed so far Mohl hardly voiced sentiments against the democratic form of government, he did so in his political writings. This is evident in what seems like a natural place for a criticism of democracy, namely, his reviews of de Tocqueville's *De la Démocratie en Amérique,* published in 1836 and 1844.

In those reviews, Mohl, considering the situation in Germany, is aware of the inevitability of the march of democracy and admits that democratic ideas already exercised great influence even in aristocratic circles.[69] Looking for a country which could serve as a model democracy, he chooses the United States over France. "There can be no doubt that for the jurist the precise research on the legal situation in the United States must be of greater interest," since the United States is "the only prototype of the by no means very magnificent and sublime peaceful modification of democratism (*Demokratismus*). Thus only she can satisfy the cool intellect. The self-consistent formation of her whole legal, governmental, and political structure, not being impeded by violence and being facilitated by several . . . internal causes, is especially useful to a comprehensive understanding of what can be expected of democracy under modern conditions." [70] Mohl mentions several American institutions that demonstrate the drawbacks of democracy.

There is, for instance, education. Whereas the United States possesses many schools for technical skills, her institutions of higher learning leave much to be desired. This results in an "intellectual equality," which, in turn, constitutes a major support for democratic ideas on equality and freedom.[71] Democracy discriminates against talent and true education. The

---

[67] The reviews can be found in "Amerikanisches Staatsrecht," 8 *Kritische Zeitschrift* 359 (1836), and in "Entwicklung der Demokratie in Nordamerika und in der Schweiz," *ibid.,* XVI, 275 (1844). The discussion of the reports of the constitutional conventions can be found in Mohl, *Staatsrecht, Völkerrecht und Politik* (1860), I, 493. A shorter version of the latter work had already appeared as "Nordamerikanisches Staatsrecht" in 27 *Kritische Zeitschrift* 283 (1855).

[68] *Das Bundes-Staatsrecht der Vereinigten Staaten von Nord-Amerika,* p. xii.

[69] "Amerikanisches Staatsrecht," 8 *Kritische Zeitschrift* 359 f. (1836).

[70] *Ibid.,* VIII, 366.

[71] *Ibid.,* VIII, 377.

statesmen America could boast of during the War of Independence were the product of an aristocratic rather than a democratic environment. Under the latter, the man with a higher education will always be considered an alien and be disliked—the subject of envy. There is no freedom of the mind under majority rule.[72] "In no nation in the world is it as little advisable, even as little possible . . . to openly fight and frustrate a way of thinking that has been devised by the majority of the people. There are no accusations and no punishments. Nevertheless, resistance against the powerful masters of the nation is resented. It results in great disadvantages to the individual's civil and social position. . . . Thus in the United States the despotism oppressing the intellectual life is greater than in the most absolutist European nations. . . . Its natural results are narrow-mindedness and a passionate clinging to accepted values, a very mediocre degree of education, a want of excellent writers, in general—intellectual mediocrity." [73]

Mohl opposes unlimited freedom of the press, as it exists in America. In his opinion, newspapers appeal to human passions, to those who instigate the masses against everything that is above an average ability and intelligence. They get people used to superficialities and make them prone to sheer political excitement. They are a "curse for any serious literary occupation." They discourage people of means to participate in public affairs for fear their wealth might stir the envy of their fellow-men.[74] Being always treated unjustly by the masses, the rich are forced to live in seclusion or to cater to the masses. As soon as the individual's success is above average, democracy frustrates the achievement of its most immediate purpose, namely, an unlimited development of individuality.[75]

General suffrage has resulted in a destruction of the American aristocracy [76] and the election to public office of mediocre people who flattered the masses.[77] Owing to an abundance of legal codes and modifications of constitutions, American democracy is characterized by legal instability. This resulted in an absence of legal security, "one of the mainstays of exertion and enterprise, a main source of prosperity." [78]

[72] "Entwicklung der Demokratie in Nordamerika und in der Schweiz," *loc. cit.*, XVI, 288.
[73] *Ibid.*, XVI, 289. Similar his remark in *Staatsrecht, Völkerrecht und Politik*, I, 456.
[74] "Amerikanisches Staatsrecht," *loc. cit.*, VIII, 378–380; "Entwicklung der Demokratie in Nordamerika und in der Schweiz," *loc. cit.*, XVI, 289–291.
[75] *Ibid.*, XVI, 286–287.
[76] Mohl obviously had in mind what Jefferson called "natural aristocracy" in a letter to John Adams of Oct. 28, 1814. *Writings* (Ford ed., 1898), IX, 424.
[77] "Amerikanisches Staatsrecht," 8 *Kritische Zeitschrift* 372–374 (1836).
[78] "Entwicklung der Demokratie in Nordamerika und in der Schweiz," *loc. cit.*, XVI, 291–292. Mohl continues: "Only permanent legislation can develop well and bear rich fruit, and completely satisfy citizens, authorities, and courts. Frequent changes in the administration, however, result in useless spending, administrative insecurity, and clumsiness, and halt improvements that have hardly begun."

Legislative omnipotence is counterpoised by communal autonomy. This softens the "legal pressure by the majority which otherwise could be unbearable." [79]

Mohl's awareness of the major problem of democracy—the majority's want of measure with resultant dangers to the freedom of the individual —also is the keynote of his study on the development of democracy in the United States.[80] Being of the opinion that "every power induces man to extend it further, even beyond the limits of the permissible," [81] he complains that of all forms of government, democracies are most bare of institutions that prevent an abuse of power.[82] "By their very nature, representative democracies do not only fail to provide sufficient protection against a violent abuse of power by . . . the majority, but are especially . . . given to such an abuse." Representative democracies turn more and more democratic, and their faults become evident only with the march of democracy. This development can be clearly recognized in their "most important example," the United States. Where the "relatively aristocratic" Founding Fathers could devise a government that was rather independent of public opinion, "the whole spirit of the people in all strata has changed slowly, step by step, but inevitably, as if it were sliding on a slanted plane, toward more democratic beliefs and institutions. The Washingtons and Hamiltons were succeeded by the Jeffersons, and those by the Jacksons and Pierces—all of whom being typical expressions of the general popular will. The Federalists were defeated by the Democrats, and the latter are fought by Nullifiers and Know-nothings. . . . Now dangers can clearly be recognized which, only half a century ago, could not have been held possible by the sharpest mind." [83] Having stressed the importance for European constitutionalism of a knowledge of American democratic development, Mohl describes the situation in the United States in passages which seem worthwhile of translation:

> The idea of popular sovereignty is by no means any longer understood and applied in the United States as it was during the separation from England and even during the formation of the present federal constitution. To be sure, representative democracy was then conceived to be a form of government in which not only the government (*Staat*), its power and form, were founded upon the will of the people, but in which also the conduct of public affairs was to be carried out as desired by and with responsibility to, the people. By no means, however, was every human being part of the people in the legal-political (*staatsrechtlichen*) sense, but only the perfect, independent

[79] "Amerikanisches Staatsrecht," *loc. cit.*, VIII, 383.
[80] *Staatsrecht, Völkerrecht und Politik*, I, 493.
[81] *Ibid.*, I, 494.
[82] *Ibid.*, I, 496.
[83] *Ibid.*, I, 499–501.

man who had a material stake in the welfare of the whole. It was considered compatible with popular sovereignty that all affairs which were especially complicated and required special training, i.e., in case of doubt, all affairs which concerned the whole and not just some local part, would not be directly dealt with by the people but by men who were specifically selected for that task according to their ability. Especially, it was admitted that elections which required a precise knowledge of persons and things would be undertaken only by people suited to the task, just as it was considered necessary to protect the law (*Recht*) and the Constitution from the arbitrariness and instability of the masses by proper institutions. However, these ideas of the great statesmen of the War of Independence and the people that had won freedom have now long been abandoned. They are considered narrow and perhaps even undignified imperfections. Now, every individual that is not disqualified for a few specific reasons is recognized as a fully qualified member of the people who can, in particular, participate in all elections. The people demand the greatest possible direct share in the affairs of the state. They are credited with possessing a quite special, nearly mysterious, ability to manage these affairs well. Consequently, popular election of all officials is requested. A tenure as short as possible for all positions is said to be a prerequisite for justice and expediency. The abolition of all barriers which could restrict the will of the temporary majority is aimed at as a necessary result of popular rule.

One was, however, not content with bringing about theoretical changes, but, on several occasions, realized these changes in practice. A number of institutions which the founders of American independence and internal liberty considered indispensable for the protection of a reasonable and lawful liberty has already become a victim of the new concept of democracy. And there can be no doubt that further demands, which not long ago would have been regarded as completely senseless, will gradually be granted. Already now, after this practice had started in the then more than half-wild State of Ohio at the beginning of this century, the judges are elected directly by the people in two thirds of all the States for the short period of a few years only. Similarly, administrative positions, which previously were filled by governors or legislatures, have fallen into the hands of general elections. The councillorships which used to be attached to the Governors in some of the States for advice on pardons and on the filling of offices, are abolished in order that the highest officials, being deprived of the support of their responsible assistants, may be completely personally exposed. People can vote who have no pertinent ties whatsoever to the State and often have not even been residents. The logical evolution of general human and civil rights has already proceeded to serious attempts at extending all active and passive political rights to women. The new States that entered the Union not only adopted democratic constitutions which essentially deviated from older patterns—the deviations being greater the later the new State was admitted—but also, the constitutions of most of the older States were amended in the same direction, often several times and always becoming more democratic. Occasionally, a weak majority has resisted this trend, as, for instance, in Massachusetts. However, in the long run, it can hardly be expected to win. To be sure, this movement exists, for the time being, in the particular States only, and the forms of the federal state have not been changed so far. However, it would be a great mistake to believe the neodemocratic spirit would not also be evident in the federal government. Aside from the fact that that government, as everything else in the United States, is absolutely under the control of public opinion, a most immediate influence is secured by the fact that elections for the two houses of Congress are indirectly or directly determined by the legislation of the particular States. Not only the House of Representatives, even the Senate has thereby gained an atmosphere which is far removed from the spirit prevailing during the first decades of the Union. Also, from Jefferson on, the majority of presidents, for reasons of a short popularity, has pursued the shortsighted and egoistic policy of following the democratic current and, if possible, of doing away with barriers that stood in its way.

The consequences of these changes are now becoming discernible, and they are by no means pleasant. There is general agreement that the statesmen now at the helm are, in both intellectual and moral respects, far inferior to their predecessors. In legislative assemblies, including Congress (at any rate, the House of Representatives), there are quite a few crude and unable men, whose behavior is not seldom a disgrace for the country, and whose reputation, as to honesty and altruism, is very bad. Who could forget the base maltreatment of Senator Sumner by another senator on the floor of the Senate? Or the scandalous fistfights among Congressmen? It is openly admitted by members of Congress that any bill could become law if sufficient money was spent on it. The waste of federal funds by officials and the aiding and abetting of fraud by popular representatives whose task is supervision is absolutely unbelievable. The wide extension of suffrage and eligibility and the admission of many incompetent people to elections brought about a highly corruptible class of professional politicians, whose influence must be bought and who, after an electoral victory, obtain public offices as "spoils." In no nation in the world has justice less prospect for victory if it collides with a great and vital interest of the crowd. No proof is needed to show how much, even in the affairs of daily life, this state of insecurity is further increased by the short-term election of judges. As can amply be seen in the discussions of the constitutional convention of Massachusetts which will be discussed below, prudent men already openly recognize that popular elections of judges for short terms have brought about the decline of the courts and decreased their respectability. The administrations of some of the biggest cities, as, for instance, New York, have fallen into the hands of the mob, and are unbelievably poor. United States foreign affairs are characterized by arrogance, disregard for the rights of the weak, a giving in by the government to unjust and imprudent demands by internal parties. They have already led to very blameworthy steps and will lead to more. In her relations with other nations, the new American democracy is as sensitive and demanding as it is inconsiderate and unjust. Her refusal to permit searches of ships that are suspected of carrying slaves, her open aiding and abetting freebooters which on their own responsibility attack weak foreign states in an attempt to conquer them, her rejection of the resolution of the Congress of Paris concerning the abolition of privateering—all these are shameless acts.

These are bad conditions, the more so since they obviously have not yet reached their climax. First, with respect to internal affairs, the modern ideas of democracy will develop further, until the many evils which will be the natural result of this development will require an examination of the righteousness of the starting point and of taking a new direction. However, in all probability it will be a long time before this turning back will take place, the more so since the allegedly freest country in the world is ruled by a tyranny of public opinion which does not suffer any opposition to momentary currents or opinions accepted by the crowd. Second, the unprecedented increase of the power of the United States, which will continue for a long time to come, provides those who exercise power and formulate policy with more and more means to put through the unjust and antisocial demands of the crowd, and the latter, with an increasingly higher opinion of itself and with a greater and greater lust for abuse. It is very dubious whether and when those hurt and threatened will join in an effort to put a halt to such a spirit.

It is absolutely necessary to obtain a clear picture of this march of ultrademocratic ideas, in order that one may not be deceived about the true state of affairs by a phraseology that has remained unchanged and by the federal Constitution that up to now has not been amended. The reading of good and honest writings on public affairs in the United States can naturally be recommended [Mohl suggests Calhoun's writings "on democratic government," Lieber's *On Civil Liberty and Self-Government*, and Cornelius de Witt's article on Jefferson in the *Revue des deux mondes*, 1858 and 1859]. However, an even clearer and more penetrating view is provided by a direct acquaintance with facts. In descriptions, the truth is easily clouded by subjectivity. Besides, it is very difficult for an American to plainly express his thoughts and fears with respect to the subject in question. To be sure, the press is absolutely free. Neither law nor police prevent the citizen from mentioning any fact or any opinion. However, it is also well-known that the general submission of opinions and of external behavior under the will of the majority makes unadvisable, perhaps even inadmissible, deviations from what is generally accepted. Everything which somehow appears like an attack upon the government (*Regierungsrecht*) and upon the excellence of the people, is considered a sin against the Holy Ghost. Especially he who wants to exert an influence in State affairs or to occupy public office, would commit political suicide if he rebuked the people for thinking too highly of themselves and told them that their progressing direct interferences in public affairs are of evil consequences. Therefore, one can expect of those concerned, who are probably well aware of the evil, only slight hints and indirect proposals. . . .[84]

This opinion on the trend of political life in the United States is not a pleasant one. However, neither does it derive from a general antipathy against the land and the people, nor was it arrived at easily. But the more one sees in the institutions of North America a new form of legal life with worldwide historical significance, the more remarkable this extension of human attempts toward an adequate order of the state is for the political scientist, the more impressive the growth of the might of the transatlantic empire is: the greater the apprehension with which one must observe the changes in the innermost nature of things. The continually growing obsession that everything done by a crowd is right and reasonable because they are doing it; the increasing reluctance of providing public officers with sufficient power to conquer illegal attempts, although they derive their competences from the people and hold office for a short period only; the more and more openly expressed animosity toward all independent positions although such positions are the price to be paid for good achievements; in a word, the progressively expanding evolution of a false democratic spirit is already now the source of great evil, and threatens with more in the future. One cannot help the conviction that what in the last analysis is a wrong conception of justice and freedom must in the end result in a condition which is internally deadly to morals, and for other states—highly dangerous on account of disregard for law and greed; a new Roman Empire, driven by the perpetual restlessness and inconsiderate activity of the crowd, inclined toward violent attacks upon those who are weaker owing to presumptuousness and a want of moral feelings, instigated by ambition to conquests everywhere. Although the government is unable to resist party-passions and inhuman and heartless racial oppression as well as insurgent desires in the interior, it is sufficiently strong and organized to let these faults appear suspicious to foreign nations. Duty and right are slowly but increasingly replaced by momentary arbitrariness, the conduct of public affairs is transferred from the hands of statesmen into those of the seducers of the people (*Volksverführer*). However, it is highly dubious whether the magnitude of the evil will bring about a cure in good time. And the opin-

[84] *Ibid.*, I, 506–511.

ion which can not infrequently be heard in Europe, that finally things will end up in monarchy, is completely wrong. Events point into the opposite direction. And it is much more probable that the history of attempts to organize the living together of human beings will be enriched by a new great example, but not by a success.[85]

IV

In summary, it can be said that Mohl's remarks on the United States, be they of a strictly legal or of a political kind, reveal him, the champion of the *Rechtsstaat,* as a true Liberal. Although he was not opposed to social change and would take into consideration the interest of the community, his main concern always remained the freedom of the individual.[86] He thus could be an admirer of the *Federalist* as well as of the *Disquisition on Government,* classics that agree on the protection of the individual as the end of government as strongly as they disagree on the nature of the American Union as a means for achieving that end.[87] As a proponent of the type of popular government that had been established by the Founders of the American Republic, he had to oppose the "ultrademocratic" trends of the Jacksonian Revolution. When American democracy marched on, Mohl did not permit himself to be swept away by the democratic tide. The "political professor" could not very well be a political opportunist.

For America, this was a blessing. It would indeed be wrong if Mohl's criticisms of America were taken the wrong way. He himself hoped that they would not.[88] Unlike his contemporary de Tocqueville, Mohl never visited the United States. Like the great Frenchman, he appreciated her merits, and yet remained sufficiently detached to recognize that "the United States is by no means a paradise inhabited by angels, and her insti-

---

[85] *Ibid.,* I, 532–533.

[86] Landsberg, *loc. cit.,* p. 408, commenting on Mohl's *Die Polizeiwissenschaft nach den Grundsätzen des Rechtstaates.*

[87] For Mohl's comments on the Federalist Papers, see especially the translation of his review of Story's *Commentaries* in 15 *American Jurist* 335 (1835); *Die Geschichte und Literatur der Staatswissenschaften,* I, 509, 548–551; *Staatsrecht, Völkerrecht und Politik,* I, 502. Mohl's comments on Calhoun's *A Disquisition on Government,* and *A Discourse on The Constitution and Government of the United States* (works Mohl referred to as Calhoun's writings "on democratic government" in the passage quoted above) can be found in *Die Geschichte und Literatur der Staatswissenschaften,* I, 568–573; *Staatsrecht, Völkerrecht und Politik,* I, 510.—Of course, even from the *Federalist* one may imply that, should the national government abuse its power and oppress the individual, the States can reassert rights they originally conceded to the national government. Cf. the author's *The Federalist—A Classic on Federalism and Free Government* (1960), pp. 281–285.

[88] *Staatsrecht, Völkerrecht und Politik,* I, 535.

tutions are not of utopian excellence." [89] At times, he would advise his German audience not to adopt institutions he found well suited to Americans, recognizing the danger of transferring historically grown forms into different environments. His honesty about a nation he had liked from the days of his youth was, as far as German interest in America is concerned, a definite asset. It gave his work the aura of objectivity, which, in turn, was likely to awaken the Germans' curiosity in, and admiration for, the United States.

There can be no doubt that ever since Mohl, American constitutionalism has had an important impact upon Germany. That impact can be recognized with respect to all the major features of American government, namely, federalism, democracy, and judicial review—features Mohl, demonstrating his clear view for the essential, had emphasized in his writings on the United States.

From the eighteen-fifties on, there has come forth abundant German literature on federalism. Waitz's classic on the nature of the federal state [90] was as unable to solve the problem of federalism as the *Federalist* had been.[91] Consequently, the discussion over national power and states' rights continued, especially after Bismarck, the founder of the Second Reich, had expressed himself as ambiguously as the *Federalist* on the nature of the union.[92] Under the Empire, Max von Seydel became the German counterpart of John C. Calhoun, just as opinions similar to those of John Marshall, Joseph Story, and Daniel Webster were voiced by Albert Haenel and Paul Laband. As in the United States, the nationalists had their way. After Germany had emerged as a unitary state with strong federal features under the Weimar constitution, the debate over the nature of the Reich continued, the major exponents of the opposing views being Hans Nawiasky and Gerhard Anschütz.[93]

An American impact can also be seen in the case of popular government. Although German democratic institutions were strongly influenced from France, American ideas of representation naturally imposed themselves in a country that was federal rather than unitary. Furthermore, the

---

[89] *Die Geschichte und Literatur der Staatswissenschaften*, I, 524.

[90] Georg Waitz, "Das Wesen des Bundesstaates," *Allgemeine Monatsschrift für Wissenschaft und Literatur* (1853), p. 494, republished in *Grundzüge der Politik* (1862), p. 153.

[91] Cf. the author's *The Federalist*, pp. 266–275.

[92] In 1866, Bismarck stated as to the nature of the North German League which was about to be formed: "Man wird sich in der *Form* mehr an den *Staatenbund* halten müssen, diesem aber *praktisch* die Natur des *Bundesstaates* geben, mit elastischen, unscheinbaren aber weitgreifenden Ausdrücken." Quoted by Gerhard Anschütz, *Drei Leitgedanken der Weimarer Reichsverfassung* (1923), p. 8.

[93] Discussions of German federalism can be found in Rupert Emerson, *State and Sovereignty in Modern Germany* (1928), and Herman Finer, *Theory and Practice of Modern Government* (1950). See also Anschütz, *Drei Leitgedanken der Weimarer Reichsverfassung*.

office of the chief executive, as far as its power and stability are concerned, came to resemble that in the United States rather than that in the Third Republic. When the office became elective under the Weimar constitution, the direct mode of election was more similar to that of the American than that of the French president. After the Germans had learned their lesson of "ultrademocracy," to use a Mohlian expression, their Basic Law of 1949 mitigated democracy by taking its guidance largely from the United States. A bill of rights which even restricted the legislature was included, and provision made for judicial review.[94]

The latter, "most distinctive feature of the American constitutional system,"[95] made its appearance in German constitutionalism at a rather late stage. When it was finally accepted, it was accepted in a most comprehensive way. Mohl, it will be remembered, great as his admiration for the American institution was, doubted whether the judges had the right to invalidate legislation under a separation of powers. German jurists under the Imperial and Weimar constitutions argued, *a fortiori*, that judicial review was not possible under a parliamentary system of government. However, after some beginnings toward its establishment were made in the twenties, judicial review became one of the outstanding institutions of the Bonn Republic.[96]

In view of that addition to German constitutional law, it is probably no exaggeration to say that German constitutionalism has been more influenced by the United States than by any other nation. Mohl, clearly envisaging the importance of the future world power for constitutional democracy, was the first great German *Staatsrechtler* and political scientist who admonished his countrymen to study American institutions.[97] Fortunately, his pleading was not in vain.[98]

---

[94] See Hajo Holborn, "The Influence of the American Constitution on the Weimar Constitution," in Conyers Read, ed., *The Constitution Reconsidered* (1938), p. 285; Paul G. Kauper, "The Constitutions of West Germany and the United States: A Comparative Study," 58 *Michigan Law Review* 1097–1102, 1102–1137, 1157–1162 (1960).

[95] Edward S. Corwin, "Judicial Review," *Encyclopaedia of the Social Sciences* (1932), VIII, 457.

[96] See Carl J. Friedrich, "The Issue of Judicial Review in Germany," 43 *Political Science Quarterly* 188 (1928); Taylor Cole, "The West German Federal Constitutional Court: An Evaluation After Six Years," 20 *Journal of Politics* 278 (1958); Paul G. Kauper, *op. cit.*, pp. 1162–1181; Hans G. Rupp, "Judicial Review in the Federal Republic of Germany," 9 *American Journal of Comparative Law* 29 (1960).

[97] See *Das Bundes-Staatsrecht der Vereinigten Staaten von Nord-Amerika*, pp. vii–xiii; the translation of Mohl's review of Story's *Commentaries* in 14 *American Jurist*, 332–333 (1835); "Amerikanisches Staatsrecht," *loc. cit.*, VIII, 366; "Nordamerikanisches Staatsrecht," *loc. cit.*, XII, 163–164; *ibid.*, XXVII, 283; *Die Geschichte der Literatur und Staatswissenschaften*, I, 249–250, 509–513, 598–599; *Staatsrecht, Völkerrecht und Politik*, I, 500–501.

[98] For German attitudes toward the United States from 1776 to our day, see Ernst Fraenkel, *Amerika im Spiegel des deutschen politischen Denkens* (1959).

VI

Justices and Scholars

11

Supreme Court Biography
and the Study of Public Law

J. W. Peltason

Biography of Supreme Court justices, as distinguished from more general historical analysis, dates from 1916 when Albert J. Beveridge published the first volume of his monumental study of Chief Justice Marshall.[1] Prior to that time there were books about Supreme Court justices, sketches by devoted sons, collections of opinions, analyses of doctrines, and chronologies of life and works, but a study in depth of the kind to which we have recently been accustomed dates from the end of World War I.[*]

In addition to the extended biography, biographically-oriented studies have also become popular, the kind usually entitled, *The Constitutional Views of Mr. Justice So and So*. These books often include outlines of the life of their subject, but their central focus is on published opinions and decisions.[2] The biographical vogue has also been reflected at the level of doctoral dissertations: between 1951 and 1954 over one-fourth of the

---

[1] Albert Beveridge, *The Life of John Marshall* (1916).

[*] This interest in biography coincides with the rise of judicial realism. It seems plausible that the realists' emphasis upon the subjective element in judicial decision-making would stimulate an interest in biography. But it is difficult to document any such relationship. In fact many biographers, while rejecting mechanical jurisprudence, have not been sympathetic to psychological or sociological approaches to the study of law: at least there is little evidence that they have been much influenced by these approaches. Biographers tend to come from the fields of history, law, journalism, and within political science from the "historical-philosophical-legal school" rather than from the behavioral side.

[2] For example, Clyde E. Jacobs, *Justice Frankfurter and Civil Liberties* (1961). Samuel J. Konefsky, *The Constitutional World of Mr. Justice Frankfurter* (1939).

doctoral dissertations in political science then underway in the field of public law were biographical in character, and of the seventy dissertations started in this field since 1957, fourteen are of this nature.[3]

As a result of all this scholarship and without attempting to list every biography, we have full-scale studies of Marshall by Beveridge,[4] Taney by Swisher,[5] Waite by Trimble,[6] Taft by Pringle,[7] Hughes by Pusey,[8] Fuller by King,[9] Stone by Mason,[10] Miller by Fairman,[11] Brandeis by Mason,[12] Field by Swisher,[13] W. Johnson by Morgan,[14] Sutherland by Paschal,[15] Davis by King,[16] and the first two volumes of the Holmes biography by Howe.[17]

Who remains as a subject for biography? Fifty-three of the ninety-five men, including those now sitting, are "available." Some such as Gabriel Duvall, Ward Hunt, Samuel Blatchford, Alford Moore, W. B. Woods, Thomas Todd, H. H. Burton, and S. Minton might have left important documents, but they are not men to inspire many scholars to devote the time and energy necessary to produce their biographies. It would be undesirable to develop scholarly one-upmanship in which students are encouraged to find a relatively obscure justice to claim as their own—a vice, so we are told, sometimes practiced by our colleagues in literature who "discover" some long forgotten writer "because all the major ones have already been taken." And this is still unnecessary, for there are major figures "unbiographed," Joseph Story, David J. Brewer, and Noah Swayne,[18] among others.

Samuel J. Konefsky, *Chief Justice Stone and the Supreme Court* (1945). Samuel Hendel, *Charles Evans Hughes and The Supreme Court* (1951). Charlotte Williams, *Hugo L. Black: A Study in The Judicial Process* (1950). John P. Frank, *Mr. Justice Black, the Man and his Opinions* (1949). Claude Peter Magrath, *Morrison R. Waite: The Triumph of Character* (1963).

[3] From the *American Political Science Review*. Beginning in 1957, the *Review* listed only those dissertations started each year. Despite the large number of such dissertations, relatively few of them have been published as yet.

[4] See footnote 1.

[5] C. B. Swisher, *Roger B. Taney* (1935).

[6] Bruce R. Trimble, *Chief Justice Waite, Defender of The Public Interest* (1938).

[7] Henry F. Pringle, *The Life and Times of William Howard Taft* (1939).

[8] Merlo J. Pusey, *Charles Evans Hughes* (1951).

[9] W. L. King, *Melville Weston Fuller* (1950).

[10] A. T. Mason, *Harlan Fiske Stone, Pillar of The Law* (1956).

[11] Charles Fairman, *Mr. Justice Miller and the Supreme Court, 1862–1890* (1939).

[12] A. T. Mason, *Brandeis, a Free Man's Life* (1946).

[13] C. B. Swisher, *Stephen J. Field, Craftsman of the Law* (1930).

[14] Donald G. Morgan, *Justice William Johnson, The First Dissenter* (1954).

[15] Joel Francis Paschal, *Mr. Justice Sutherland, a Man Against The State* (1951).

[16] W. L. King, *Lincoln's Manager: David Davis* (1960).

[17] Mark DeWolfe Howe, *Justice Oliver Wendell Holmes, The Shaping Years, 1841–1870*, I (1957); *The Proving Years 1870–1882*, II (1963).

[18] For Story there are only a few articles and W. W. Story, ed., *Life and Letters of Joseph Story* (1851). Professor Alan Westin is at work on a biography of the first Mr. Justice Harlan.

What does Supreme Court biography add to our knowledge about American constitutional development and the American judicial process? What are biographers' objectives and what are their intellectual assumptions? By these questions we do not mean to inquire into the motives of the authors, but into the advantages and disadvantages of viewing public law through a biographical lens. (John A. Garraty quoted one commentator: "only three motives for writing biography; one wishes either to erect a monument to a departed loved one, or to set an example for future generations, or to make money.") [19]

To paraphrase Garraty, whereas science's tendency is to generalize, biography's tendency is to particularize.[20] Speaking in general terms, biography has attracted scholars who are not primarily interested in developing generalized theories about the role of the Supreme Court in the American political system. To them a biography is not so much a case study from which generalized knowledge can be developed or in which hypotheses can be tested, but a description of the life of a certain individual, an intellectual exercise carrying its own utility. And, of course, judicial biography is useful for purposes other than the systematic study of public law and does serve objectives other than to contribute data for the development of more generalized explanations of behavior.

Biography has an inspirational function. As Professor Charles Fairman writes, "The practical reward of knowing judicial biography is obvious: the great jurists are wise counsellors." [21] One could quibble by pointing out that of all public officers, judges would seem least in need of biography in order to spread their wise counsel. Their duty as jurists requires them to write detailed explanations for each of their decisions; one can secure the benefit of their wisdom without having to read their biographies. Nonetheless, the nonjudicial deeds and views and the examples in the life of a great man who also happens to be a judge undoubtedly inspire, challenge, and enlighten.

Biography is also an excellent medium for instruction. To personalize great events and to write history in terms of individual challenge and response is to make history attractive. The *United States Supreme Court Reports* are not likely to be the reading fare for large numbers of people, but the life and works of a particular justice may invite their attention and through a biography they may become acquainted with major constitutional disputes and leading Supreme Court decisions.

Judicial biography is also a convenient framework for the study of ideas and for discussion of public policy, that is, as a branch of intellectual history and of political philosophy. In this use of biography, the concern is

[19] John A. Garraty, *The Nature of Biography* (1957), p. 105.
[20] *Ibid.*, p. 116.
[21] Charles Fairman, "Mr. Justice Bradley," in Allison Dunham and Philip B. Kurland, eds., *Mr. Justice* (1956), p. 70.

with ideas, not the judge, and the materials under study are the published records. Since many of the major American ideological conflicts have taken place within the context of constitutional disputes, Supreme Court biography is a useful device to delineate these conflicts. Moreover, the constitutional philosophy of an individual jurist seldom represents his own idiosyncratic position but symbolizes a much wider consensus. A Supreme Court justice of stature is a spokesman for and representative of important segments of our society. To analyze the thought of a Chief Justice Marshall, a Justice Sutherland, or a Justice Holmes is to deal with a fighting faith, with ideas that have consequences.[22]

Biography is also justified as a way to hold judges to account: a political mechanism of democracy. Professor Edmond Cahn has written along these lines . . . "anonymous hands may become irresponsible hands and . . . no man is fit to judge unless the people can ultimately pass judgment on him." [23]

Devoted sons are not the only persons concerned with saving reputations, demonstrating greatness, and exonerating conduct. Historians have been especially attracted to serving as spokesmen for History, sometimes reviving reputations and "proving" that prior scholars underestimated the contributions of a particular individual, sometimes "proving" that earlier historians overvalued a particular individual. Although it may have no immediate relevance to the study of public law or to our understanding of the judicial process to "prove" that Justice Frankfurter is being misunderstood or that Justice Black's position is most likely to preserve democracy, perhaps judges are in special need of scholar-champions. Unlike Presidents and Senators, they may not take to the public platform to justify their actions.

Biography is also history and history is essential to a comprehensive understanding of the American judicial process. The eyes of a Supreme Court justice are important vantage points through which to view the world. And one does not have to accept the "hero-in-history" position to recognize that our Constitution would have been different if different men had been appointed to the Court. But biography has its dangers as a technique for writing history, and it is an especially dangerous method for dealing with the history of the judiciary. By its concentration on an individual jurist, it may lead to an exaggeration of his role, give a misleading notion of his area of discretion, and by divorcing him from the context in which

[22] For example, Wallace Mendelson, *Justices Black and Frankfurter: Conflicts in the Court* (1961). In this volume Professor Mendelson illuminates competing concepts of judicial policy and makes his own case in behalf of the tradition represented by Justice Frankfurter.
[23] Edmond Cahn, "Eavesdropping on Justice," in *The Nation*, Vol. 184, July 5, 1957, p. 15.

he decides, it may minimize the subtle but powerful conditioning limits within which he operates.

The relatively large numbers of legislators have discouraged such a biographical approach to the study of the legislative process and have contributed to a depersonalization of legislative history, to the advantage of such history. Under these circumstances there is less of a danger that we will get explanations of legislative decisions by examining the views of the individual congressmen and concluding that a particular law was passed because a majority of the congressmen felt it was in the public interest. But the relatively small number of Supreme Court justices invites just this kind of superficial analysis and explanation.

Justice, then Professor, Frankfurter once lamented ". . . American legal history has done very little to rescue the Court from the limbo of impersonality." [24] The contrary seems to be the case. American legal history, especially when dealing with the Supreme Court and constitutional issues, seems to be infused with the cult of the great judicial personality. For example, scholars frequently explain the expansion of the national government's functions as an outgrowth of John Marshall's decision in *McCulloch* v. *Maryland* or attribute the great political and legal battles of the end of the nineteenth century to a conflict between Chief Justice Waite and Justice Field. And the rise of judicial realism reinforced this tendency to view constitutional disputes as involving only differences among sitting jurists. For realism exposed the fact that judicial decisions are not controlled by past precedents and emphasized the wide area of judicial discretion. (Obviously there is judicial choice-making, but only within restricted channels, the channels being established not by precedent but by the political system.)

This concentration on the individual jurist and on the Supreme Court as an isolated institution conforms to the canons of conventional constitutional interpretation which furnish judges and their biographers (especially if they are students of constitutional law) with categories to "explain" decisions. But these explanations are often nothing but stylized choices between ready-made tautological models: they give no indication of the degree to which the positions taken by the Court reflect segments of the total system; they lead to correlations of trivial significance. Thus we get explanations, though they are more elegantly stated, of the decisions of the Supreme Court of the 1890's, such as: the Court struck down many welfare laws because a majority of the justices felt these laws violated the Fourteenth Amendment and they felt the laws violated this Amendment because they were conservatives, and so on. Or the Supreme Court's 1954 decision in *Brown* v. *Board of Education* reversing the Plessy

[24] Felix Frankfurter, *The Commerce Clause Under Marshall, Taney and Waite* (1937), p. 6.

decision is "explained" by saying that the individual jurists who were sitting on the Supreme Court in 1954 felt that racial segregation in public schools violates the Fourteenth Amendment because of its discriminatory impact on Negro school children.

The focus on individual jurists leads to even more circularity. Obviously if the goal is to explain the behavior, say, of Justice Black, his values are important and are related to his decisions. Yet to say that Justice Black's votes against laws restricting free speech grow out of his concept of democracy, valid as it may be and useful as it is, it hardly adds much to our understanding of the judicial process, no more than to explain Justice Sutherland's conservative decisions as an outgrowth of his conservative philosophy.

Although the biographical concentration on a single jurist may reinforce this tendency to isolate the Supreme Court from the total system and to consider its decisions as flowing from its own self-contained world, biography need not do so. Beveridge's *Life of Marshall* is an excellent example of a biography which is history, which treats Marshall, his Court, and his great decisions as part of the ongoing conflicts of which they were both cause and consequence. Similarly, Swisher's studies of Taney and Field are essentially excellent histories, the justices are in context.

Judicial biography could also be used to study psychological variables, to provide case histories exploring the relationship between personality and decisions. There is a growing body of literature attempting to develop profiles of the relation between political attitudes and personality patterns. As yet no judicial biographer has used this literature. Although it would be dangerous to place much reliance on this data as applied to a single judge, biography could serve as a monographic source. But it may be that to relate behavior of a judge to his personality requires more sophisticated training in disciplines other than history, law, political science, or journalism, the backgrounds of almost all the judicial biographers.

Most judicial biographers make little attempt to describe the man behind the robe except in formal, heroic terms. When biographers do deal with the private, as distinguished from the public man, it is at the surface level. A child is born, a child dies, a man is married, these events which loom large in the life of a man, even a judge, are mentioned in passing or dismissed in a paragraph or two. Relations with a wife, children, and associates are usually treated in delicate terms. One gets the impression that no Supreme Court justice ever had a fight with his wife or a cross word with a son—perhaps this is what is meant by a "judicial temperament."

The failure of biographers to concern themselves, except in terms of chronology, with the private lives of their subjects is probably not a loss for students of public law.* Personality studies might conceivably be fruitful for understanding essentially political phenomena if we could learn from such studies whether judicial offices attract or repel people with particular characteristics, as Professor Lasswell alleges is the case for administrative and legislative offices [25]—and whether, if so, this phenomenon has systematic consequences for policy choices. Yet despite all the conventional wisdom dispensed at gatherings of bar associations, judicial biographers have been unconcerned to determine whether great judges are by temperament of an order different from lesser men, or have failed to investigate the relation between personality and behavior.†

These then are some of the uses of biography. But questions remain. Do judicial biographies tell us something about Supreme Court decisions which cannot be acquired from reading the decisions themselves? Do the biographies tell us something about how judicial decisions are made? Or to paraphrase Professor Cahn and use his words in a context other than he intended, are biographical studies "mere Pablum to satisfy idle curiosity or do they furnish useful and valuable aids in understanding the judicial function?" [25a]

The juxtaposition in biography of life and works would seem to rest on an assumption that the works of a man can be better understood in terms of his life and his life is more meaningful in terms of his work. Beveridge specifically asserted: "John Marshall's greatest opinions cannot be fully understood without considering his previous life and experiences. An account of Marshall the frontiersman, soldier, legislator, lawyer, politician, diplomat, and statesman, and of the conditions he faced in each of these capacities, is essential to a comprehension of Marshall the constitutional jurist and of the problems he solved." [26] Yet when it comes to explaining the behavior of any particular judge, the interrelations between his background and his decisions has yet to be demonstrated. In fact, when Beveridge dealt with Marshall's great decisions, he ignored Marshall's background. Volumes III and IV of Beveridge's work which deal

---

* As might be expected one of the best pictures of the private life of a judge is by a novelist-biographer, Catherine Drinker Bowen. In her *Yankee From Olympus* (1944) she gives Holmes a three-dimensional quality. On the other hand, her treatment of Holmes as a judge is superficial.

[25] Harold Lasswell, "Political Constitution and Character," in 46 *Psychoanalysis and the Psychoanalytic Review*, pp. 14, 15 (1960).

† There are exceptions. For example, Beveridge explains Marshall's ability to dominate the Court as an extension of his general qualities of inspiring others and his sensitivity to their feelings. Other biographers have commented on how the personality of the Chief Justice has effected the level of dissent on the Court.

[25a] Cahn, *op. cit.*

[26] Beveridge, *op. cit.*, I, v–vi.

with Marshall's years on the Supreme Court are independent histories, comprehensible without any knowledge of Volumes I and II which cover Marshall's pre-judicial experiences.

When biographers do try to relate background materials to specific decisions, their conclusions are questionable. For example, a biographer of Justice Frankfurter wrote: "It would be quite natural for him to feel sympathy for those seeking to gain or retain American citizenship, since he himself had attained that status derivatively through the naturalization of his father. . . . [But in fact] he has probably leaned over backwards to avoid the charge of discrimination in favor of those with a similar foreign background." [27] Thus, no matter how Justice Frankfurter decides these cases, for or against naturalized citizens, his background could be used to explain the decisions. And such explanations ignore the fact that other justices with different backgrounds have both agreed and differed with Justice Frankfurter. Perhaps the proper conclusion is that to know whether a justice is a naturalized or natural-born citizen tells us nothing about the kind of decisions he is likely to make in citizenship cases. Along these same lines Professor Swisher said of Justice Field, "Through his associations [while in Washington serving on the Supreme Court] he came to know the points of view and the political, economic, and social philosophies of the representatives of prominent political groups and economic interests. If he came to know these types, however, he was virtually cut off from farmers, laborers, and small, independent property owners who made up a large part of the population. He saw them around him but he did not meet them socially, he did not come into intellectual and emotional contact with them. These limitations may have been the basis for the bias in outlook of which he was accused in the years to come." [28] Yet precisely the same environmental conditioning is the lot of all Supreme Court justices. It could be just as readily concluded, if in fact Field's associates were among more conservative gentlemen than say Holmes, that the biases caused the associations as it could be said the associations caused the biases.

These comments are not intended as criticism of the biographers but as indications that socio-economic variables are of limited utility in studying judicial behavior. Ninety-five justices provide too few instances for statistical correlations. Of the few scholars who have tried to relate background to behavior, Professor John Schmidhauser has made the most valiant attempt. His study provides much useful information, but perhaps its greatest significance is that it suggests that such studies offer little

[27] Helen Shirley Thomas, *Felix Frankfurter, Scholar on the Bench* (1960), p. 250.
[28] Carl B. Swisher, *Stephen J. Field, Craftsman of the Law* (1930).

promise in understanding the course of Supreme Court decisions.[29] *

Some time ago Robert K. Carr wrote, "It is entirely possible that a careful examination of the personalities and the economic and social backgrounds of the eighty men who have served on the Supreme Court would prove to be as valuable and as realistic an approach to the American Constitution as the more usual law school approach which lays so much emphasis upon the study of cases, the rule of *stare decisis,* and of fixed legal principles." [30] This may be so, but fixed legal principles or biographical explanations are not the only alternatives, and the equivalence in utility between the two approaches may be at a low level. For when it comes to the use of background data to understand the decisions of Supreme Court jurists, we are left with the nonuseful, self-evident generalization that judges, like all men, are products of their heredity and environment and that their behavior as judges is conditioned by their experiences as men.

But biography does have one unique and major contribution: to describe what happens behind the scenes, to get at those factors in the immediate environment of the judges which influenced behavior, in other words, to describe the intimate world of the judge.

Briefs, oral arguments before the Court, and the written opinions and decisions are the only materials normally available to students of the judicial process. What happens between presentations to the Court and the handing down of its decisions is a closely guarded secret. As Professor Frankfurter wrote, "The intimacies of the conference room—the workshop of the living Constitution—are illuminations denied to the historian," [31] a fact he decried. And to study the judicial process without getting at this lacuna is as incomplete as it would be to study the legislative process by only looking at the formal speeches of the legislators and their votes. Scholars working on the legislative or executive process have a wealth of information as to the workings of the Congress or the Presidency or the state legislatures or the governors. But students of the judiciary have only what the judges or their papers reveal, and this component is chiefly available via biography.†

[29] John R. Schmidhauser, "The Justices of the Supreme Court: A Collective Portrait," 3 *Midwest Journal of Political Science* 1 (1959).

* Schmidhauser concludes somewhat tentatively, "It is not at all clear that the social and political background factors in themselves may serve as reliable indicators of precise patterns of judicial behavior." (p. 48.) However, he suggests that it would be wrong to conclude that background factors have had no influences. (p. 49.) The problem is that beyond this generalization it is difficult to determine what the influence is.

[30] Robert K. Carr, *The Supreme Court and Judicial Review* (1942), p. 235. Quoted by John R. Schmidhauser, *op. cit.,* p. 1.

[31] Frankfurter, *op. cit.,* p. 9.

† Of course, full scale biography is not the only way to use these materials. For example, Professor Walter F. Murphy's "In His Own Image: Mr. Chief Justice Taft

Unless a judicial biography provides information about the life of the Court as a functioning institution, and most good biographies do, its usefulness to those interested in the study of the American judiciary is somewhat restricted. Therefore, it is difficult to understand the vehemence of some who criticized Professor A. T. Mason for using in his magnificent biography of Harlan Fiske Stone the Stone papers to provide an extraordinarily detailed account of the Supreme Court at work. Mason is not the only biographer to be concerned with these questions. He differs from the others only in the detail he had available to use and in that he revealed information about the struggles within the Court involving justices who were still serving on the Court.

As a result, Mason's biography is far more than a description of the events in the life of Harlan Fiske Stone. It is more than an interpretation by Mason of Stone's previously published constitutional views. As Alan Westin wrote in a review critical of Mason for using the materials which made such a book possible: "For a view of how the Supreme Court justice decides a case, how he is acted upon and moulded by the conference and in his relationships with fellow Justices, how legal doctrines are developed and undeveloped within the Court, how ambition, conviction, and self-restraint interplay in the mind of a judge . . . this is an unsurpassed source book." [32]

Samuel J. Konefsky pointed out that Mason's critics have chosen "to treat as a grave defect what is probably the book's chief value and unparalleled contribution." [33] One is tempted to go further and say that Mason's critics have chosen to treat as a grave defect what is probably the chief value and unparalleled contribution of the biographical approach. True, as Westin argues, these materials are not necessary in order to secure "a warm and balanced portrait of a man and a judge," [34] but then despite Harlan Fiske Stone or any other Supreme Court justice's special qualities, to secure a warm and balanced portrait of him—a quite legitimate goal—is only of incidental relevance to the study of public law and is more an exercise within the realm of competence of the literary scholars than students of political science. Similarly, Allison Dunham's criticism of Mason seems to miss the point. Dunham wrote: "It seems to me that for an evaluation and understanding of Supreme Court decisions and opinions these materials [letters and memoranda concerning cases and Court matters] serve no useful purposes. In deciding whether X v. Y is

---

and Supreme Court Appointments," in Philip B. Kurland, ed., *The Supreme Court Review* (1961) is built chiefly on research into the Taft, Stone, Sutherland, McReynolds, Coolidge, and Hughes papers.

[32] Review, 66 *Yale Law Journal* 465 (1957).

[33] Review, 41 *American Political Science Review* 1135 (1958).

[34] Westin, *op. cit.*

a good or bad decision, or whether the rule it establishes is likely or un-likely to survive, it does not help us to know that the Court did not even discuss the issues written about in the opinion, or that the opinion was modified to accommodate views of colleagues on the Court or sensibilities of coordinate departments, or that a judge thought the approach or con-clusion finally adopted by his colleague was suggested by a law clerk. Un-like most decision-makers in and out of government, judges by convention are required to state publicly reasons for conclusions reached, and these stated reasons influence or fail to influence the law and other judges. There is no contribution to the advancement of knowledge in this area by reason of publication of these letters." [35]

If one's purpose is to decide whether Justice Stone's decisions dealing with intergovernmental tax immunities are sound or that his dissent in the *Butler* case enunciates good principles, or whether the footnote in the *Carolene Products* case is likely or unlikely to survive, then Dunham is correct: the publication of the letters and memoranda serve no useful purpose. But if these are one's purposes, then biography serves no useful purpose. To argue about the soundness of principles requires no consider-ation of the life of the individual who enunciated the principles. And as to Dunham's final point, that only the reasons stated in published opin-ions influence or fail to influence the law and other judges, how is one to know if this be the case if he is denied access to materials that might reveal other factors influencing judges?

Edmund Cahn has objected to the use of these materials on the ground that their publication will result in unfairness and divisiveness. As an ex-ample of unfairness he cites Mason's publication of a memorandum pre-pared by Justice Jackson. In this memorandum Jackson persuaded Chief Justice Stone to take the responsibility for writing the Court's opinion in *Smith* v. *Allwright* from Justice Frankfurter and assign it to Justice Reed. Apparently Stone was persuaded that Jackson might be right in feeling that this controversial decision might be more acceptable to the South if written by Justice Reed, a white Protestant from Kentucky, rather than Justice Frankfurter, a Jew from Massachusetts. Said Cahn, "The publi-cation of this memorandum is as unfair to Jackson and Stone as to Frank-furter." [36] But why is it unfair to reveal that the justices had the eminent good sense to recognize some obvious political facts of life! Clearly such a revelation does not square with some prevailing myths about how courts operate. Perhaps some feel that we must maintain the myth in order to retain the public's confidence in our courts, a kind of Platonic Golden Lie. But if Supreme Court justices consider questions of tactics in their

[35] Review, 24 *University of Chicago Law Review* 797 (1957).
[36] Edmond Cahn, "Eavesdropping on Justice" in *The Nation*, Vol. 184, January 5, 1957, p. 15.

assignment of opinions and in their choosing of what to say and when to say it, there is nothing scandalous or unfair in providing specific examples.

The chief record available to us of the inner history of the Supreme Court is the personal papers of the individual jurists. Yet some justices have destroyed their papers [37] and others have chosen to edit them,[38] deleting what they think should be kept from the public. As Mark DeWolfe Howe, Holmes' biographer, writes, Holmes "was careful to destroy all papers within his control which record those events and moods that he considered private. It is clear, I think, that he thought it none of our business to know more of his life than he chose to make public. . . . As a consequence, my responsibility has been primarily that of interpreting his published writings." [39] However valuable Howe's interpretation of Holmes' published works, it will not be a substitute for Holmes as a source of information of what went on inside the Supreme Court during the important years he served in such a central position. Fortunately, in the Holmes-Pollack and Holmes-Laski letters which Professor Howe edited, Holmes revealed "inside information" of great value.

It is disappointing that Holmes, the teacher of humility, saw fit to determine which of his papers the public should be allowed to see. One can agree with Westin, "the primary responsibility in choosing judicial papers rests on the Justice himself," [40] but of all persons, the justice is probably the least qualified to determine which of his papers should be made public or even when it should be done. Nor would the Court as a corporate body, as Edmond Cahn suggested, be any more appropriate to establish policy to govern the disposal of confidential notes.[41] As Hannah Arendt has written: "Action reveals itself fully only to the storyteller, that is, to the backward glance of the historian, who indeed always knows better what it was all about than the participants. . . . What the storyteller narrates must necessarily be hidden from the actor himself, at least as long as he is in the act or caught in its consequences, because to him the meaningfulness of his act is not in the story that follows." [42]

Karl Llewellyn has pointed out: "It is well to remember that neither secrecy of the court's deliberation or later secrecy about what went on

[37] Westin (*op. cit.*, p. 488) gives as his source, *Location of the Personal Papers of Justices of the United States Supreme Court*, Case File, Memorandum, 1956, Library of Congress.

[38] Philip B. Kurland, "Personal Thoughts about Some Problems of Judicial Biography," 36 *Notre Dame Lawyer* 490 (1961).

[39] Mark DeWolfe Howe, *Justice Oliver Wendell Holmes, The Shaping Years* (1957), p. vi.

[40] Westin, *op. cit.*

[41] Cahn, *op. cit.*

[42] Hannah Arendt, *The Human Condition* (1959), p. 171. I am grateful to Professor Murray Edelman for calling this quotation to my attention and for his other useful comments.

during that deliberation rests in the nature of things or in any ordinance of God. The roots of each are either practical or accidental, and it is only either ignorance or tradition which makes us feel that we have here something untouchable, semiholy arcanum. . . . I personally suspect that our own practice of secrecy began when decision began to be postponed beyond the close of argument, with an eye to avoiding misapprehension and disappointment, and then to avoiding financial speculation. And I suspect the carry-over into later secrecy about past deliberations to represent partly a closing of ranks to protect the court from criticism or attack, and in later years a similar closing to allow free discussion with no possible repercussions in a re-election campaign. . . . Our modern fetish of secrecy reminds me of the shock German lawyers displayed at the notion of such dangerous things as published dissenting opinions." [43]

One may argue about the proper timing for the release of judicial papers, both to protect reputations and to avoid creating conditions in which justices will hesitate to speak freely in private conferences and letters. One may concede Cahn's point that there is a public interest in free and uninhibited comment among Supreme Court jurists. But the public also has a right to the judge's files. To borrow a phrase from the justices, when a man becomes a member of the Supreme Court of the United States, his files become "affected with a public interest"; they belong to the nation, not to the judge.

The use of the files of one judge may lead to biases in our understanding, but so may the withholding of these papers, and as John Frank observed, Professor Mason's breaking of the barrier may well result in other justices making available similar materials. "We can therefore expect from this path-breaking work an opening up of the field of Supreme Court history beyond anything that had heretofore been imagined." [44] It is not impossible that A. T. Mason will be known in history as the man who made judicial biography worthwhile.

---

[43] Karl Llewellyn, *The Common Law Tradition* (1960), p. 324.
[44] John P. Frank, Review, 9 *Stanford Law Review* 621 (1958).

Appendix

Alpheus T. Mason

John Davies

One of the biggest chairs in the whole University is the McCormick Professorship of Jurisprudence and it takes a big man to fill it. The two previous giants in the earth sitting thereupon were Woodrow Wilson and Edward S. Corwin, and their worthy successor is Alpheus Thomas Mason, one of Princeton's most successful teachers and author of ten stout volumes, climaxed last month by the 914-page, 3-pound 1-ounce *Harlan Fiske Stone: Pillar of the Law.* . . . This jumbo biography and history of the Supreme Court has been greeted with critical acclaim—"the best biography ever written of a Chief Justice," quoth the *New Republic,* "one of the most important judicial biographies yet written," said the *Saturday Review*—and it seemed to us that since Mason at the age of 57 had reached the summit of a teacher-scholar's career, here was an apt subject for an ALUMNI WEEKLY interview.

But on the morning he talked to us it was not in a vein of self-appreciation but depreciation, all in a mood of smiling irony: "I might have made something out of myself if I had played my cards differently." (He has been at Princeton 32 years). It seems he had received a letter from a relative, which read in part, "I am frankly disappointed in you. . . . By this time, you should be a dean." "There it is," he told us, "the assumption that the really successful teacher is the one able to rise above and beyond it—in other words, stop teaching," and in his bantering familial reply referred to the contrasting Japanese custom of emphasizing teaching rather than administration. Quite seriously he quoted Justice Stone (who used

This article first appeared in the February 8, 1957, issue of the *Princeton Alumni Weekly*, and is reprinted here through the courtesy of the editors of that publication.

to be Dean of the Columbia Law School) that administration is "a necessary evil to be tolerated and justified only as it makes more potent the educational influence." An easy-going and informal person who sprawls over his office furniture, Mason is an individualist who says quite frankly that bureaucratic red tape and committee activities are not his primary interests; one of his many books was entitled *Bureaucracy Convicts Itself*.

He thinks that allied with all this administrative kudos has been a decline in esteem for the teacher and productive scholar. An indication of this may be the discontinuance of the pre-war practice of publishing the faculty research output in university presidents' annual reports. "The academic discoverer," he drawled, "has been eclipsed by the academic operator who's skilled in peddling so-called research projects and in the tactics of foundation solicitation, 'projectitis.' In teaching as in research, the eminent scholar gets lost by being picked as an administrative researcher to adorn a big project and supervise *other* people. Just as you said last week about my friend Holly Whyte's book on business bureaucrats."

A *lone wolf*

One suspects his principal intellectual influence came through Louis D. Brandeis—of whom Mason wrote a 713-page biography—a brilliant Justice who believed in a world of competing individuals through whose rivalry the organization itself would prosper. Mason is a lone wolf researcher who writes about individuals, his forte being the "old-fashioned" field of biography. "My own observation is that once team work is elaborately formalized under a directing head whose primary function is fund raising, the product declines both in quantity and quality. Harold Laski once wrote to Justice Holmes on the subject: 'Most of the expenditures upon cooperative enquiries in the social sciences, where A directs B, C, D, etc., coordinating their results is piffle. . . . An asistant can tell you something, but not much, of what to look for, but the intuition which turns the key in the lock only comes from constant brooding over the materials.' "

The tandem drive and the twin glamor of high-powered management and group research lead directly away from teaching. Mason does his teaching in the grand manner and after 30 years he still works hard at it. Like one of his old students, Robert F. Goheen, he is a partisan of the preceptorial method and has written an article for PAW on its technique. He likes to use a table for precepting, so everyone can sit face to face (PAW two weeks ago showed him and a group of alumni around the same table at last year's Alumni Day precepts, to the next round of which he looks with high spirits.)

His special course, naturally, is "Con Interp" (Constitutional Interpretation), for generations the toughest course in the University, sought out by the most diligent students and just as zealously avoided by the free-loaders. Participation in one class this year became so intense "I positively had to insist on decorum." Should Princeton establish a program to prepare for law school, we asked. "Absolutely not, training in the liberal arts—moral, aesthetic and intellectual values—is what the civilized man needs—and that includes lawyers. Justice Stone had something to say on that too: emphasis should be on 'the intellectual discipline which the student derives from courses and by particular teachers, rather than particular subjects.' In my own judgment, the best criterion is simply to avoid undergraduate courses with an authoritarian tinge—beware of textbooks and lecture courses telling what to think, rather than those encouraging thought and stimulating intellectual independence."

Alumni in law schools

On this subject Mason can speak with authority, because of the brilliant record Princeton men have made in law schools. At Harvard Law, for instance, two years ago 35 students had all A's, of whom 6 were alumni, including the top 2; last year 3 out of the top 4 were Princeton. The reason for their success, he thinks, is the preceptorial method, "the ability to walk up to a particular problem and see it from a number of angles, to understand that reasonable men can differ on the same case to the extent of 5 or 6 different opinions—just as the Supreme Court does occasionally."

Mason vs. Pusey

Would he care to comment on the altercation at which Judge Medina hints on this page, between himself and Mr. Merlo Pusey? (The chorus of approval on the Stone biography from the reviewers was disrupted by a single Bronx cheer from Pusey, biographer of Charles Evans Hughes, who said Mason's "rantings" drove him "*ad nauseam.*") He would care to comment indeed; not all scholarly arguments are fought with creampuffs. It seems that Pusey's biography was in reality directed by Hughes himself. The Chief Justice supplied his biographer with a finished manuscript covering his entire career. Mr. Pusey refers to this material as "Notes," but Mason points out "everything was neatly arranged by chapters, the subject acting as his own Boswell." Mason wrote an article in the *Vanderbilt Law Review* stating these facts; Corwin fired the same shot in another journal. "Mr. Pusey was not pleased."

"Justice Stone made no such plans for a self-portrait. There was no selective mirror of censorship. He died in harness, with no opportunity to rearrange his papers or burn any. The Stone family gave me unrestricted access to his files and correspondence. On me alone rested the responsibility of determining how he should stand before the bar of history and scholarship—so far as I can represent it."

What does Mason intend to do next? "Well, as the old Swiss proverb has it, 'there are no eggs laid in last year's nest.' " He will give the Edward Douglass White lecture series at Louisiana State next month, out of which will grow another book on the Supreme Court. Then he will probably do a biography of another great jurist whose name should not appear in print until Mason's mind is made up. "But you shouldn't be talking to me anyway," off he started again and out went the tongue into the cheek, "you're wasting your time. I'm an old-fashioned has-been from an older era, not an academic promoter or assembly-line researcher." He reverted to teaching and again quoted Justice Stone, who still believed after several years on the bench: "I am quite sure that my work as a teacher will be far more influential and lasting than anything I ever do as a judge. . . . Teachers are the big doers because they influence the whole course of human thought and action."

This was where we came in, the tape on the recorder had run out after an hour and a half, and we left with the thought that the saber-toothed tiger (undergraduate teacher-individual scholar) may be doomed to extinction, but there's a lot of life left in this specimen.

The Art of Precepting

As an aid to younger members of the faculty, the social science and humanities departments this year arranged for several forums on the preceptorial system as it has evolved at Princeton. One of the participants was Professor Alpheus T. Mason of the Department of Politics, who gave his views, based on 25 years of experience on the faculty, on "The Art of Precepting." As a frank analysis of the ingredients necessary for a good preceptorial and of the type of preceptor and student required to make the system work, his remarks on that occasion should be of interest to all concerned with Princeton's plan of study.—ED.

Anyone who has had the depressing experience of sitting for fifty minutes amid the stony silence of from seven to nine undergraduates, stubbornly refusing to allow themselves to be lured, prodded or cajoled into any semblance of intellectual discourse, may well want to forget the whole thing—much less talk about it. Such a preceptorial experience—and it is not an uncommon one—may well raise doubts as to whether there is anything one can say that will prove helpful.

Precepting is an art. It does not permit or require rigid conformity to any particular set of rules. Here, certainly, John Stuart Mill's dictum is quite applicable: each person's "own mode of laying out his existence is the best, not because it is best in itself, but because it is his own mode."

As conceived by Woodrow Wilson, the preceptorial system was designed drastically to change educational methods, to dignify student-teacher relations, to change the attitude of the student toward his work, and alter the teacher's attitude toward his job. It was meant, Wilson said, to make of the undergraduate "a reading man instead of a mere pupil receiving instruction." "The governing idea," he declared, is that students

This article first appeared in the February 3, 1950, issue of the *Princeton Alumni Weekly*, and is reprinted here through the courtesy of the editors of that publication.

"are getting up subjects with the assistance . . . of preceptors who are their guides, philosophers and friends."

In short, the preceptorial system was intended to raise education from a lowly business, in which pupils study lessons and teachers hear recitations, to the more elevated level of cooperative enterprise—teachers and students united in exploring worthwhile subjects.

That is the ideal toward which we strive. As ideal we may approximate but never quite attain it. Even on those rare occasions when one feels that he has been reasonably successful, one is powerless to explain how or why it all happened on that particular day or in that particular group. The sparks that started it all off are as variable as they are elusive. The most one can do is suggest certain pre-requisites that may help ignite the indefinable something that sets discussion ablaze.

(1) *Physical setting:* Our rooms are not always conducive to the preceptorial method. Students sitting along four walls like birds on a pole, with the preceptor behind the authoritative desk, once removed from his fellow explorers, is not quite the proper setting. A table around which all meet face to face provides a more favorable atmosphere.

(2) *Size of the group:* President Eliot of Harvard used to say that seven was the proper size for a group discussion. He considered seven the right number because, as he said, "that number of men can sit around a small table, talk with each other informally without waste of words or any display or pretense, provide an adequate diversity of points of view and modes of dealing with the subject in hand, and yet be prompt and efficient in the dispatch of business." A large number, Eliot held, and experience bears him out, tends to hamper both the flow and the quality of discussion.

(3) *Make-up of the group:* Membership in a preceptorial conference ought not to be constituted solely on the basis of grades or on an alphabetical seating list. "God has not classified men's ability," Wilson remarked in 1905, "either alphabetically or according to their performance in examination." Successful discussion is more likely to come out of a group that is socially and intellectually congenial or from one made up of friendly protagonists.

Obviously Wilson's ideal—a student transformed from mere pupil into reading man, a teacher raised from schoolmaster to philosopher, guide and friend—makes heavy demands on both student and preceptor. The student must be present not only physically but intellectually. He must have read the assignment and feel inclined to discuss it.

But how can this high-toned relationship of teacher and student embarked on an exciting cooperative venture be sustained if the student does not abide by his side of the bargain—that is, if he absents himself or fails to do the reading? Does the preceptor take no notice of this untoward situation? Certainly not. For he is then faced with a condition, not a theory. He must, I think, insist that students be both regular in attendance and in reading their assignments.

Here, however, delicacy is required of the highest order if the preceptor is not to slip back down to the base level of schoolmaster. It is one thing to make a mental note of a student's absence; it is something else ostentatiously to record it in the conventional schoolmaster's class list. When a student is absent or has failed to do the required reading, it is one thing to express, with a bit of good-natured chiding thrown in, grave disappointment that discussion had to proceed without the benefit of his contribution; it is something else to scold or upbraid a fellow-seeker after knowledge.

I am reminded of my old professor of English Composition. Three instruments were his stock in trade: the textbook to which he clung tenaciously; the forbidding black book containing the class lists; and the pencil with which he inserted, without disguise, the grade at the conclusion of each student's recitation. I may have learned some pedagogy in his classroom, but preciously little English Composition.

The preceptorial system demands, I think, some pretty definite things on the part of the preceptor. Above all, he must come to know his preceptees—by sight and name, at least. The preceptor who, after a few meetings, does not know his men—the section of the country they come from, something of their family background, etc.—is to them no friend— perhaps no philosopher either—but a stranger still. The preceptor must also read the weekly assignment. He must at least read what the preceptees read! He should, moreover, work out in advance the course which the session might well take. I do not believe that discussion *qua* discussion is all that Wilson had in mind. He meant systematic exploration of the assigned reading, and that, by and large, is the only thing the group can profitably do. Of course, I don't mean to rule out digression, now and then, into interesting by-ways, but I do say that aimless talk is obviously a waste of valuable time. To achieve the proper balance, the preceptor must have a delicate sense of when to let the reins down, and when to pick them up. But who knows how to achieve this?

A fairly well mapped procedure will not only help in keeping discussion on the main track, but it will also supply a much-needed prop for the hapless preceptor confronted, as he will be sooner or later, with those forbidding human bumps on a log who doggedly refuse to take Wilson's higher road, leading to that academic paradise where the undergraduate is transformed from a mere pupil receiving instruction into a "reading man" in search of **knowledge.**

Bibliography
of Alpheus T. Mason

Books:

1. *Organized Labor and the Law,* with especial reference to the Sherman and Clayton Acts (1925).

2. *Brandeis: Lawyer and Judge in the Modern State* (1933).

3. *Brandeis and the Modern State* (1936). Foreword by Norman Hapgood. Revised and enlarged edition of the earlier book on Brandeis. Published in a 100,000-copy edition by the National Home Library Foundation (1938).

4. *The Brandeis Way:* a case study in the workings of democracy (1938).

5. *Bureaucracy Convicts Itself:* the Ballinger-Pinchot Controversy of 1910 (1941).

6. *Brandeis: a Free Man's Life* (1946); Centennial Edition, 1956.

7. *The Rise and Fall of a Railroad Empire* (with Henry Lee Staples) 1947.

8. *The Democratic Process: Lectures on the American Liberal Tradition* (with Carl J. Friedrich and Arthur M. Schlesinger, Jr.) 1948.

9. *Free Government in the Making* (1949); 2nd edition, 1956.

10. *The Supreme Court: Vehicle of Revealed Truth or Power Group, 1930–1937* (1953).

11. *American Constitutional Law* (with William M. Beaney), 1954; 2nd edition, 1959; 3rd edition, 1964.

12. *Security through Freedom* (1955).

Included here are all the publications (exclusive of book reviews) of Alpheus T. Mason between 1924 and 1964.

13. *Harlan Fiske Stone: Pillar of the Law* (1956).

14. *The Supreme Court from Taft to Warren* (1959). Paperback edition, W. W. Norton Company, 1964.

15. *The Supreme Court in a Free Society* (with William M. Beaney) 1959.

16. *In Quest of Freedom* (with Richard H. Leach) 1959.

17. *The Supreme Court: Palladium of Freedom* (1962).

18. *The States Rights Debate: Antifederalism and the Constitution* (1964).

19. *Corwin on the Constitution: Essays in American Constitutional History* (with Gerald Garvey) 1964.

20. *William Howard Taft: Chief Justice* (1964).

Articles:

1. Legal Justification for Injunctions in Labor Disputes, 23 *South Atlantic Quarterly* (January 1924), 40–50.

2. The Right to Strike, 23 *South Atlantic Quarterly* (July 1924), 197–211.

3. The Labor Clauses of the Clayton Act, 18 *American Political Science Review* (August 1924), 489–513.

4. The Trades Disputes Act of 1927, 22 *American Political Science Review* (February 1928), 143–154.

5. The Right to Strike, 77 *University of Pennsylvania Law Review* (November 1928), 52–72.

6. Ours—a Government of Laws and not of Men, 13 *Constitutional Review* (October 1929), 197–205.

7. The Labor Decisions of Chief Justice Taft, 78 *University of Pennsylvania Law Review* (March 1930), 585–626.

8. Organized Labor as a Party Plaintiff in Injunction Cases, 30 *Columbia Law Review* (April 1930), 466–488.

9. Labor Turns Tables, *The Nation* (July 1930), Vol. 131.

10. Labor Turns to the Injunction, 231 *North American Review* (March 1931), 246–251.

11. Mr. Justice Brandeis: a Student of Social and Economic Science, 79 *University of Pennsylvania Law Review* (April 1931), 665–706.

12. Mr. Justice Brandeis: Exponent of Social Intelligence, 25 *American Political Science Review* (November 1931), 965–980.

13. Mr. Justice Brandeis and the Constitution, 80 *University of Pennsylvania Law Review* (April 1932), 799–842.

14. *Report on a Survey of Administration and Expenditures of the State*

of New Jersey, Chapter 10. Published by The School of Public and International Affairs, December 1932.

15. Labor, the Courts and Section 7A, 26 *American Political Science Review* (December 1934), 999–1016.

16. The Supreme Court of Yesterday and Today, 1 *New Jersey State Bar Association Quarterly* (December 1934), 25–41.

17. Has the Supreme Court Abdicated?, 238 *North American Review* (November 1935), 353–360.

18. The New Labor Law and the Workers, 14 *Personnel Journal* (December 1935), 216–222.

19. Politics: Science or Art?, 16 *Southwestern Social Science Quarterly* (December 1935), 1–11. Reprinted in Richard Snyder and H. H. Wilson, eds., *Roots of Political Behavior: Introduction to Government and Politics*, 1949.

20. The Limits as to Effective Control of the Employer-Employee Relationship, 84 *University of Pennsylvania Law Review* (January 1936), 277–309.

21. Labor and Judicial Interpretation, 184 *Annals of American Academy of Political and Social Science* (March 1936), 112–124.

22. Politics and the Supreme Court: President Roosevelt's Proposal, 85 *University of Pennsylvania Law Review* (May 1937), 659–678.

23. Prospects for Democracy, Alumni Lecture. Published by Herbert L. Baker Foundation, June 1937.

24. The Dilemma of Liberalism, 2 *Journal of Social Philosophy* (April 1938), 223–235.

25. In Government We Mistrust, 7 *The American Scholar* (Summer 1938), 239–249.

26. The Conservative World of Mr. Justice Sutherland, 32 *American Political Science Review* (June 1938), 443–477.

27. A Birthday Tribute. Radio address delivered on the 82nd birthday of Mr. Justice Brandeis (Columbia Network, November 13, 1938). 72 *United States Law Review* (November 1938), pp. 634–636.

28. Moulding of Social Insurance Opinion, 2 *Public Opinion Quarterly* (October 1938), 333–356.

29. Social Statesmanship of Mr. Justice Brandeis, 4 *Journal of Social Philosophy* (January 1939), 240–272.

30. The Democratic Approach to Politics. Published by the Princeton Alumni Association of Cincinnati, 1939.

31. Springs of Democracy, leading article, "Calling America," special number of Survey Graphic (February 1939), 128.

32. The Philosophy of Savings Bank Life Insurance, 20 *Savings Bank Journal* (March 1939), 12.

33. Facts versus Facts, 20 *Savings Bank Journal* (April 1939), 12.

34. Proved Facts and Practical Fancies, 20 *Savings Bank Journal* (May 1939), 12.

35. William Howard Taft, 1857–1930, 34 *Illinois Law Review* (March 1940), 884–889.

36. Dictatorship, *New Century Dictionary Book of Facts* (1941), 244.

37. Louis Brandeis: People's Attorney, *American Mercury* (April 1947).

38. Variations on the Liberal Theme. Publications of the Brandeis Lawyers' Society (April 1947), 1–14.

39. Phenomena of America's Highest Office, *Philadelphia Inquirer* (March 23, 1947).

40. 1947 as a Symbol of Hope, *Philadelphia Inquirer* (December 1, 1946).

41. Phi Beta Kappa Address, *Dickinson Alumnus* (May 1947).

42. Laski on Democracy, 14 *Law and Contemporary Problems* (Spring 1949), 394–404.

43. Business Organized as Power: the New Imperium in Imperio, 44 *American Political Science Review* (June 1950), 323–342. Reprinted as PS-185, Bobbs-Merrill Reprint Series in Social Sciences.

44. Welfare Capitalism: Opportunity or Delusion, 26 *The Virginia Quarterly Review* (Autumn 1950), 530–543.

45. The Nature of the Union Reconsidered, 65 *Political Science Quarterly* (December 1950), 502–521. Reprinted in Abraham Eisenstadt, *American History: Recent Interpretations*, 1962, 214–227.

46. In Defense of Individual Freedom, 51 *Columbia Law Review* (February 1951), 147–169.

47. Harlan Fiske Stone Assays Social Justice, 99 *University of Pennsylvania Law Review* (May 1951), 887–918.

48. American Individualism: Facts and Fiction, 46 *American Political Science Review* (March 1952), 1–18.

49. The Federalist—a Split Personality, 57 *American Historical Review* (April 1952), 625–643.

50. Harlan Fiske Stone and FDR's Court Plan, 61 *Yale Law Journal*, (June 1952), 791–817.

51. Charles Evans Hughes: an Appeal to the Bar of History, 6 *Vanderbilt Law Review* (December 1952), 1–20.

52. Extra-Judicial Work for Judges, 67 *Harvard Law Review* (December 1953), 193–216. Reprinted in Arthur Sutherland, Jr., ed., *An Introduction to Law*, 1957.

53. Inter Arma Silent Leges, 69 *Harvard Law Review* (March 1956), 806–838.

54. The Core of Free Government, 1938–1940, 65 *Yale Law Journal* (April 1956), 597–628.

55. The Supreme Court: Temple and Forum, 48 *The Yale Review* (Summer 1959), 524–540.

56. Myth and Reality in Supreme Court Decisions, 48 *Virginia Law Review* (December 1962), 1385–1406. Reprinted in William H. Nelson, ed., *American Political Thought: Theory and Practice,* 1964.

57. Federal-State Relations in the United States: Union not Unity. Selected Problems of Social Sciences and Humanities. Skopje, 1963. Papers from the Yugoslav-American Colloquium, Ohrid, Macedonia, August 27–September 2, 1962, 103–111.

58. The Constitution of the United States (with William M. Beaney), 7 *Collier's Encyclopedia* (1963), 228–257.

59. Must We Continue the States Rights Debate?, *Rutgers Law Review* (Fall 1963), 60–76.

Lectureships and Seminars

1. Liberal Summer School, Cambridge, England, Summer 1935.
2. Henry Wells Lawrence Memorial Lectures, Connecticut College, 1948.
3. Northwestern University Centennial Lecture, 1951.
4. Gaspar G. Bacon Lectures, Boston University, 1953.
5. American Studies Seminar (auspices Rockefeller Foundation and Stanford University), Tokyo University, Summer 1953.
6. The Messenger Lectures, Cornell University, 1955.
7. Edward Douglass White Lectures, Louisiana State University, 1958.
8. William W. Cook Lectures, University of Michigan, 1962.
9. Yugoslav-American Colloquium (auspices State Department and Indiana University) Lake Ohrid, Macedonia, Summer 1962.
10. Yugoslav-American Colloquium (auspices State Department and Indiana University) Zadar, Dalmatia, Summer 1963.

The Authors

GORDON E. BAKER is Associate Professor of Political Science at the University of California, Santa Barbara.

JULIAN P. BOYD is Professor of History at Princeton University.

HAROLD W. CHASE is Professor of Political Science at the University of Minnesota.

GOTTFRIED DIETZE is Professor of Political Science at the Johns Hopkins University.

ANDREW HACKER is Associate Professor of Government at Cornell University.

JOHN W. HOPKIRK is Associate Professor of Political Science at Pennsylvania Military College.

WOODFORD HOWARD is Assistant Professor of Political Science at Duke University.

SAMUEL KRISLOV is Associate Professor of Political Science, University of Minnesota.

RICHARD H. LEACH is Associate Professor of Political Science at Duke University.

DONALD R. MATTHEWS is Professor of Political Science at the University of North Carolina.

J. W. PELTASON is Dean of the College of Arts, Letters, and Sciences, and Professor of Political Science at the University of California, Irvine.

JAMES W. PROTHRO is Professor of Political Science at the University of North Carolina.